Lance & Le Tour
The Complete History Of Cycling's Most Uneasy Alliance
Matt Lamy

For Manda, Adam and David
and Sue and Arf – a real cycling hero

Published by IPC Media 2009
Copyright © 2009 Matthew Lamy

Matthew Lamy has asserted his right under the Copyright, Designs and Patents
Act 1988 to be identified as the author of this work.

First published in Great Britain in 2009 by IPC Media, Blue Fin Building,
110 Southwark Street, London SE1 0SU

ISBN 978-0862-963-286

Acknowledgements

Obviously my greatest thanks goes to those people who agreed to be interviewed for this book – it was a privilege talking to them all. Whatever cycling fans may think of Lance Armstrong himself, there can be little argument that the individuals interviewed in the following pages are fully deserving of the title 'expert'. I must also thank Sean Weide, press officer for the Rock Racing team, and Philippe Maertens at team Astana for setting up interviews with some of Armstrong's former and current team-mates.

In terms of the production of this English-language edition, my eternal gratitude goes to Dan Thomas for proof-reading the final product. Even before Dan assumed a hands-on role with this project, his constant distracting emails when I should have been working, and his encouragement when I should have been despairing, helped keep me sane. I also owe the eternally-youthful Huw Williams a great deal for his wonderful cover design and for laying out the pages – there might not be any pictures involved, but we quickly found out that books still need the eye of a designer. My thanks also goes to my two publishers: Katsuya Debari at American Book and Cinema in Japan for originally giving me the opportunity to write this book; and Keith Foster at IPC Media for allowing me to see this book in a language I can actually read. My agent, Miyo Kai at Timo Associates, deserves great praise for instigating the project in the first place.

I am also extremely lucky to have some good friends who have offered their opinions and encouragement along the way. Nigel Wynn, a fellow 'full-time dad and part-time bike journalist', has been a constant source of positivity and cups of tea if I ever needed a break from my twin (no pun intended) jobs. And Luke Edwardes-Evans's 20-plus years in cycling journalism means he has forgotten more than most people ever know about bike racing, but I'm glad I've put his knowledge to good use. He also makes a mean bacon and egg roll.

Finally I have to say thanks to the most important people. Firstly my mum Sue, who was both a proof reader and a source of general encouragement. Secondly my dad Arthur, without whom I would never have been interested in push-bikes. Thirdly my wife Manda, who was my sounding block throughout, and another proof reader at various moments. And fourthly and fifthly my two boys Adam and David, who stuck rigidly to their afternoon nap routine and let daddy get in at least a couple of hours' work each day.

Contents

Introduction

"For while we cannot guarantee that we shall one day be first, we can guarantee that any failure to make this effort will make us last"
John F. Kennedy

A few years ago I read a book called *Moondust* by Andrew Smith. The book told how Smith travelled across America trying to track down many of the people – astronauts, engineers and managers – behind NASA's quest to put man on the moon. As I conducted the last few interviews for *Lance and Le Tour* I came to realise that there were many similarities between the subject of Smith's book and the focus of my interest – and I don't just mean that both are overshadowed by men called Armstrong.

The very final interview I did for *Lance and Le Tour* is actually the one that appears in the first chapter – it is with Mark Gorski, the original general manager for the US Postal team. What caught my imagination while talking to Gorski was his memory of the formation of US Postal. Gorski told me: "I ran into Thom Weisel [the major backer of what would become the US Postal team] in March 1995. Thom was really lamenting saying: 'I want to try and build something even bigger than we had at Team Subaru-Montgomery.' So I just listened to him and when I got back on the plane later that day to go back to Colorado I wrote out a proposal to him. And I remember the final paragraph of this proposal said that our ultimate objective for doing this would be to become the first American team to win the Tour de France."

In my mind, Gorski's stating of that audacious goal had echoes of the equally impossible mission John F. Kennedy instigated in May 1961, when he said: "I believe that this nation should commit itself to achieving the goal, before this decade is out, of landing a man on the moon and returning him safely to earth." The comparison of those two statements might sound incongruous, but in its own sporting context the idea that an American team could succeed and rule at a fiercely French event, in a fiercely European sport, was just as grand as Kennedy's moon dream.

Neil Armstrong's first step on the moon in 1969, and Lance Armstrong's first step onto the top podium of the Tour de France 30 years later, were the results of two great American projects. Sure, in cycling, Greg LeMond had already become the first American to win the Tour, but as Jim Ochowicz says later in this book, LeMond did that as part of a European team, with European team-mates and European sponsors. Lance Armstrong's achievement was supported by American colleagues, in an American organisation, with American funding.

Both projects suffered their share of close-calls and near disasters. The Apollo 11 crew may have reached the moon partly on a wing and a prayer, but as I researched this book I realised that at many points things could have been so different for Lance Armstrong. Gorski revealed that Armstrong came within a whisker of never winning his breakthrough Tour prologue in 1999 when his chain momentarily slipped off its cogs; and then he might never have won that 1999 Tour if his closest rival Alex Zülle hadn't been held up by an accident on a slippery seaside causeway two stages later. Fast forward four years later, in a tumultuous 2003 Tour where Armstrong was pushed to the wire, another of my interviewees, Armstrong's team-mate Victor Hugo Pena, revealed how Armstrong concealed a debilitating bout of diarrhoea from both his team and the public early in the Tour, then rode to the end of a crucial mountain stage up Luz Ardiden with a bike that had split apart.

Of course, both the moon and the Tour each have their own conspiracy theorists, the people who say that Neil Armstrong's first steps on that powdery surface were actually filmed in a television studio, or that Lance Armstrong never won seven consecutive Tours without cheating. I didn't begin writing *Lance and Le Tour* with any intention of proving Lance Armstrong's honesty one way or another. But, with the great majority of my contributors being people who had put their hearts and souls into 'Project Lance', the side of the fence this book should take was decided for us.

Then there are more parallels. The moon is an inhospitable, alien world, but I am only half joking when I say the same could be said about turn-of-the-millennium France, especially for any American invader trying to reign at the nation's most celebrated sporting event.

Finally there are the elephants in the room, those two men called Armstrong, neither of whom are known for having particularly familiar relationships with writers or the media.

Despite starting out as a study of the entire moon programme, Smith's journey across the US became something of a quest to find just one man: Neil Armstrong. I remember Smith recalling how, throughout his journey, people would say to him: "Have you spoken to Neil yet?"

Unlike Smith, from the outset my book was indeed supposed to be about just one figure. But as I spoke to those who have spent time alongside him, I grew to realise that the 'Lance Armstrong story' is about more than just one unnaturally determined Texan. Behind the headline there are dozens of other personal tales that combine to explain how Lance Armstrong has become the icon he is today. (That said, I was also overwhelmed by the number of times I was asked: "Have you spoken to Lance yet?")

So *Lance and Le Tour* is about Lance, and it is about the Tour, but it's also about the people who helped him climb mountains, or chase down rivals, or build him bikes, or even write or take photographs of him. In many cases they gave all of themselves because they believed they were working for a bigger goal – they were working for 'Project Lance'.

As Mark Gorski told me: "When we started we thought we might as well aim big. We thought we might as well shoot for the moon."

Matt Lamy
Caterham, UK, August 2009

1999: The Greatest Comeback
With Mark Gorski, US Postal Team General Manager 1995-2003

On July 3rd 1999, on a podium in Le Puy du Fou, a 27-year-old American pulled on the Tour de France's yellow jersey for the first time, and began writing cycling history.

It was a warm summer afternoon when Lance Armstrong covered the first 6.8 kilometres of the 1999 Tour faster than the other 179 best professional cyclists in the world. Yet, less than three years earlier he had been staring death in the face with advanced testicular cancer that had spread to his lungs and his brain. But if his immediate past was hardly imaginable, this first yellow jersey marked the beginning of a future where Armstrong's dominance over professional cycling would be even more incredible. This moment was the true birth of Lance Armstrong, the icon.

Armstrong's road to that first presentation of the yellow jersey has become part of modern sporting legend. There is the story about his upbringing with a determined and protective mother, but a father who had long gone. Then there is his success in amateur and professional bike racing, where Armstrong was crowned the youngest world champion in history and became one of the biggest stars in American cycling. And then there is the moment when it was all wiped away by that cancer diagnosis. Armstrong may have beaten the disease but he didn't just restart winning bike races – the two cancer-free years leading up to that moment on the Tour prologue podium had probably been the hardest of his life.

Armstrong finished cancer treatment at the end of 1996 and began the process of recovery in early 1997, but chemotherapy had left him with reduced muscle mass, a whole different body shape, and a fragile psyche. In addition to that, by the summer of 1997 he had been all but dumped by his existing racing team, the French Cofidis organisation, with few other squads interested in hiring a recently-recovered cancer patient. The only team that expressed any real interest was the fledgling US Postal, a reasonably new American-based team funded by cycling-mad tycoon Thom Weisel and run by former pro rider and Olympic gold medallist Mark Gorski.

"We sat down with Lance at the Interbike trade show in Los Angeles in September 1997," remembers Gorski. "It was there that Lance announced to the world that he was going to try and make a comeback, and when he and his agent Bill Stapleton really set out to have discussions with any of the teams that would be willing to talk to him. It was a tough go, there were not a lot of teams that were interested or willing to spend a significant amount of money to really take a chance on Lance. At the time, the notion that anybody could come back from cancer to win even one stage in the Tour, or even just ride near the front of the peloton, was crazy.

"Thom and I talked at length about whether signing Lance was something we wanted to do. Without a doubt it felt like the right thing to do, we wanted to support Lance in his ambition and desire to try to make a comeback, and it would be great public relations and there would be a lot of focus on Lance. But in terms of actually getting results and winning races, and ultimately winning the Tour, well that wasn't even part of the equation. Lance hadn't even been close to being a general classification rider in the Tour before, and our feeling was that maybe the ultimate goal would be that he could win a stage at the Tour."

Despite the professional cycling community having limited expectations, Armstrong and Stapleton still felt their services were worth a decent wage.

"At that time – October 1997 – we had already made our rider selections for the 1998 season, and our budget was completely full," Gorski says. "We had an opportunity to sign Lance, yet we really didn't have the funding for it. So for two weeks I went out to our key sponsors at that time – US Postal Service, Visa, Trek and a couple of others – saying we needed to raise $200,00 to $250,000 for a base salary for Lance.

"But the key was that Lance and Bill were really pushing for a really strong bonus programme that would give Lance a significant benefit if he performed well. That was based on UCI points, rather than specific victories, and it was a key sticking point in negotiations. I remember Thom and Bill and me sitting in a meeting talking about this, and Thom blurted out: 'OK, I'll underwrite the bonus payments.' I remember being shocked and thinking, 'Oh my God, I can't believe Thom's said that.' At that time, in late October 1997, nobody really knew if that meant paying up $500 or $500,000 in bonuses... In fact it ended up being nearly a million dollars."

In October 1997, a year after discovering he had developed cancer, Armstrong held a press conference to say he was healthy, he was happy, and he was back ready to race as a member of the US Postal squad. But it wouldn't be plain sailing. "At the initial training camp in January 1998 nobody was really sure where Lance would fit in," Gorski remembers. "Clearly Lance had been a team leader in the past, and in any other situation Lance would have come back and assumed leadership of that team, but it wasn't quite that way in the first year after his comeback. It was more like an experiment."

Armstrong spent the last part of 1997 training in Santa Barbara, California, before moving with fiancée Kristin Richard to a flat in Cap Ferrat, southern France, in January 1998. He went to work, racing and training with the other members of the US Postal squad, but it quickly became clear that Armstrong had problems.

His first comeback race was a five-day Spanish stage race called the Ruta del Sol where he finished 15th. "At the Ruta del Sol Lance did fine, he did OK, he was just finding his legs," Gorski says. "Then he went to Paris-Nice. The first stage of Paris-Nice was a cold, raw day, and Lance just climbed off the bike. He said he wasn't ready for that. In a way that just served to reinforce the doubt in everyone's mind. It did feel like a grand experiment and no one knew where it was going to end up.

"There were clearly peaks and valleys in the first few months of his comeback. When Lance climbed off at Paris-Nice I honestly did not know if we would see him again. Then he went back to Austin, Texas. He wasn't training hard, and I remember speaking to him regularly by phone in those weeks after Paris-Nice. I just said to him: 'Do what you need to do.' I did not say anything other than: 'We're supportive of you, we believe in you, we know how hard this is and we know this is tough mentally and physically.' But I was thinking, he might not come back, this might be it. I think it could have easily resulted in Lance trying to come back to pro cycling but finding he just wasn't ready to do it."

Despite his pre-cancer sporting glory, and despite the success of his cancer treatment, professional cycling was within a whisker of losing Lance Armstrong.

In the aftermath of his decision to quit, Stapleton and Armstrong's personal coach Chris Carmichael tried all they could to reverse his decision. Stapleton suggested he should have one more big race in the United States – the US Pro Championships in June - before finally hanging up his wheels. Armstrong agreed to wait, and spent the next few weeks relaxing at home in Austin while Stapleton, Carmichael and his other friends surreptitiously continued to try to change his mind. Carmichael flew to Austin in April to create a training regime for Armstrong that would prepare him for the US Pro Championships. They decided to head away from Austin, to a town called Boone in North Carolina, where they would spend a week going through an intensive programme. As a riding partner they invited former 7-Eleven pro Bob Roll to also come along. That week had the effect Carmichael was hoping for – it rekindled Armstrong's passion for cycling.

"On occasion I would drive the team car and direct the team, and I remember Lance came from Carolina in the first week of May 1998 to a race in Atlanta, Georgia, and he seemed to be coming back," Gorski says. "He was pretty aggressive in that race and he was showing signs of the old Lance. And then later at the US Pro Champs in Philadelphia, Lance really played a huge role in the final few kilometres to set up the victory for George Hincapie, and Lance finished fourth. It was a big morale booster for the team and for George. What I think none of us knew was that Lance was privately progressing through his comeback on his own schedule. He went from Philadelphia to the Tour of Luxembourg, rode a great race there and won; then did well at a smaller stage race in Germany."

As well as getting back to racing Armstrong also found joy in his private life and married Kristin. He didn't attend the 1998 Tour de France in July, which was probably a blessing. But in September he did race at the year's last Grand Tour, the Vuelta a Espana, where, quite amazingly, he finished fourth overall. That was a better result than Armstrong had ever achieved in a Grand Tour, even before having cancer.

More important than the result itself, though, was the fact that Armstrong had developed a new friendship with a former pro cyclist from Belgium called Johan

Bruyneel. Bruyneel, who was widely respected in the sport as a canny rider, had retired from the peloton and Armstrong suggested he should join US Postal as a directeur sportif.

"When we were at the World Championships in 1998 in Holland where Lance finished fourth, Johan came up and we met formally to confirm his position on the team for the 1998 season," Gorski remembers. "Discussions between Lance and Johan, and myself and Johan, began in August or September but it was at the Worlds that we signed an agreement for him to join as a directeur sportif for the 1999 season.

"Without a doubt it was Johan's idea to go all-out for the Tour win the following year. Lance's breakthrough in the Vuelta in 1998 set the stage for that, and I think there were conversations between Johan and Lance during that Vuelta where Johan planted the seed in Lance's mind that he could win the Tour. But truth be told, I think that it was really just a dream, so why not dream big? But Lance still didn't have a track record at that point to say: OK, this is something that he can obviously do. It was still a huge unknown."

Armstrong and Bruyneel spent the winter months extensively riding the course of the 1999 Tour, repeatedly going up mountain climbs so that Armstrong knew exactly where he could attack and where he could relax. And for the first half of the season they didn't worry about the Classics, Armstrong's pre-cancer area of specialism, they would simply ride the events that would prepare Armstrong best for an overall challenge at the Tour. In fact, before July 1999, Armstrong only won one event that season, a time trial at the Circuit de la Sarthe stage race.

"It was a new way of approaching the Tour. I think the Johan and Lance approach to everything was just unique," Gorski says. "It was so thorough, methodical, well thought-out, and the amount of time and energy and effort they put into the planning of success is phenomenal. Visualisation, preparation and knowing a course, knowing every turn, is critical in cycling, but I don't think that it had been done in that way, with that level of thoroughness before."

The 1999 Tour de France wasn't just a comeback for Armstrong, it was also a comeback of sorts for the race itself after the Festina affair in 1998. Although the Tour organisers ultimately failed in their attempts to keep out riders or teams that they felt would bring their event into disrepute, there were still plenty of high-profile athletes missing from the 1999 Tour – in fact, it was the first edition for half a century where no previous Tour winners were among the starting list. The reigning champion, Marco Pantani, had decided that that year's route didn't suit him and was also mired in controversy having been asked to leave the Giro d'Italia earlier in the year for having a high haematocrit reading – seen as an indication of possible doping. The 1997 winner Jan Ullrich was suffering from loss of motivation and a knee injury caused at the Tour of Germany. And the 1996 Tour champ Bjarne Riis had a knee and elbow problem after an accident at the Tour of Switzerland - injuries that would eventually force the Dane to retire from cycling completely.

Perhaps the expected pre-race favourite for the overall victory was Alex Zülle, a Swiss star, double Vuelta a Espana winner and a former member of the Festina squad that had been expelled from the Tour in 1998. Zülle had served his ban and had left Festina for the Spanish Banesto team, which had supported Miguel Indurain to his five Tour wins and knew what it took to succeed at the biggest race in the world.

Also expected to be in the mix was world time trial champion Abraham Olano, who led the powerful ONCE squad; and Ivan Gotti, who led the Polti team and had taken his second Giro d'Italia title earlier in the year.

Despite their individual successes, none of these riders really knew what it took to win the Tour de France, so the way was open for a new champion. But on the eve of the race, within the US Postal management, the idea that Armstrong could be that champion was taking a back seat to crucial housekeeping duties.

"As the sort of business manager – the general manager of the team – it was a stressful lead-up to the prologue for me," Gorski remembers. "We were negotiating with Lance and Bill for his contract, we actually revised his contract for the remainder of 1999 and for 2000 and 2001 literally in the two or three weeks leading up to the Tour, and the days leading up to the Tour, and even the hours leading up to the start of the prologue, it was crazy. After Thom went through that financial experience with Lance's bonus payment in 1998, Thom said, 'We've got to find insurance to underwrite this.' So I spent months working with insurance underwriters negotiating policies that would cover bonus payments to Lance for 1999, and ultimately 2000 and 2001. And I was also undergoing negotiations with Lance on salary and bonuses, which were very substantial – into the seven figures.

"I will never forget it was two o'clock in the morning on July 3rd – the day that Lance took the yellow jersey at the prologue – and I was in the team hotel in Nantes going through everything and actually signing Lance's agreement and executing it – faxing it to Bill at his offices in Texas – and at the same time executing this insurance contract. I had to use the fax machine at reception at the hotel because it all needed to be done, signed and executed before the start of the prologue, which was just hours away. And ultimately there were millions of dollars of bonus payments that resulted from all of this.

"The funny thing is that I was with Lance in the team vehicle – we didn't have a bus at that point, we just had a campervan – and we were going over to the opening ceremony for the Tour, but Lance and I were in the middle of these massive negotiations. We would check in with each other about this business stuff but at the same time he was getting ready for maybe the biggest day in his life in cycling. So there were all these other currents going on."

Still, these problems didn't affect Armstrong's prologue performance. "I remember being in our team campervan and Lance was the last rider to depart," says Gorski. "I think George Hincapie and Kevin Livingstone were there in the camper and Johan Bruyneel was in there as well. Lance put his time trial suit on, and his last words to all of us were: 'Get ready to watch the show.' And as he walked out we just looked at each other and shook our heads, and said: 'He is one of a kind.' The level of confidence and showmanship all wrapped in one human being... there's just nothing like him. And what a show he gave us."

Much has been written about Armstrong in the years since that moment, but Gorski remembers it could have all been so different. "I was in the car behind Lance with Johan and Jeff Brown, who was the mechanic, and there was a pretty good grade climb near the end of that prologue. We were watching like hawks and we could see Lance was debating whether he should stay in the big ring or drop into the little ring as he was climbing, and he decided to go to the little ring. As he shifted, for a brief moment, the chain actually went off the ring. Our hearts were in our mouths. I remember looking at Jeff, whose job it was to make sure that the derailleurs are tuned properly to stop that happening, but Lance jammed the shifter and corrected it almost instantaneously. He averted disaster but if he had lost his chain off of the ring it could have made the difference between winning and losing that prologue. That was the key moment.

"Then there was the explosion of emotion when he crossed the line and reached where we all were. That will be a memory that I will always treasure. I've heard Lance say publicly that in all his seven Tour wins that 1999 prologue was the most meaningful moment. I think that all that had happened in the prior two or three years – from Lance's cancer diagnosis to chemotherapy to the struggle of the comeback, the ups and downs – meant that that moment was very significant. But even then no one knew what was going to come next. Nobody had any clue that it might mean winning the Tour, winning two Tours or winning seven Tours. All it meant was that this guy came back from his deathbed to win the prologue at the Tour de France.

"But right then I remember crying, breaking down in tears: tears of just disbelief, of joy. It was amazingly emotional for me."

The result of that opening day meant Armstrong led the race by seven seconds from Zülle with Olano third at 11 seconds. "I gave everything and I felt good," Armstrong said to the press afterwards. The Tour organisers were also happy because, after the trauma of 1998, at last they had a feel-good story at their race. They wouldn't always be so pleased to see Armstrong's name in the headlines, but right now everything was fine.

The first proper road stage of the 1999 Tour saw a bunch sprint finish and Armstrong remained in the yellow jersey. Stage two, though, highlighted just how quickly Armstrong had assumed the mindset of a Tour favourite. Part of the day's route took the riders over the Passage du Gois, a cobbled causeway that is submerged by the tide for part of the day and which links the French mainland with the island of Noirmoutier. Armstrong had done his homework and knew that this presented a possible danger spot, so he made sure he was at the head of the race when the riders reached the Passage. He was right – there was indeed misery on the slippery causeway. While Armstrong and the riders at the front carried on regardless, other overall favourites – notably Zülle and Gotti – were caught up in the carnage. Despite desperately chasing to get back with the leaders they had lost 6-03 to Armstrong by the finish.

"That was an amazingly interesting day," Gorski remembers. "I was driving the second team car and the Passage du Gois ripped the race apart, and handicapped Zülle a lot. But Lance was riding the race as though he were a Tour favourite and he knew he had to be near the front. Lance became consistent in not making mistakes throughout his future Tours, and the Passage du Gois was a great indicator of things to come. That was where preparation and planning came in. That was the result of Johan talking on the radio and drilling into the heads of the riders that they had to be at the front, and they had to keep Lance at the front."

The next few stages would be the preserve of the fastmen, with Tom Steels taking his second win on stage three, and Italian sprint legend Mario Cipollini taking four wins on the trot on stages four, five, six and seven. With the sprinters picking up time bonuses Armstrong had slipped down the rankings but stage eight, the Tour's first major individual time trial, would show if he was really serious about winning this Tour.

From the moment he rolled off the start ramp in the town of Metz, Armstrong set best times at all the checkpoints along the course. His newly-developed high-cadence pedalling technique caused his legs to pump like the pistons of a speeding locomotive, but the attention to detail in his position and equipment – the streamlining of his exclusive Giro time trial helmet – meant this power was allied to a form that simply slipped through the air. Armstrong began to catch riders that had started ahead of him, most impressively Olano, the reigning world time trial champion, resplendent in his rainbow jersey. The Spaniard had rolled down the ramp two minutes before Armstrong, yet he was overtaken by the US Postal rider. Armstrong even caught the Belgian sprinter Tom Steels, who had had a massive six-minute head start. The Texan was imperious.

At the finish line Armstrong recorded a time of 1-08-36, which was 57 seconds quicker than second-placed Zülle and 2-04 ahead of Festina's Christophe Moreau in third. Overall, it meant Armstrong was back in yellow, 2-20 in front of Moreau in second and 2-33 ahead of Olano in third. Zülle's good ride had lifted him to 34th in the overall standings but he had lost yet more time to Armstrong and was 7-08 off the lead. Gotti's Tour challenge, though, was now all but over having lost more than 15 minutes overall to Armstrong.

"I think the convincing way in which Lance won that longer and much more important time trial – the prologue is never going to determine the outcome of the Tour – played a key part in the outcome of the Tour, both psychology and in terms of the time differentials," Gorski says. "I think that day was when the rest of the world woke up and said Lance Armstrong is a serious contender for this Tour and he can win it. I think everyone then started to really understand Lance's determination, including his own team-mates, and that was where his success quickly started to reinforce itself in his own team-mates' idea of how serious this was and what they were a part of."

The Tour riders had a rest day next, but then it was into the territory that traditionally decides the real winner of the race: the mountains. Perhaps surprisingly they seemed to hold no fear for Armstrong.

"Coming into the Tour my coaches and people in the team thought that my strength would be in my climbing and not my time trialling," he said. "If that holds true then I might be able to hold on." It was enough to send a chill up the other riders' spines.

At the heart of the team, Gorski doesn't remember having quite the same level of confidence: "I do think that there was a huge question mark still. That transition in any Tour – from long flat stages and time trials to the mountains – is such a dramatic change that a lot of guys falter. So there were levels of doubt. The more traditional European media who still had doubts about Lance were wondering how this was going to end up. I think Johan's confidence in Lance, and Lance's confidence in himself, probably let him feel he was going to be fine in the mountains. Lance was certainly not lacking in confidence."

The first mountain stage, stage nine, ran 213 kilometres to the ski station at Sestriere and took in the fearsome climbs of the Col du Télégraphe and Col du Galibier, as well as the final climb up to the summit finish. Although Armstrong may have been buoyed by the sight of roadside spectators waving the stars and stripes, there were plenty of potentially less pleasant surprises in store. The terrain itself was hard, but Armstrong had done his homework and knew – perhaps better than anybody else in the peloton – just what he was facing. However, the real unknowns came from his rivals, and it became clear that the Spanish teams, Banesto and Kelme, were preparing to ambush Armstrong for his yellow jersey.

Added to this was a weather system taking a turn for the worse, with torrential rain causing small rivers to flow down the slopes.

"We were worried about the Spanish squads," Gorski says. "When you know the heritage of the Tour and the great climbing prowess of Spanish riders over the years and the variety of the Spanish teams, there was always that threat. I think there was also this notion that there could be collusion between some of the Spanish teams. There was definitely a worry that there would be a barrage of attacks from the Spanish teams and they would be working together. I remember Johan being very concerned about that. You had Banesto, ONCE and Kelme with such a lot of climbing firepower between them that, if tied together and launched as one collective unit, could have done some serious damage."

On the road Banesto's Jose Luis Arrieta and Saeco's Laurent Dufaux had made an early break and led the field by a substantial margin by the time the big names reached the first big climb, the Col du Galibier. Up until this point the US Postal team had managed to protect Armstrong, with Tyler Hamilton and Kevin Livingstone working particularly hard. But on the Galibier Armstrong faced his first concerted challenge when Kelme's Joaquim Castelblanco and Fernando Escartin – a rider who Armstrong viewed as a potential overall threat, especially in the mountains – and Banesto's Manuel Beltran broke away. Polti's Richard Virenque, trying to amass more points in his quest for a fifth King of the Mountains title, also joined the three Spaniards, but there was no obvious sign of panic from Armstrong. Livingstone upped the pace of the chase and the four escapees were brought back into the fold.

On the Col de Montgenèvre, the penultimate climb of the day, the yellow jersey group included some big names but Armstrong found himself without any team support. Despite this he remained unruffled and allowed Virenque to lead the group over the summit of the climb to take maximum mountains point. Rather than wait for the final climb, perhaps the expected place for the attack on Armstrong, Gotti and Castelblanco managed to open a 30-second gap on the tricky, slippery descent of Montgenèvre.

But on the lower slopes of the road to Sestriere Armstrong decided to turn on the power. His legs spinning rapidly, the race leader simply flew away from his companions. Zülle and Kelme's Carlos Contreras tried desperately to bridge to the Texan but almost immediately Armstrong opened a gap of 11 seconds. Within a kilometre of his initial acceleration Armstrong was with Gotti and Castelblanco. Slowly Zülle managed to inch his way up to the back of the trio, but Armstrong again took his place at the front of the group and lifted the pace once more. Pumping his legs harder, rocking his bike from side to side, Armstrong sprinted away.

The conditions were still hazy, and the rain was still spitting, but it made no difference. As the summit grew nearer Armstrong bobbed in and out of the saddle, sprinting through a crowd that was cowering under raincapes and sheltering under umbrellas. Increasing the gap to his rivals all the way to the finish line, Armstrong zipped up his yellow jersey, looked up to the open heavens and punched the air. Zülle bravely managed to arrive just 31 seconds down, while Escartin and Gotti rolled in to finish 1-26 in arrears. Overall Armstrong was now in complete command: 6-03 ahead of Olano, 7-44 ahead of Moreau, and 7-47 ahead of Zülle. It seemed Armstrong really could climb.

"There were a lot of people who felt that my climbing was suspect. I gave a response to them today, but I wasn't trying to shove it in anybody's face. I felt good and I saw an opportunity," Armstrong said at the finish. What probably made his rivals worry most wasn't simply the time gain but the manner in which Armstrong rode the first mountain stage. He never looked in trouble, he never looked fazed. While the other favourites thought the hills would be where they could regain time on the Texan, instead they were facing the possibility of being even further away from the yellow jersey.

"Part of what played into the epic nature of that first day in the mountains was the weather, the rain, the mountain itself," Gorski says. "But I remember Kevin Livingstone did an amazing job on the Galibier and played a key role that day. Kevin was critical to Lance's getting to the important point on stages in the mountains and still being fresh."

Stage 10 was another trip through the Alps, and it ended on perhaps the most celebrated summit in cycling: Alpe d'Huez. But before they reached those hallowed hairpins the Tour riders would have to negotiate 220 kilometres of tough terrain, including first the hors catégorie Col du Mont Cenis and then the Col de la Croix de Fer. Like the day before, US Postal's troops kept order at the front of the race for as long as they could, making Armstrong's journey to the day's battlefields as comfortable as possible. Unlike the day before, the weather was warm and rain-free.

At 77 kilometres, on the descent of Mont Cenis, a break escaped consisting of just two riders, Française des Jeux's Stéphane Heulot and Big Mat's Thierry Bourguignon. With this stage happening on July 14 - Bastille Day - every French rider wanted to take the win, and these two were being more than a little hopeful. Back among the overall favourites very little happened until the bottom of Alpe d'Huez, where Armstrong still had Tyler Hamilton with him as support, although Hamilton was sporting multiple bandages following a crash on the previous day's dangerous descent of the Col de Montgenèvre.

As the road steepened Banesto's Manuel Beltran launched himself off the front of the group in an attempt to test Armstrong. Like the day before, Armstrong didn't panic, in fact he didn't even react. The Casino team's Benoît Salmon and Kelme's Alberto Contreras tried to bridge to Beltran. Then Escartin attacked to join his team-mate Contreras. Hamilton could finally do no more and signalled to his team leader that he was now on his own. Then Mapei's Pavel Tonkov attacked, but still Armstrong just watched.

Finally the yellow jersey was spurred into action. Legs windmilling, he picked up his rivals one by one. Soon it became a game of cat and mouse. Tonkov attacked again, then Zülle, then Armstrong reacted. The group reformed, and it was a powerful collection of riders – Escartin, Contreras, Beltran, Zülle, Tonkov, Virenque, Telekom's Giuseppe Guerini and Armstrong - all there together.

With just over four kilometres to go, and with Heulot still leading the stage but now by just 15 seconds from the group of favourites, Telekom's Guerini made an inspired bid to free himself of the frontrunners. He soon passed Heulot and assumed the stage lead, while Tonkov tried to react but could not make it stick. Armstrong didn't look quite as impassive as he had on the previous day's stage, with noticeable beads of sweat forming on his brow. Perhaps sensing the yellow jersey's discomfort, Tonkov took off again.

With just a kilometre to go, Guerini was flying with a 20-second gap to Tonkov. He looked destined for a glorious stage victory, when disaster struck. A spectator trying to get an action shot from the middle of the road didn't get out of the way in time, and the two collided. Guerini tumbled to the ground. He was helped back aboard and, adrenalin coursing through his veins, he sprinted away. Guerini had lost time but the crash had left him reinvigorated. With his mouth open he powered on, maintaining his gap and even had the time to savour his moment of glory. Tonkov crossed the line in second place, 21 seconds down, while Escartin, Zülle and Armstrong finished four seconds after that.

"Today I didn't need to attack, I didn't need to win. All I needed was to keep my rivals in check and be steady," Armstrong said after the stage. Overall it left Armstrong with a gap of 7-42 to Olano in second place, while Zülle had battled up to third place overall, 7-47 behind. Escartin, who was becoming quite a challenger in the mountains, was up to fifth at 8-53.

The next five days would see four transition stages taking the Tour from the Alps to the Pyrenees, and end with a rest day in the shadow of the hills before the race entered its second mountain range. Each day saw the US Postal team patrolling the front of the peloton, letting a break of its choosing get a gap, and then leaving it up to the Spanish squads, ONCE and Kelme, who were vying for the teams competition prize, to chase the escapees down. Despite the fact that the US Postal boys had never been in this position before, they controlled the peloton like masters.

"We had guys that were relatively inexperienced but they really did a very good job riding for Lance and a lot of that was down to Johan," Gorski says. "The dynamics of protecting a team leader – whether it be at a one-day race, or small stage race, or even the Tour de France – don't really change but at the Tour you've got a lot more big teams to contend with, the pressures are much more significant, and the stage is greater and more difficult. I think our guys knew what to do but had probably never been in the position to protect a leader before. Now they were faced with supporting someone through the last two weeks of the race, which was a pretty daunting task."

For the overall leaders nothing changed, except for a moment of lapsed concentration for Olano on the uphill finish to stage 12, when he lost two more seconds to Armstrong and Zülle. That meant that the overall placings had Armstrong still in yellow, Olano second 7-44 down, and Zülle in third – now just three seconds behind Olano – at 7-47.

But something crucial had changed in the race, and that was the atmosphere around Armstrong. The media, and French newspapers especially, were becoming more vocal about how they believed Armstrong was taking performance-enhancing substances. They simply could not understand how a man who had been so close to death just two years earlier could be winning the most gruelling sporting event on the planet. Armstrong was furious and refused to speak to the press. Instead, the US Postal team announced they would be holding a press conference on Monday's rest day, in Saint Gaudens.

"I can emphatically say that I am not on drugs," Armstrong told the media. "I thought a rider with my history and my health situation, and also the previous results of my career, I would have thought it shouldn't have been such a surprise that I am leading the Tour. OK, I was surprised to have certain good days, but I'm not a new rider. I know there has been some looking and prying and digging, but it's been a week and nothing has been found. You're not going to find anything. There's nothing to find."

With the press conference doing little to clear the air, but at least allowing Armstrong to assert his innocence, the racing was back under way on stage 15 to Piau Engaly. This was seen as the most special stage of the race – the 'Queen' stage – because it took in some of the most famous and fearsome climbs in Tour history: the Col de Menté, the Col de Portillon, the Col de Peyresourde, the Col de Val Louron Azet, and ended on the road up to Piau Engaly, a new finish town for the Tour.

From the start the Spanish riders attacked and Escartin and Saeco's Laurent Dufaux managed to join an earlier break of ONCE's Andrea Peron and Telekom's Alberto Elli, which was up the road from a group including Armstrong and Zülle. Sensing he had let Escartin get away, Armstrong increased his pace on the climb of the Col de Louron Azet, with Zülle trying to stick to his rear wheel. As had become the norm at this Tour, the Swiss star yo-yoed off the back, then returned to the front, but on the climb of the Col de Louron Azet Armstrong wanted somebody to work with, so he ended up waiting for Zülle at certain points. By the summit Escartin had a lead of 2-53 over the yellow jersey.

The descent into Saint Lary Soulon saw a regrouping among the chasing favourites, while Escartin ploughed on ahead, now alone. At the base of the climb to Piau Engaly Zülle came to the front to set the tempo, but it wasn't for long. Still anxious not to give Escartin too much time Armstrong upped his cadence and dropped Zülle and the rest. The Texan, looking in complete control, quickly picked up Dufaux and seemed to take a breather, allowing Zülle – showing yet another display of pure bravery in a race that he graced with sometimes hardly believable fortitude – and Virenque to climb back up to him. They all worked together to try to bring down Escartin's advantage but, racing on roads close to his home nation of Spain, the Kelme leader was flying to the stage victory.

Into the final kilometre and Virenque decided to attack, with Zülle following. They managed to get a small gap on Armstrong, but he still had them well in sight. Escartin took the line 2-01 ahead of Virenque and Zülle, with Armstrong another nine seconds further back. Overall Armstrong had a reduced lead of 6-19 over Escartin, who had moved up into second place overall, with Zülle in third at 7-26.

Although the outcome was no disaster, it was the first small sign of weakness on Armstrong's part in the whole Tour. Speaking to reporters at the finish he laid some of the blame on his tactics at the start of the final climb: "I paid for my aggression at the bottom of the climb. The others didn't look so good and Johan Bruyneel told me to attack and ride my own race. But I paid at the end."

Despite that, Gorski says the situation was well in hand at US Postal: "Fernando Escartin was a great climber but he was a very poor time triallist. If it had been Zülle or someone that could also deliver a stronger time trial at Futuroscope there may have been a perception of danger. But at that point I don't think that there was serious concern. Obviously there is concern all the way to the Champs-Elysées. It's not over until it's over and you can't allow yourself to relax until you reach the finish line. But confidence was high and Lance was feeling good."

The final chance – and by now it really was only a slim chance – for any of the other Tour riders to mount a challenge on Armstrong would come on the last of the big Tour mountains on stage 16. The route took in some more famous Tour climbs – the Col d'Aspin, the Col du Tourmalet and the Col d'Aubisque – although it was hard to see the peaks in all their glory as a heavy blanket of low-lying cloud had enveloped the Pyrenees.

The riders set off in sunny, warm conditions, but by the time the race reached the Col du Tourmalet a break had already been established featuring Alberto Elli, ONCE's David Etxebarria and Pavel Tonkov. Kevin Livingstone, again taking on the role of Armstrong's chief pace-setter, led the chasing group on the climb, but the trio at the head of the race stayed in front over the summit. Their lead even grew on the descent as groups behind reformed, and on the next climb, the Col du Soulor, Armstrong switched his concentration to preventing Escartin and Zülle getting even a sniff of a gap. Through thick mist the descent of the Soulor was hair-raising, but the favourites managed to survive it intact, and Escartin took over pace-setting duties for the Armstrong group on the final 'real' climb of the Tour, the Col d'Aubisque.

The three leaders – Elli, Etxebarria and Tonkov – who had maintained a gap of over two minutes on the climb finally succumbed to the small group of overall leaders on the descent and 12 riders – including Armstrong, Zülle and Escartin – entered the outskirts of Pau together. With the three main yellow jersey combatants all marking one another it allowed others in the group to go for the stage victory. Etxebarria won the day from five other riders, while Armstrong, Escartin and Zülle rolled in as part of another pack of six riders 21 seconds behind.

Overall nothing had changed, except Armstrong was one day, and the last of the big climbs, closer to taking victory in Paris.

At the end of the stage the doping question hanging over Armstrong would still not go away and the Texan spent two hours talking to the media. Specifically, Armstrong had been found to have the substance triamcinolone, a corticosteroid, in his body. This substance, although on the banned list, was found in an ointment called Cemalyt, which had been used by Armstrong to treat saddle sores. To clarify the matter US Postal's management asked the UCI to publicly release confidential details about the dope tests Armstrong had undertaken while at the race. The UCI issued a statement confirming that all of Armstrong's tests had produced negative results and stated that the use of Cemalyt was permissible.

Gorski remembers the situation well. "Lance always took on the media head-on. I remember he used a cream for saddle sores and it had cortisone in it, and I remember being with Johan in the middle of the night trying to sort this out with the UCI and having to present the doctor's prescription for it – all the stuff you have to go through to live within the extensive drug testing rules that cycling has. There definitely was some stress around it – I remember that clearly.

"We were in Pau and I remember the press conference on the rest day there. Lance really dealt with the press personally and head on, but he wasn't a spinmeister, he didn't have a team of PR people around him to answer the tough questions for him."

Despite Armstrong's best efforts, some parts of the press are still convinced that Armstrong cheated during his first Tour victory. But it's worth remembering the 1999 Tour de France could not have started with a more anti-doping sentiment and the race organisers were absolutely determined, perhaps more than at any other point in the race's history, to stamp out drugs. All 180 riders who took the start line of the prologue had to undergo a dope test to check that they weren't cheating. However, the samples Armstrong gave at the 1999 Tour would come back to haunt him six years later when L'Equipe newspaper claimed a retest of Armstrong's blood contained traces of the banned blood-booster, EPO. So Armstrong, just two weeks into his first Tour de France victory bid, was already under suspicion for doping.

With at least the challenge of the Tour mountains completed, if not the quest to prove his innocence, Armstrong had a reasonably clear run-in to Paris and the final yellow jersey. The only arena where he might face some opposition was the stage 19 individual time trial based in Futuroscope, but Armstrong had already proven that he had little to fear in races against the clock. Before reaching Futuroscope, though, the race spent a couple of days travelling up the west coast of France on stages 17 and 18, which saw no changes to the overall rankings.

And so to stage 19, the final individual time trial of the 1999 Tour. For Armstrong it wasn't quite a formality, but being more than six minutes ahead of his nearest rival meant his overall lead was all but assured. More relevant was the battle between Escartin in second at 6-19, and Zülle in third, 1-13 further back. Escartin wasn't a noted time triallist and Zülle would be itching to claim the runner-up position on the Paris podium.

Interestingly enough it was Armstrong's team-mate Tyler Hamilton who set the time to beat, covering the 57 kilometres around the Futuroscope theme park in 1-09-51. It was a figure that was still standing at the top of the timing sheets even as Armstrong rolled down the start ramp. But Armstrong was quickly up to speed, his legs spinning at a rapid cadence, and at each time-check along the course he was registering the fastest result. Zülle, who had begun six minutes ahead of him, was also going well and was only slightly down on Armstrong's times, but Escartin, who had started three minutes in front of the race leader, was caught and passed by Armstrong at the 20-kilometres-to-go point. Escartin, a weak rider against the clock, tried to hang on to Armstrong's shadow but it was in vain.

Zülle crossed the line in 1-08-26, taking the top spot from Hamilton. Meanwhile Armstrong was beginning to tire but he still managed to beat Zülle's marker, just, by nine seconds, with a time of 1-08-17.

"I remember even Johan encouraging Lance to be careful and use some caution," Gorski says. "Near the end there were a couple of fairly technical tight corners and Lance just blasted through them. With Lance there is always a sense – and certainly there was at that point in his career – of him wanting to prove something, and the way he won that final time trial was further evidence of that. I think it was all just consistent with Lance and his personality and his approach.

"In hindsight, after a few years of reflecting on it, I think that was such an enormous statement to the rest of the peloton. In a way he put the rest of the peloton back on their heels to such an extent that he completely psyched them out, he was so aggressive. And I think there was a reluctance for a long time, maybe until Jan Ullrich really battled Lance in 2003, to take on Lance head-on, to truly challenge him."

That result not only cemented Armstrong's aura as an aggressive winner but it also put him among a select band of Tour de France legends – alongside Eddy Merckx, Bernard Hinault and Miguel Indurain – as the only men to have won all three of the Tour's individual time trials in a single edition of the race. More immediately for Armstrong, it also meant that barring accident, the overall victory was his. He led by 7-37 to Zülle, who was now securely in second place, and 10-26 to Escartin, whose time trial had dropped him down to third. All Armstrong had to do was roll into Paris and up the Champs-Elysées.

And the final stage did pass easily enough with Australian fastman Robbie McEwen taking the sprint win on the Champs-Elysées. But one man – the man in yellow – and his blue US Postal stormtroopers, were probably celebrating the most.

"I think even in those last few days, Lance didn't want anyone to really talk about final victory," Gorski remembers. "It was almost like you didn't want to jinx it by talking about it. He didn't want to hear anything about yellow hats or socks or handlebar tape, anything that was planning for victory. So I think there was an enormous sense of relief and then 'OK we're there, it's actually happened.' But even on those final laps around the Champs-Elysées I remember not really being comfortable until he crossed the line. Then when it was finished there was just a flood of emotion. There was a sense of accomplishment and this historical event that we had embarked upon and were part of overwhelmed everyone I think.

"That night we did the first of many dinners and celebration events in the private ballroom in the Musée d'Orsay, which was a very special event and became one that we did regularly in later Tours. But to me, I just don't know how any of the later victories could stand up against the 1999 Tour for emotion and the newness of it, and I guess the profound nature of the accomplishment.

"From my perspective, being so close to the action that year, it was special because we weren't the New York Yankees yet, we were a smaller operation, with a smaller budget. We didn't have the luxurious amenities that the bigger teams did at that point. There was almost a Cinderella element to it all in that first year. It was never a Cinderella story again. It was more expected from then on."

Still, the question about whether Armstrong was doping or not lingered, and if Zülle hadn't lost six minutes on stage two we might have seen a very different race. And of course there was no Ullrich or Pantani.

"I'm sure in the minds of some of the media having no Ullrich or Pantani took the gloss off of Lance's win," Gorski says. "The fashion in which Pantani won the Tour in 1998 – he just danced up the mountains – was phenomenal, although in hindsight we can only speculate as to how and why he was doing that. So you could certainly have suggested during the 1999 Tour that if Pantani was there he would have left Lance two or three minutes behind on a couple of the key mountains stages and it would have been a totally different race. I definitely heard that argument from the media, but if key riders thought that, nobody was saying it.

"That wasn't something anyone wanted to say to Lance Armstrong, who was dominating the Tour, and looked like he might dominate it for some time to come. Nobody wanted to piss him off."

The Festina Affair

With Luke Edwardes-Evans, editor of *Cycle Sport* magazine 1998-2002

By August 1999 Lance Armstrong was known by the world at large as the miracle man who had beaten cancer and gone on to win the Tour de France, but among the cycling media he wasn't seen in quite the same light. During the course of the 1999 Tour Armstrong was the subject of more press suspicion and treated with less respect than any other previous potential yellow jersey. The reason why he was under the microscope to such an extent lay not with Armstrong himself – although to win the Tour de France just two years after being gravely ill certainly caused suspicion among cynical reporters – but was rather the result of what had happened at the Tour the year before.

On July 8th 1998 the Tour de France and the world of professional cycle racing changed forever. Three days before the Grand Départ in Ireland, the world's biggest team, Festina, found itself embroiled in the darkest scandal ever to hit cycling. Willy Voet, a Festina soigneur, had been stopped by customs officials in northern France en route to Dublin and was found to have 400 bottles and capsules of doping products in his team car. Festina wasn't just the world's biggest team; despite its Swiss sponsor it was also seen as France's biggest team too. In its ranks were French heroes Richard Virenque, at that point a four-time Tour de France King of the Mountains; Laurent Brochard, reigning world road champion in 1998; and young French prospects Pascal Hervé, Christophe Moreau and Didier Rous. They represented the best French cycling had to offer, but the revelation that they had cheated woke French cycling to its problems.

Voet's arrest would go on to overshadow that year's Tour de France and, in its own way, the ensuing career of Lance Armstrong. For Luke Edwardes-Evans, who was editor of *Cycle Sport* magazine at the time, the first rumblings of scandal gave little indication of the size of the controversy to follow.

"I went over and stayed in Dublin because there was a big pre-Tour dinner; a huge thing with Tour director Jean-Marie Leblanc and all the officials, famous people, and mayors and governors I suppose," Edwardes-Evans says. "There was no inkling at that point that Willy Voet had been arrested, nobody knew a thing about it. I think it was on the night of the prologue or maybe the day after that when the news really started coming out. I think the Irish hosts were a bit upset that a scandal had hit and taken the gloss off their moment, but it wasn't really until the race got back over to France that the whole thing blew up."

And blow up it did. A week later Festina's team boss, Bruno Roussel, and the squad's doctor, Eric Rijckaert, confessed all. The Tour organisers took immediate action and banished the squad from the race. A week after that, on July 23rd, nine Festina riders were held at Lyon police headquarters where they were given medical exams. All but two – Virenque and Hervé – admitted to taking drugs. Later, the results of these medical examinations showed that eight of the nine Festina cyclists, including Virenque, had used EPO and four had used amphetamines. Over the following days and weeks the true extent of the doping problem in top-level cycling became clear, and it was shocking.

"I think I was shocked by the scandal because of the level of it, by how embedded it was and by the fact it involved the whole culture of cycling," Edwardes-Evans says.

"Everybody knew that riders doped, and we knew a little about EPO, but nobody knew the extent to which it was endemic and institutionalised in the sport. That was really what the Festina scandal was about. It was about a systemic programme of doping, organised and instituted by the teams. It later transpired that the Festina manager, Bruno Roussel, was doing it in some ways to protect the riders from themselves. But what was shocking was that it was set up like the holiday payment scheme for employees in a normal company. The riders would put money in from out of their salary, but it didn't go towards a weekend in Blackpool, it went towards a doping programme run by the team."

Although many people had heard of EPO, the Festina affair was the first real public appearance of the drug in the pro peloton. EPO, or exogenous erythropoietin to give it its full name, was designed to treat anaemia caused by chronic kidney disease, cancer and other critical illnesses, but in cyclists' hands it could be used to boost red blood cell count, or haematocrit level, to make the blood more efficient at delivering oxygen to muscles. The drawback to its use by sportsmen is that if taken unchecked the blood can get so thick it stops the heart from pumping. It is now believed that EPO has been in wide use among the pro peloton since the early 1990s, but an effective test for the drug did not appear until the Sydney Olympics in 2000.

"The Festina affair was the great EPO scandal," Edwardes-Evans says. "We did know about some of these things to do with EPO, like the deaths of Dutch riders in the early 1990s, and everybody knew that cyclists took loads of dodgy substances, from steroids to amphetamines, to help them win or even just finish races. But the thing about EPO was that it is like a designer drug for cyclists. It appeared to be almost this perfect liquid that you could inject that would turn you into a cyclist that had come straight off Mount Olympus.

"And because it wasn't like steroids that gave you spots and a big chin and huge muscles, it seemed almost like a pure cycling drug. That made it a double-edged sword because it wasn't a dirty-sounding drug, and yet it instantly made everyone ride another level higher. The riders just got thinner and faster the whole time. I think they realised that as long as their aerobic capacity was high all they had to do was increase their power-to-weight ratio and they would fly up the climbs – that's how you saw these big guys just flying up the climbs at the time. EPO was like the wonder drug and that was scary."

The difference between the old, slightly haphazard approach to drug use, and this new ultra-modern, hi-tech system of doping was one of the things that most shocked veteran cycling fans.

"We knew people took drugs before but there was always something slightly crazed about it, that it wouldn't always work and cyclists were slightly mad, and doping tied in with that kind of bandit image, which is appealing for some," Edwardes-Evans says. "So a rider might take some amphetamines or something, and they might get round the final bend or they might just crash on through a plate-glass window on the other side. But EPO was pure science that could create a perfect cyclist, and riders didn't need to take anything else.

"Once you realised that EPO use was institutionalised and the riders could take it, and they had doctors on the team to keep them hydrated through the night to stop their blood getting too thick and giving them a heart attack, then it was pretty frightening. It was frightening because you had to think: well why would they want to stop this? This is something that makes you 25 per cent better and it doesn't seem to have any side-effects. And even now you don't hear of people keeling over because they have taken EPO."

The Tour organisers were among those most shocked by the magnitude of the scandal and acted instantly to defend the integrity of their race. Not only did they expel Festina but they increased drugs tests. Then the French police stepped up its attempts to investigate doping among cycling teams, and even raided other squads' hotels on the 1998 Tour. That resulted in more Tour squads going home during the 1998 race, with the TVM and ONCE teams angrily deciding to leave early.

After the Tour, the French state also acted decisively in the field of sports legislation – making it the case that if teams were found to have been involved with doping they would now be breaking a law in France. But while this was all good in the quest for clean racing, it also meant that all eyes would be on the Tour in 1999, and especially on its eventual winner.

"The Festina affair definitely affected France a lot more than anywhere else," Edwardes-Evans says. "After the Festina affair the French looked into using civil law to prosecute people who were using doping products illegally, and I definitely started to think that this was the only way you were going to be able to scare people enough into not doping. It had got to a stage beyond just some riders taking some dope to finish a race, it had become a large organised business. There were obviously people making a lot of money selling these products into cycling. It had become part of the infrastructure of the sport, and the only way to deal with that was to introduce civil law and the police into it.

"Cycling has always existed in its own little bubble, even more than most other sports, it has been an enclosed world. So you needed to get these guys to understand that what they were doing wasn't acceptable to the general public, and the only way to do that was to get the police bashing down their doors.

"But whoever won the Tour the year after the Festina affair was going to come under the spotlight from the French press, which is what would happen to Armstrong when he won in 1999. Armstrong was always going to be scrutinised and questioned about his performances by the French press because of what happened in 1998.

"He was a perfect target for the French, particularly because of France's antagonistic attitude to America. There were also commercial issues at work with the French press's approach to Armstrong. It wasn't that attacking him would sell more copies of their papers or magazines, but it certainly wasn't going to make them sell fewer. However, if a magazine like *L'Equipe* attacked French riders it did lead to fewer copies being sold. So Armstrong was an easy target really, and he was a gift to *L'Equipe* when they wanted to run anti-doping stories."

In fairness to the French cycling community, it wasn't all about finding a new non-French target. The steps they took, and the attitude many people involved with French cycling adopted, was fully committed to dope-free sport.

"I think it is largely right to say that France did take a massive step towards having clean cycling in the wake of the Festina affair," Edwardes-Evans agrees. "It was a big wake-up call for France and the Tour de France. It was cultural as well as commercial. Even teams who were old-fashioned – old-school teams with old-school directeurs – somehow they changed the way they behaved. Obviously some didn't, like the Cofidis team [who would be the subject of another major, although not institutionalised, doping scandal in 2004], but France did change, and in fact even Italy got quite serious in the wake of the Festina affair."

The fans may have been shocked and the riders might have had lots of beady eyes now trained on them, but perhaps the people most affected by the Festina scandal weren't the cyclists, or the spectators, but the dedicated cycling reporters. These were people who spent their whole lives following professional cycling but who had, en masse, managed to completely miss what was happening under their noses in their specialist sport.

"I think the biggest fallout from Festina wasn't just that there were drugs in sport and it went so deep, but that so many journalists and reporters who had followed this sport for so many years had been duped by the riders," Edwardes-Evans says.

"There was a reaction among cycling reporters that they had been caught out big time. I think that a lot of journalists may have known doping in the sport was bad, but even they couldn't imagine it was as bad as it was, and they were sort of embarrassed that they hadn't blown the whistle in a bigger way. I think from then right up to the present day there is that feeling among cycling journalists, that they are no longer going to be taken for a ride." Which may go some way to explaining the press and Armstrong's fractious relationship.

But for everybody connected with professional cycling there was a huge feeling of relief when the 1998 Tour circus finally finished its three-week trot around France and the eyes of the world could move on to another sporting event.

"Personally I was relieved when the 1998 Tour came to an end," Edwardes-Evans says. "It was stressful, it wasn't fun being into cycling. It was hard for everyone involved with the business and there were a lot of people who wanted to talk to us and do interviews, and the race itself was a mess with riders protesting and leaving the race. You almost wanted to get back to the quiet time, or anything other than the Tour de France.

"Looking back I suppose it was quite ironic that Marco Pantani won the 1998 Tour. There was an amazing stage where he attacked Jan Ullrich, it was one of the best stages I have ever seen. It was just amazingly dramatic, and yet what fools we were to watch that and hope that it was genuine. Knowing what we know about Pantani now, it can't have been."

Although the saviour of the Tour in 1998, Pantani was thrown out of the Giro d'Italia in 1999 for failing a blood test and would spend most of the rest of his career haunted by the shadow of doping. He died of a cocaine overdose in 2004.

Despite the shockwaves from the Festina affair that reverberate in professional cycle racing even now, Edwardes-Evans remembers things calming down quite soon after the Tour ended, and he believes that, perversely, cycling may have even gained a bigger exposure from the scandal.

"Everything went back to normal pretty quickly," he says. "I don't entirely know how the fans were affected, but I don't think it made a lot of difference. I think fans stuck with the sport. Even after all the doping stories of the last few years, Festina is still the biggest single scandal involving a whole team.

"But in a strange way since 1998 cycling does seem to have become a more global sport. The scandals may have actually brought people into the sport. But if you're going to look at things that way you've got to say that Lance Armstrong has brought a lot more people into the sport through simply being Lance Armstrong, not because of spikes in coverage due to drugs scandals."

2000: No Fluke

With Viatcheslav Ekimov, Armstrong's US Postal/Discovery Channel team-mate
2000-2005

So was Armstrong's 1999 Tour de France victory a fluke, or the start of something amazing? If the previous year's race was slightly light on top favourites, this time around Armstrong would have to defend his title against a couple of truly big threats: Jan Ullrich and Marco Pantani, the 1997 and 1998 yellow jerseys respectively.

For Armstrong himself the intervening year was a succession of new experiences. Whether it was the home-coming parade through Austin, the special appearance on the pitch of a Texas state college American Football match, the chat shows he was a guest on, the products he was now promoting, or the award ceremonies at which he was being honoured, Armstrong's story had captured the imagination of the United States public and he was rapidly becoming an A-list celebrity. October 12th, 1999 also saw him become a father with the birth of his first child, Luke David Armstrong.

In Armstrong's wider family at US Postal, there were also a few changes, but probably the biggest was the introduction of Russian hardman Viatcheslav Ekimov. Ekimov had been one of the first major signings to the fledging US Postal in 1997, but he had missed out on Armstrong's 1999 glory year.

"I was with the US Postal team from the start," Ekimov says. "But I left at the end of 1998 because I couldn't get an agreement with the management. For 1999 I went to an Italian team, Amica Chips. That was quite a good year for me. I took five victories, and I was pretty happy with my physical condition but I was a little upset with the financial situation in that team.

"I remember being at a stage of the Vuelta a Espana in Valencia, 1999, and we were sharing the same hotel as the US Postal team. One evening I sat down at the bar with Johan Bruyneel and Johan said that if I wanted to, I could come back to the team. I said: 'Listen Johan, I was trying all of 1998 to stay in US Postal but I couldn't make it happen.' But then Johan told me that the situation had changed and now it was Lance who organised the team, it was Lance who ruled the team. So I said OK, and the same evening I signed another contract and I was back."

Ekimov noticed plenty of differences when he met the new-look US Postal squad. "We had a training camp in America in the winter time, and when I went there I realised it was a different team already. After Lance's first victory at the Tour de France in 1999 the team was already completely set up as a much bigger concern. The bikes were at the training camp, the clothes were there, the mechanics were there, the soigneurs were there: it was a big, big presentation of the team. The first year I was in US Postal, 1997, we drove everywhere in a really small American truck with an American licence plate and Volkswagen cars. But in 2000 the team was organised in the image of a big European team."

Armstrong's personal preparation for the 2000 Tour was just as meticulous, having competed at the Tour of Valencia, Catalan Week, the Tour of Aragon, Paris-Camembert and the GP Gippingen. Again he rehearsed the Tour's crucial mountain stages, but his training was interrupted by an accident on the descent of the Col du Soulor. Armstrong's tyre blew while riding at full speed. Not wearing his helmet, Armstrong crashed head first into a wall, causing him to be hospitalised overnight and knocking him out of action for some weeks. Still, it meant that when he did return to Tour reconnaissance work he did so with renewed gusto, and was back in fine form for the Grand Départ.

Ekimov had also been looking forward to the start of July. "I knew straight away I would be riding the 2000 Tour de France with the team. For me there were two highlights that season: there were the Classic races in the wintertime, and there was the Tour de France in the summer. My job at the Tour was to protect Lance on the flat stages. George Hincapie and I liked to call ourselves bodyguards, we were always at the side of Lance. If the peloton was on the right side of the road we would be on the left side of the road, just to prevent crashes. In later years we were joined in that role by Pavel Padrnos, so it meant there would be three big guys riding in front of Lance, protecting him."

Despite the presence of Pantani and Ullrich, to the new boy Ekimov, Armstrong exuded enough confidence to look like the runaway race favourite. "I didn't have any doubt that Lance would win in 2000. Right from the start he looked so good. Every day he gave us the feeling that he was going to win this race. The only thing that we, his team, had to do was avoid making mistakes in the early stages until we got to the first big mountain stage."

The 2000 Tour began in familiar surroundings for Armstrong with an individual time trial around Futuroscope, the scene of the previous year's final time trial and where Armstrong had sealed his first overall victory. The opening race against the clock this year wasn't classed as a prologue due to its length – at 16.5 kilometres it was long enough to be called a full time trial. As the reigning Tour champ Armstrong was the last rider to roll down the Futuroscope start ramp. And just as he had caused a big surprise with his comeback ride in the opening time trial in 1999, another rider was causing a shock in 2000. Cofidis's David Millar, a young British rider competing at his first Tour de France, had recorded a staggering time of 19-03, edging out the previous time-sheet-topper, Laurent Jalabert of the ONCE team, by 13 seconds.

Out on the course Telekom's team leader Ullrich, resplendent in the rainbow colours of the world time trial champion, was looking smooth and powerful. Even back in 2000 Ullrich had already developed a reputation for coming into the Tour not quite at peak fitness, but at Futuroscope the German hero looked lean, fit, and meaning business right from the first stage. At the four-kilometre checkpoint Ullrich had recorded the same top time as Jalabert and Millar, and he even managed to catch and pass Mercatone-Uno's Pantani, who had started a full minute ahead of him. But Ullrich couldn't beat Millar's time and he crossed the line at 19-17, putting him third behind Jalabert.

Meanwhile that familiar leg-pumping, high-cadence action of Armstrong was tearing round the course. Just like in 1999 Armstrong looked quick, but there was no cool, calm posturing – his grimaces showed that the American was determined to leave every ounce of power he had out on the course. At the eight-kilometre checkpoint Armstrong was three seconds slower than Millar: it would have to be a sprint to the line. Armstrong's thighs hammered up and down but it wasn't enough. He crossed the line in 19-05, two seconds behind Millar. Jalabert was third at 13 seconds, and Ullrich was fourth at 14 seconds. Pantani recorded a time 2-16 slower than Millar, leaving him in a pretty poor 136th place.

Ekimov finished in an impressive seventh place, but that year's Tour time trials were of particular interest to him. "It was an Olympic year, and I knew that I was going to be in the Olympic team for Russia in Sydney, so the Tour de France had the last real time trials where I could compare my form against the other top riders. Even though I was working for Lance over those three weeks, on the mountain stages I was just keeping a little in reserve, just so I could save my legs for the second time trial as well," Ekimov says.

Stages two and three were flat affairs but stage four in Nantes saw the Tour organisers reintroduce the team time trial, having stopped the discipline after the 1995 Tour de France. The team time trial is a specialised event where each squad takes to the course independently, and a good performance here can result in massive time gains over rival squads. Because the 1999 Tour had been run without the event it meant that this was the first opportunity for the new, improved, Armstrong-led US Postal to cement its place among the other top-level teams in the purest test of squad strength.

Of the main overall contenders it was the white and pink Telekom team of Jan Ullrich that registered a time first, clocking 1-27-01 as they powered their way, teeth gritted, to the finish line in Saint Nazaire. Out on the road the ONCE riders were storming round the course, all nine team members still together, and looking in perfect control. They smashed Telekom's time with a 1-25-35, putting them securely at the top of the time sheet.

As the squad leading the team classification before the stage, US Postal were the last to depart, but the strength with which they had ruled the race in 1999 seemed to be disappearing. They started quickly enough but as they reached further into the stage the organisation began to fracture. A team's time is only registered when its fifth member rides over the finish line, but by the time US Postal crossed the mammoth Pont de Saint Nazaire bridge, 59 kilometres into the stage, they had dropped some of their number and were down to a dangerously low six riders.

Ekimov remembers the situation well: "The team time trial was a real fast race, there was a tailwind the whole way and it was pretty straight. Lance was accelerating so much and the team was very nervous, so we couldn't find a good rhythm or a good steady pace. We just kept going faster and faster and faster, then the weakest guys started cracking and sitting on the wheel of the others. Then guys like me had to take more turns at the front, more pulls, and longer pulls, and then we started cracking as well. Then finally we couldn't do much, and we realised there were only six of us still alive on that bridge. It was just a terrible day for us.

"Later on I came up with the idea that we should have longer pulls. Instead of going to the front then the next rider coming around straightaway, each rider should pull at the front for 200 or 300 metres. That way the guys who aren't pulling can save a little energy and then they can pull faster or longer when they do come to the front, and we wouldn't lose so many riders over the distance. Lance had a little bit of doubt about my idea and Johan had a little doubt, they said it wouldn't be as fast. I agreed it wouldn't be as fast but I said it would be more steady and more economical, and we would save losing so many team members over the stage distance. I learnt this technique from racing on the track – I was in the Russian pursuit team that won gold at the 1988 Olympics. So the first time US Postal used my tactics, we won the team time trial stage by over a minute. Then the following year the rest of the peloton started using long pulls."

In the end, despite looking ragged on the road US Postal rallied on the final stretch and clocked 1-26-21, 40 seconds quicker than Telekom, but 46 seconds slower than ONCE. That deficit to ONCE was reduced to 26 seconds when the Spanish squad was given a time penalty for sheltering one of its riders on the Pont de Saint Nazaire. Overall it meant Laurent Jalabert was in yellow, his team-mate David Cañada was second at 12 seconds, and Armstrong was in third at 24 seconds. Ullrich was down to 12th at 1-07 and Pantani, whose Mercatone-Uno team had finished the stage in a respectable ninth place, was up to 79th overall at 5-26.

The following few stages of the 2000 Tour de France would take the race south towards the Pyrenees. Stage five saw little change to the overall standings although a 12-man break on stage six succeeded in claiming a 7-49 advantage on the main field by the finish. Telekom's Alberto Elli took over the yellow jersey and the other top places overall were filled by his fellow escapees. Stages seven, eight and nine saw only a little movement on the overall rankings with the pre-race favourites slipping down the order but the relative time differences between them remaining unchanged.

The skies over the town of Dax looked ominous for the riders taking the start line of stage 10 for the 2000 Tour's first foray into the mountains, a 205-kilometre trek to Lourdes Hautacam. The grey clouds delivered drops of heavy rain, while further out on the course, on the high peaks, there were reports of snow and fierce winds. For Armstrong, a man who privately revelled in the worst conditions – and who won his 1993 world title in nothing short of a monsoon in Norway – this was manna from heaven. But ahead of him and his rivals were four of the Pyrenees' toughest climbs: the Col de Marie Blanque, the Col d'Aubisque, the Col de Soulor and the summit finish at Hautacam.

From the start of the day Armstrong looked strong. Ekimov remembers: "That first day in the mountains, to Hautacam, it was a rainy day, a cold day, and it had an uphill finish. But Lance just did it, easily. I had been riding at the front of the peloton and then we reached the Pyrenees where there was a short climb, but it was quite steep. I felt completely flat, in fact I was more than flat, and I was dropping like a stone from the front group, which was then down to about 25 or 30 riders.

"At that moment I remember hearing Lance say to me: 'OK, everything is fine – I'll see you at the finish.' I couldn't believe what I heard. I wished I could have been in his shoes that day because I had no power left and he was just starting to race. In my head I was so proud to have this guy in the team. I came up the Hautacam half an hour after being dropped, but I knew the result already because Lance had looked so good earlier."

It was on the climb of the Col d'Aubisque that the first action among the leaders took place. The US Postal squad took to the front and raised the pace for Armstrong, but rather than put the other favourites in trouble the tactic rather backfired and left Armstrong without any team-mates in a group of 22 race favourites, including Ullrich, Pantani and last year's runner-up, Alex Zülle of Banesto. Ahead on the road was another small, dangerous group of seven top climbers that included Polti's Richard Virenque. And at the front of the race, having escaped with Lotto's Jacky Durand back near the start of the stage, was Kelme's Javier Otxoa.

By the summit of the Col d'Aubisque Otxoa had a lead of 10 and a half minutes on the Virenque group and almost 12 minutes on Armstrong and companions, but it wasn't until the start of the final climb, the Hautacam, that the favourites really started testing each other. Pantani took to the front and raised the pace, then dropped back a little. Then suddenly the little Italian exploded off the front of the group. Without missing a beat Zülle chased and was quickly onto Pantani's wheel, and just behind Zülle came Armstrong. Ullrich, meanwhile, seemed to have missed the move. The trio of Pantani, Zülle and Armstrong regrouped, then Zülle dropped back and Armstrong turned on the power. Pantani desperately tried to follow but he couldn't. Armstrong spun his small gear and simply sprinted away up the hill.

Within minutes Armstrong had latched on to the back of the Virenque group. His face a mask of concentration and determination, Armstrong then tore through the pack to take up pace-making duties at the front. He lifted the tempo a little higher still, causing Virenque and the others to shatter and fall away. Only Banesto's Jose-Maria Jimenez was able to hang on to the rear wheel of Armstrong, who was now scything through the heavy rain and catching Otxoa at an alarming rate. The stage leader just had three kilometres to go, and Armstrong was over four minutes behind, but Otxoa was struggling just to turn the pedals. In contrast, Armstrong calmly had his eyes fixed on the road ahead. Under the final kilometre banner Otxoa was almost home and not very dry, and with a gap of a minute and a half to Armstrong, all he had to do was keep turning those pedals. He did, to take a glorious stage victory. Armstrong sprinted across the line 42 seconds later.

If the day was one for Otxoa, then the Tour was looking like another one for Armstrong. His rivals crossed the finish line in dribs and drabs. Zülle came in 10th, 3-05 behind Armstrong; Ullrich came in 13th, 3-19 behind Armstrong; and Pantani, the man who had started the attacks on the Hautacam, finished 21st, 5-10 behind Armstrong. Overall, Armstrong took the yellow jersey and his hold on it was already looking firm. Ullrich was in second place 4-14 down, and Festina's Christophe Moreau was in third at 5-10. Zülle was 13th at 7-22 and Pantani 25th at 10-34.

Making his mark on the first day in the mountains was something Armstrong did in his first Tour victory in 1999, and it was something that would become his trademark in the Tours to come. For now, though, he was just pleased to have gained an advantage on the other favourites. "I had no desire to win the stage, my ambition was solely to put time on my rivals," Armstrong said afterwards.

Stage 11 saw no real action among the big names, then the riders had the Tour's first rest day.

The great challenge of stage 12 was clear, and it could clearly be seen on the horizon from the start – the final climb up the Giant of Provence, Mont Ventoux. This fearsome, brutal hill – so big it acts as a waymarker for aircraft flying over the region – is made up of two distinct sections. The first, the base, is a lush green forest. The second, the route to the summit, is a barren, pale, entirely treeless moonscape. Earlier in the year, at the Dauphiné Libéré race – traditionally used by the stars as a final warm-up event for the Tour – the hill had not been particularly welcoming to Lance Armstrong, and it was the Texan's US Postal team-mate Tyler Hamilton who had reigned supreme.

Despite the horror of the scenery they were heading towards, the day started out bright and sunny for the riders, although the biting cold and fierce wind kept spirits from lifting too high. As expected, it was the tree-lined early slopes of the Ventoux that saw the first attempt to separate the frontmen. Hamilton and Armstrong's other faithful mountain lieutenant Kevin Livingston took their places at the front of the leaders' group and set such a strong tempo that riders like Kelme's Fernando Escartin and Zülle began to drop away. Even the world's greatest climber, Pantani, was obviously suffering.

At the front Ullrich, looking fit and strong, rode in Armstrong's wheel tracks, followed by Virenque, Roberto Heras of Kelme and Festina's Joseba Beloki. Pantani and Jalabert began to yo-yo off the rear, then slowly claw their way back to the Armstrong group, while the early stage leader, Kelme's Santiago Botero, was caught and swallowed up by Armstrong and company. Livingston was setting a pace that would push Armstrong's rivals to breaking point, but suddenly Heras had other ideas and attacked. Armstrong responded and followed, causing another selection among the favourites.

As the leaders entered the bleached boulders of the Ventoux's second phase, with just over six kilometres to race, an elite front group of cycling's stars had formed, with Pantani hanging onto the back. Three kilometres later Virenque was setting the pace but as the Frenchman accepted a drink from the roadside, Pantani, who had seemed barely able to keep up, launched a powerful attack. Heras jumped on his wheel and the pack regrouped briefly before Pantani set off again, this time sprinting out of the saddle harder and for longer. Heras and Ullrich took up the role of pacing the group back to Pantani, but the Italian went away again, this time getting a gap and making it stick.

Armstrong, who had been speaking on his radio back to Bruyneel in the team car, decided it was time to up the cadence. He jumped out of the saddle and spun away from his rivals. Soon he was alongside Pantani, seemingly asking the Italian to join him. Initially Pantani dangled just a little too far behind Armstrong, but then managed to match his rhythm and drew parallel. With two kilometres left to race it appeared that the stage win would come down to a straight sprint between these two, matching each other pedal stroke for pedal stroke, grimace for grimace, side by side. As the line drew near Armstrong backed off and let Pantani take the win. That gesture would have unexpected ramifications in the days to come.

In third, 25 seconds behind, was Beloki, while Ullrich trundled his trademark big gear into fourth place at a loss of 29 seconds. Overall Armstrong now led Ullrich by 4-55 while Beloki had moved up into third place at 5-52. Pantani was 12th at 10-26.

Ekimov explains the rationale behind Armstrong's final decision that day: "Sometimes these situations happen. Sometimes to find a friend in the peloton you should give a stage away, instead of taking the stage and making more enemies. Pantani was on a really good day that day. He probably didn't like to win a stage that somebody gave him, but he always respected any agreement between riders and he was a man of his word. I don't know the exact details of what happened on the Ventoux, but I know in cycling history these situations happen."

Stage 13 happened to fall on July 14th, Bastille Day, so the French riders were itching for the honours even more than normal. Unfortunately Spaniard Vicente Garcia Acosta of the Banesto team broke home hearts by beating two French break colleagues. The overall favourites all rolled in together, 10 minutes back.

The 2000 Tour's three days in the Alps began in pretty imposing style on stage 14. The wind was blowing, the temperatures were low, and the peloton had to face three almighty climbs: the first-category Col d'Aloss and Col de Var and then, after 200 kilometres, the mighty hors catégorie Col d'Izoard. Then they had to descend before the uphill finish at Briançon.

When racing got under way in many respects it seemed little had changed since the riders left the Pyrenees – Hamilton and Livingston were setting the pace at the front of the field and Pantani was attacking. The Italian – known as the 'Pirate' because of his fondness for wearing bandanas and his swashbuckling approach to cycling in the hills – was in particularly boisterous spirits because the roads they were about to cover were the scenes of his great comeback ride earlier in the year at the Giro d'Italia. Now, with the Tour de France skirting the border with Italy, Pantani wanted to show the world what he could still do. But before his legs could do the talking on the hills, it seemed as if his mouth had done some talking to Italian journalists, and it was reported that he was unhappy with the way Armstrong had 'gifted' him the win on the Ventoux. It looked like the beginning of a classic feud.

As the leaders started the climb of the Col d'Izoard the stage was being led by Santiago Botero, who had been part of an earlier break, the remnants of which were still scattered along the course ahead of the yellow jersey group. Pantani went to the front of the group of favourites and put in a hard effort, causing Ullrich, Virenque and Moreau to fall away. Together – again – Pantani and Armstrong worked onwards, picking up early escapee Robert Conti of Vini Caldirola. Armstrong raised the tempo again, his Oakley sunglasses perched nonchalantly on top of his head, and simply rode away from Pantani and Conti. Having made the break, and having looked on a mission to catch whoever else was in front, for some reason Armstrong slowed to let Pantani – and Ullrich, and Virenque, and others – catch up, regroup, and go over the top of the d'Izoard together.

From the summit it was another 20 kilometres to the stage finish in Briançon, starting with a fast, tree-lined descent. Virenque made a bid to escape the Armstrong group, dicing with danger on the smooth bends, while Pantani and Armstrong were spotted seemingly having a friendly chat. Up ahead Botero, on a supremely brave ride, struggled up the difficult final incline to the finish. Saeco's Paolo Salvoldelli, another earlier escapee, fought his way to second, 2-30 behind. And just behind Salvoldelli, Pantani attacked his group once again, coming in third at 2-46. Escartin, Virenque and Moreau came in at 2-49 and just behind them, at 2-51, came Armstrong, Heras, Beloki and Ullrich. Overall Armstrong still led Ullrich by 4-55, Beloki was still third at 5-52, while Pantani had moved up to ninth – and was still dreaming of being in the top three overall – at 10-13.

After the racing Armstrong was asked about his chat with Pantani: "I read some stuff in the papers this morning that Marco had said, that I thought was a little wrong so I asked him about it. He said he hadn't spoken to the press in a year, so he didn't know how the story had got in there. I believe him... whatever."

Stage 15 was the last stage before the Tour's second and final rest day, so fatigue was figuring highly, and with an ascent of the hors catégorie Col de la Madeleine then a stage finish at the high-mountain resort of Courchevel, it would be a tough day in the saddle.

By the final climb to Courchevel the stage was being led by a five-strong group containing Cofidis's Massimiliano Lelli, Kelme's Javier Otxoa and Santiago Botero, Banesto's Jose-Maria Jimenez and Mapei's Daniele Nardello. Botero attacked, with Jimenez and Nardello managing to react, but Otxoa and Lelli were lost. Further back Pantani tried his luck but Armstrong's trusty mountain lieutenant Livingston matched him. Pantani raised the pace again, and again he was matched by Livingston, Armstrong and Virenque. Ullrich, visibly suffering, fell back, then Livingston reached his limit, leaving just Pantani, Armstrong and Virenque together. Soon Virenque could take no more either so Armstrong took to the front and raised the pace. Pantani matched him, both of them rocking their machines from side to side in perfect harmony – harmony on the road at least, if not in the press.

At the front Jimenez attacked Nardello and Botero, splitting the leading trio, while Armstrong and Pantani closed in from behind. They soon joined up with Botero, who had his Kelme team-mate Roberto Heras for company, and that seemed to be the signal for Pantani to launch off the front again. Armstrong, for once looking strained, let Botero and Heras take up the work of setting the pace, but they made little impression on catching Pantani, who was flying. Soon the 'Pirate' had caught Nardello, passed him, and set about catching Jimenez. Armstrong, who had finally taken to the front of his little group, dropped Heras and Botero and also caught up with Nardello, but by then Pantani was long gone.

With four kilometres to go Pantani was just 20 seconds behind Jimenez. As both riders passed through the town of Courchevel Pantani spotted the stage leader, upped the gear again, and sprinted past, pushing his way upwards through the excited crowd. Three kilometres later, and still out of the saddle, Pantani entered the final kilometre, his face a picture of pure determination, or anger.

He took the line, too exhausted for flamboyant celebrations, simply lifting a hand to acknowledge the cheering crowd. Jimenez bravely continued at his own pace, crossing the line in second place 41 seconds down. Armstrong and Heras came in 50 seconds behind Pantani.

Overall the upper order had changed little, but the time differences were significantly altered: Armstrong led; Ullrich, who had suffered on the final climb and lost 2-31 to the Texan, remained in second place but was now 7-26 behind; while Beloki in third was just a further two seconds back at 7-28. Pantani's performance had raised his standing to sixth overall, 9-03 behind Armstrong.

With a rest day to follow, there was a chance for the riders to recharge their batteries before taking on the final day in the Alps: stage 16 from Courchevel to Morzine. But before the riders could cross the start line of the 2000 Tour de France's final mountain stage there was the small matter of the Pantani and Armstrong soap opera to catch up on. The rest day had offered both parties a chance to vent their spleen to the attendant media. Talking about how Armstrong seemingly slowed for everybody on the Izoard Pantani said: "It stuck in my craw because it was excessive. He may be the leader but he should still show some respect. Yesterday [stage 15] it left a bad taste in my mouth when I was alone with Armstrong."

Despite reigning glorious in yellow, Armstrong wasn't above a comeback and said: "In hindsight, after the last few days, Pantani's actions, his words, are very disappointing to me because I thought he had more class than that."

Come the start of stage 16 Pantani was hell bent on making the final Alpine stage as difficult as possible for Armstrong. Almost from the gun he escaped on a crazed kamikaze attack, his goal not to win the stage or rise up the overall rankings, but simply to blow the race apart. Rather than pace themselves for the early parts of the route it meant the bunch, and particularly the US Postal boys, had to set about chasing from the outset. Pantani led the race alone over the Col des Saisies but he had been joined by Escartin and Polti's Pascal Hervé 50 kilometres later as they crested the Col de la Colombière. From the top of the Colombière it was another 50 kilometres to the top of the final climb, the Col de Joux-Plane before the drop to the finish at Morzine.

Ekimov remembers Pantani's bizarre behaviour well: "Marco was always a guy that liked to win races, but he also liked to win stages in a nice manner, so nobody could say he had been on somebody's wheel or had any excuses. He was a fighter. So that was probably his tactic, to make something unusual happen that nobody could even predict. He was trying to win in other ways during the course of that Tour but it hadn't worked particularly well, so that was probably why he tried unusual things like that attack."

While Hamilton and Livingston, as usual, set the pace for the yellow jersey group on the climb of the Colombière, team Telekom took up chasing duties on the descent having seen Christophe Moreau – a possible threat to Ullrich's second position overall – join the three escapees. That resulted in Pantani and his companions finally being swallowed up by the start of the Joux-Plane, but as soon as the leading group hit the lower slopes it split apart again, with Ag2r's Andrei Kivilev, Vini Caldirola's Guido Trentin and Bonjour's Didier Rous escaping off the front. Just behind them Armstrong, Virenque, Heras and Ullrich rode together. Heras set the pace, while Ullrich yo-yoed off the back of their select group. Heras then attacked leaving Armstrong and Virenque to ride together while Ullrich bravely tried to hang on.

At the front Trentin had freed himself of his two breakaway companions, but Heras had also quickly caught and climbed past them. As Heras spun serenely on in the lead, back down the slope Armstrong was suffering. Virenque and Ullrich – who had now composed himself – lifted the tempo and were almost surprised to see the previously invincible Armstrong in trouble. The duo rode away while Armstrong contorted his face in desperation.

A bit further on Virenque lifted the pace again, and this time Ullrich couldn't respond. The Frenchman joined Heras and they rode together over the top of the

Joux-Plane with Ullrich just 28 seconds further back. Armstrong appeared at the summit in a group 1-33 behind Ullrich. His overall lead was safe with just the descent to Morzine remaining, but race watchers were still shocked to see the superman finally display some weakness.

On the run downhill Ullrich tried to catch the leaders but demon descender Virenque led Heras at top speed. It was too quick for the Spaniard as they came into Morzine and Heras ploughed into the barriers, severely buckling his front wheel. Seizing his chance Virenque sprinted to the stage victory. Ullrich caught and just passed Heras – who had had to wait for a replacement bike – and came over the line 24 seconds down. Heras was right behind the German, while Armstrong finally arrived with a small group 1-37 after Ullrich. Overall Armstrong still led the race, but now by just 5-37 to Ullrich, and Beloki in third had closed to 6-38. Pantani, the aggressor of the day, lost 13-44 on the stage, putting him in 14th place overall at 20-46.

After the stage Armstrong admitted things had gone badly wrong: "That was without a doubt the worst day that I've ever had on a bike. I think most of us know what it's like when you run out of energy and you run out of food. I had a lot of emotions: I was hungry, I was light-headed, I was nervous, I was scared. If things had got really bad I could have lost the Tour de France today. I don't know what Pantani was thinking – he's just a little shit-stirrer."

For those in US Postal, seeing their team leader in trouble wasn't a pleasant experience. "That was my first experience of Lance having a bad day," Ekimov says. "He usually had one bad day in each Tour de France, but that was my first real experience of it. Later on, in later editions of the Tour, we knew from the start that one day he would crack, but it would be for just one day. That year, I didn't lose my morale or my confidence in Lance, but I didn't expect it to happen at all – to see Lance go from being in such form and setting off fireworks in the peloton, to the next day struggling. But these things happen."

Stages 17 and 18 saw the abandon of Marco Pantani but otherwise there were no changes to the top of the overall standings. The final test for Armstrong, and the final chance for anybody to unseat him, came at stage 19's individual time trial. One man in particular was fired up for the event. With the 58.5-kilometre course starting in Germany it was a chance for that nation's favourite cycling son, and the reigning world time trial champion, Jan Ullrich, to make a mark. Armstrong had good reason to go for a spectacular ride himself – he hadn't yet won a stage in this year's Tour and he was planning to put that right.

As with the first time trial in the 2000 Tour, David Millar set an impressive marker, before being superseded by Laurent Jalabert, then Tyler Hamilton put in a quite amazing time – in fact, at that point the third fastest time trail in the history of the Tour.

To rapturous applause from his home fans, and wearing the coveted rainbow jersey, Ullrich set off down the start ramp and immediately found his rhythm. Three minutes later Armstrong sprinted onto the opening straight and launched his bid to win the stage. Ullrich looked smooth, but Armstrong looked powerful, and at the 20.5-kilometre time-check the American was five seconds quicker than the German. At the 44-kilometre checkpoint his advantage had increased to 25 seconds. Ullrich was storming around the course, catching his three-minute man Joseba Beloki and finishing with a time of 1-05-26, more than two and a half minutes quicker than that supreme ride by Hamilton.

Yet Armstrong was going faster still. His body rolling, Armstrong appeared on the finishing straight and he crossed the line with a time of 1-05-01, 25 seconds quicker than Ullrich, and an average speed of 53.986kph. More importantly, he had claimed his stage win. Overall, with two flat stages left in the race, Armstrong's yellow jersey was now all but assured with a 6-02 gap to Ullrich and a 10-04 gap to Beloki in third.

Stage 20 was a simple – if supremely long – 248-kilometre flat course where all the overall leaders finished in the pack together. And with just one stage remaining it was time for the US Postal boys to start partying.

"The last evening in Paris after the race was always more of a big day with the sponsors, the team was no longer feeling like a family because there were a lot of other people there," Ekimov says. "So the evening before the last day was more of a team dinner, and we had wine and a good time. We spent a long time around the table laughing and joking because we all knew the next day was just a quick race around Paris, and we knew the sprinters' teams would take control and all we had to do was just be there in the peloton."

The final stage broke with the regular custom of running into Paris and actually started in the shadow of the Eiffel Tower. The riders then headed away from the city centre before returning to complete the customary circuits of the Champs-Elysées. Despite some early attacks the stage and the 2000 Tour finished with a sprint finish and Mapei's Stefano Zanini took the line just ahead of the green jersey winner, Telekom's Erik Zabel.

Ekimov was overwhelmed by the experience: "Of course it was exciting being on the Champs-Elysées with the winning team. Everybody was proud to be in that team and proud to cross the finish line. It's also traditional that the team of the yellow jersey leads the first lap on the Champs-Elysées, and the rule is that nobody goes round you. So we went onto the Champs-Elysées in single file while the rest of the bunch stayed behind us. We all knew that those pictures would be seen all over the world, so we were very proud."

Surrounded by his US Postal team-mates Lance Armstrong safely crossed the line and was the Tour champion again. He had proved 1999 was no fluke – if anything, the 2000 edition of the race was dominated even more fully by the American. The final general classification times stood with Ullrich in second at 6-02 and Beloki third at 10-04.

After the race the new double-champ had this to say: "Last year I didn't know what it meant to win the Tour de France... now I have figured it out. So I knew what I was riding and the significance of the jersey on my back. It's fantastic." Then Armstrong took to the podium, baby Luke in his arms, and wife Kristin looking the epitome of American cool in Paris by his side.

But for both Armstrong and Ekimov the 2000 season still had some major challenges remaining. The first was the Grand Prix Eddy Merckx, a two-up time trial where Armstrong and Ekimov would be partners.

"I felt really good that day because after we finished the Tour de France I did probably one criterium, but for the rest of the time I was back in my house in Spain taking it easy but maintaining my form for the Olympic Games," Ekimov says. "I met Lance for the Grand Prix Eddy Merckx. He wasn't in that good shape, he was probably still tired from the Tour de France and the post-Tour criteriums, so our performances were pretty even. I even felt I could dominate Lance a little bit that day. But we rode together as a team and we got first place, and that was the goal."

Then came the Olympic Games in Sydney in September, which were a bit of a disappointment for Armstrong, whose preparation had been severely compromised after being hit by a car in the South of France only a few weeks before the Games. The accident resulted in Armstrong fracturing one of his vertebrae, and he only managed to finish 13th in the road race, although he did win the bronze medal in the time trial.

But Sydney was also the scene of Ekimov's greatest achievement in cycling. "Getting the gold medal in the time trial was totally a surprise for me," Ekimov says. "I went to Sydney with good legs and the dream was to be in the top five. Getting a medal with Lance in the race, with Ullrich in the race, with Christophe Moreau in the race, was something I couldn't even think about. Then all of a sudden I got gold. I surprised myself big time. I cannot explain how it happened."

Buoyed by a big finish to the 2000 season, Ekimov reprised his role as Armstrong's bodyguard for US Postal at the 2001 Tour and was also named the Russian Cyclist of the Century. But then, with little more to prove, he decided to finish his career at the end of the 2001 season. "That was a time when I started to lose motivation. Every year would be the same: I would do the Classics season and then came the summer where I would be pulling for Lance at the Tour. So I just started losing morale. At the same time it was the start of a new professional Russian team, who offered me a good role as manager. But things didn't go so well and I just got disappointed with the whole project. So I called Johan in February 2002 and asked him if there was any chance I could ride for US Postal again. He was laughing so hard. We met each other in Valencia, we had lunch, and I rejoined the team."

In the years that followed Ekimov was one of Armstrong's most loyal domestiques, helping him win a total of five Tour titles. The one Tour where Ekimov didn't accompany his team leader was Armstrong's final race, in 2005. In May that year, while training with Armstrong in Texas, Ekimov fell, breaking his collarbone and fracturing his spine. "Crashes are always bad if they happen to you, there is no good crash," Ekimov says. "But I knew it would be Lance's last Tour, and I was going to miss it, so I was doubly disappointed, especially as at the end of my career my only goal was to be in Lance's team at the Tour de France."

That said, Ekimov carried on with Discovery Channel even after Armstrong's retirement, completing one further Tour de France in 2006. On the last stage of his final Tour the peloton decided to let Ekimov, one of the true legends of the peloton, have the honour of being the first man onto the Champs-Elysées.

"I broke the tradition on the final day of the 2006 Tour when the peloton let me go ahead and lead the race onto the Champs-Elysées, just so I could show myself as the retirement guy. That was big respect and I even had tears in my eyes. It was a really special moment," Ekimov says.

After retirement Ekimov became a directeur sportif at Discovery Channel, then when Johan Bruyneel took on the job of team boss at Astana in late 2007 Ekimov followed there as well. It meant that in 2009 he ended up working again with his old team-mate Lance Armstrong.

"Lance and I are really good friends," Ekimov says. "But I've never tried to gain from that friendship, I'm proud just to have it."

Why The French Press Went Hunting Armstrong

With Jean-François Quénet, leading French cycling journalist and author of the yearly
Livre d'Or du Cyclisme

Lance Armstrong had a good relationship with the American press, even in his pre-cancer career. But among European reporters, and particularly the French media, his sometimes brash personality didn't go down too well. That said, his return to the sport after surviving cancer, and specifically his success at the 1999 Tour de France prologue, was heralded as a wonderful story by the media of all nationalities.

The French newspaper *L'Equipe* – which would go on to be the source of many of Armstrong's problems with the press in the following years – ran a headline the day after his prologue victory rejoicing in his performance. It said 'Revenu de si loin', which literally translated means 'Comeback from so far', highlighting – with no cynicism intended – the extraordinary feat Armstrong had achieved following his cancer treatment.

French cycling journalist Jean-François Quénet remembers that period well: "I was covering the Tour for *Ouest-France*, France's largest selling newspaper, and I remember there was a little bit of surprise among the reporters who were not fully specialised in cycling, but not among the cycling writers. You must remember that the 1999 Tour was a race with no favourites: there was no Marco Pantani, no Jan Ullrich, nobody really big was racing, so Armstrong's success wasn't that strange.

"In the morning of that prologue, *L'Equipe* published who it thought were the biggest favourites to take the stage, giving the riders a five-star rating. *L'Equipe*'s number one favourite, with five stars, was Lance Armstrong. I also covered the Circuit de la Sarthe [a smaller French race held in the Pays de la Loire region] in 1999 where Armstrong got, I think, his only win that year before the Tour. So on the short time trial we knew he could do well. The prologue was mostly seen as something important because it was a sign of his comeback from cancer."

Armstrong's honeymoon with the cycling press was, however, brief and within just a few days his performances were coming under suspicion. But Quénet says there wasn't anything specific that caused the cynicism to increase. "The prologue is not enough to cause suspicion because it is too short to evaluate the level of performances. But the full individual time trial was a different matter. Armstrong won that by almost a minute from Zülle, and I remember that was when the suspicion started. But it was not necessarily about or against Armstrong personally, the suspicion was about the Tour de France and the bike riders in general one year after the Festina affair."

Further into the 1999 Tour a specific allegation against Armstrong did present itself when reporters at another French publication, *Le Monde*, got word that Armstrong had had a positive dope test. Although exact details of the test were scant, *Le Monde* ran a story saying that the banned substance triamcinolone had been found in Armstrong's sample during a doping test. Armstrong went on French national television countering the accusations saying the substance had been present in a skin cream, called Cemalyt, which he had been using, and wasn't an indication of doping.

"I remember that all came to the fore on a mountain stage," Quénet says. "*Le Monde* is an evening paper so the story probably came out at 1pm and I remember after that stage French television came up to Armstrong and said: 'This is what *Le Monde* newspaper is saying about you, what do you have to say?' And Armstrong said: 'I don't know, I don't know, I have no comment.' The next day he then came to the media van to give a press conference and he said: 'It's not a doping affair, it's a question of cream.' It was actually cream for a sore arse. But after that, rather than pick on Armstrong, the press actually blamed the UCI, because we were well aware of the Laurent Brochard affair at the World Championships in San Sebastian two years before where exactly the same thing had happened.

"But every day during the 1999 Tour when Armstrong came to the daily press conference there were questions about drugs. Every day there were questions about what he was on. After one stage I remember him on a television interview blaming *L'Equipe*'s reporter Pierre Ballester, who was not far from him at the time, and Armstrong said words to the effect of: 'The problem at this Tour is unprofessional behaviour from some journalists like Pierre Ballester who is here, and it is they who carry on this suspicion.' At that time Ballester and Armstrong were still talking to each other – Ballester had written a lot about Armstrong before cancer – and so Ballester went to Armstrong's hotel and he had a very harsh interview with Armstrong, like a man-to-man talk, and Ballester then reproduced everything in *L'Equipe*.

"So the conflict between the media and Armstrong was there every day, but I wouldn't say it was exclusively the French press and nobody else."

In 1999 things came to a head after Armstrong's amazing stage win on the road to Sestriere. *L'Equipe* ran a headline that translated as: 'On another planet', suggesting there was something not natural about Armstrong's performance. The questions just wouldn't go away, and in the end Armstrong decided to simply stop speaking to the press for a while during the 1999 Tour.

Where Armstrong had been particularly unfortunate was in the fact he was the first rider to win the Tour de France after the Festina affair. As Luke Edwardes-Evans said in chapter two, whoever won the yellow jersey the year after the Festina affair was going to come under intense scrutiny from cycling reporters who felt they had been made to look stupid with the discoveries of the year before. And the fact that Armstrong had been so close to death only a couple of years earlier meant they found his story even harder to believe.

Quénet is anything other than a Armstrong groupie, but even he agrees Armstrong had some right to feel aggrieved at the way he was dealt with by the media: "Never before had a Tour leader been treated like that. Because this all happened after the Festina affair. Before the Festina affair there was press about drugs, but after the Festina affair there were some non-sport journalists coming to the Tour just to target drug scandals. That all happened because of the Festina affair, not because of Armstrong. But it's important to say it wasn't just the French press picking on him, it was all the press, from every country. The Belgian press, the American press, everybody was looking at the Tour through the eyes of the Festina affair. "

So Armstrong's circumstances may have been uniquely unfavourable for his relationship with the press, but he has often done little to help matters. To be fair, he might have been excused a little animosity towards those in French cycling, considering how the only French team he had ever joined – Cofidis – all but ripped up his contract after his cancer treatment. Over time, after that first Tour victory, his contact with the press improved, although it has generally been on his terms. In future years, while Armstrong would give interviews to selected reporters, rumours also began to circulate that the US Postal team bus had a rogue's gallery of photographs of journalists who had been classed 'personae non grata', and who shouldn't be spoken to. Armstrong has since denied that situation ever happened, but many of those in the cycling media are convinced the rumours were genuine.

"Armstrong's relationship with the press certainly did improve," Quénet says. "But Armstrong selected his journalists. You know he has always wanted to control everything. So he gave some press conferences where everybody could come and ask questions, but they were not very interesting, and he also had his what you might call 'accredited' journalists. He wouldn't give an exclusive interview to just any journalist, only the ones that he was used to dealing with, only the ones that knew the rules.

"In France, when he won his first Tour in 1999, for *L'Equipe* there were probably a few different journalists covering Armstrong. But in 2000 or 2001 *L'Equipe* appointed Jean-Pierre Bidet to do the Armstrong coverage. Bidet became an Armstrong-accredited journalist. He was never fooled by Armstrong, he always knew what he really thought about Armstrong, but he knew the limit of what he could write. He did a pretty good job because he was never playing Armstrong's game or saying how great Armstrong was, his comments were quite neutral or distant, but he got interviews from Armstrong and he knew the limit – he couldn't criticise him too much.

"Then you had other reporters like Yves Perret from the *Dauphiné Libéré* newspaper – Armstrong usually rode the Dauphiné Libéré race so that was another newspaper 'accredited' by Armstrong – and Armstrong would answer to Perret all the time and give him some exclusive interviews as well.

"So let's say if an unknown journalist asked Armstrong for an interview, it was very hard to get one, and there was a blacklist of journalists who criticised him too, so those journalists – which I have always been a part of – would never get an exclusive interview with Armstrong either. Personally I never asked for it, I never chased an exclusive interview, and I was very happy to work distantly, only go to the press conferences and not deal with him directly, which meant I could write everything I wanted."

Quénet's approach to dealing with Armstrong is a perfect example of the way the wider French press started viewing him. While they weren't all creating big-scandal, doping-story headlines, Quénet says there were still probably more reporters hostile to Armstrong in the French press than from other countries. And the reason for that, again, wasn't entirely Armstrong's fault.

"Armstrong came to prominence at the same time as the biggest anti-American feeling in France," Quénet says. "It was the period when Jacques Chirac was president of France, and Chirac had been smart in covering his own weaknesses by blaming America for everything. There has always been a bit of anti-American feeling in France – which is unfair because without the Americans, France would have been part of Germany since World War Two – but it's easy to excite the French public with an anti-American feeling. So when Jacques Chirac was doing a pretty bad job as president he was blaming America for his failure.

"Then there was the Iraq war. The French people hated George Bush like they have never hated any other American president, and Armstrong was always being seen with Bush. He said he was from Texas like Bush and he introduced himself as a friend of Bush. So a friend of the president of the USA who had just started a war in Iraq wasn't someone who was going to be appreciated by the French general public.

"Plus there were all these drugs suspicions, and at the same time French riders were not doing well at the Tour. While it was obvious that French riders were doing well before the Festina affair, after the Festina affair most of them stopped taking drugs and it appeared they were not competing with the same weapons. They were so far away from Armstrong that it was easy for the French public to think the French riders looked so bad because Armstrong was doping. It seems like a bit of a caricature, but you must remember that was what the French public was thinking at the time."

Although at one point, between the 2000 and 2001 Tours, Armstrong even suggested he wouldn't compete at the race because of the negative publicity he was getting from the French press, things only really started to deteriorate as

Armstrong's reign at the Tour de France entered its record-breaking phase. In June 2004, just two weeks before his attempt at an unprecedented sixth Tour de France victory, Pierre Ballester and Irish writer David Walsh of the *Sunday Times* released *LA Confidentiel – les secrets de Lance Armstrong*. The book contained a catalogue of circumstantial evidence linking Armstrong to doping, including interviews with people previously close to the Texan. The publication of the book didn't exactly put Armstrong in a good mood and the anger it caused him may explain how he managed to go on and dominate the 2004 Tour so completely. It also initiated a raft of legal cases.

But for Armstrong worse was yet to come. In something of a final flurry, less than a month after Armstrong had completed his final Tour de France victory in 2005 and headed off into retirement, *L'Equipe* ran a front page with the headline 'Le Mensonge Armstrong', which translates as simply 'The Armstrong Lie'. *L'Equipe* reporter Damian Ressiot revealed that some urine samples from the 1999 Tour de France had been retrospectively tested as part of a programme to help the anti-doping authorities improve their procedures, and 12 of the retrospectively tested samples had shown EPO use. Although the samples were labelled anonymously they were identifiable by a number and Ressiot believed he had connected Armstrong's number with six of the samples containing EPO.

Armstrong's reaction to the story was particularly interesting. On his website he stated: "Yet again, a European newspaper has reported that I have tested positive for performance-enhancing drugs. *L'Equipe*, a French sports daily, is reporting that my 1999 samples were positive. Unfortunately the witch hunt continues and the article is nothing short of tabloid journalism. I will simply restate what I have said many times: I have never taken performance enhancing drugs." In the end an investigation by Dutch lawyer Emile Vrijman, who had been commissioned by the UCI to look at the handling of urine tests from the 1999 Tour, exonerated Armstrong.

Quénet says that to some extent Armstrong was a victim of his own success and dominance. "By the end of his career there was a feeling that enough was enough. Seven years of Armstrong was too much, people in France couldn't stand him any more. The press couldn't stand him any more, the public couldn't stand him any more. He was too much of a dictator because he was controlling the peloton, nobody could break away without the permission of Armstrong. No reporters could approach him if they weren't 'accredited' to do it. He was so much of a boss that people got sick of it.

"Only in 2003 were there any doubts that he might not win the Tour, but really in seven years there was no opposition, nobody really threatened him, there was no race. So it wasn't because he was Armstrong, or because he was an American, or because people suspected he might be a dope cheat, it was simply the fact that the last two years were just too much, the racing had become boring."

There could be no complaints of Armstrong dominating the press in his retirement, though, as he gave precious few interviews to the sports media in the years after the 2005 Tour. However, after September 2008 – when he decided to announce his comeback – he has also vowed to be much more open with the press, and has been interviewed by publications he previously avoided. Generally he has been much softer, friendlier even, with the specialised cycling media. In return, and with their ability to criticise him compromised by the fact Armstrong has said his return is inspired by a desire to promote cancer awareness, the French and wider European press has had to be fairer to him.

"After his comeback Armstrong did appear to be softer with the press, certainly he was softer at the Tour Down Under in Australia in January 2009," Quénet says. "That was different to races in Europe because at the Tour Down Under everything is based in just one hotel – the Adelaide Hilton – and everything happens there. So whether he wanted it or not, he was closer to the press than ever before. And it was obvious that he wanted to be more friendly to anybody in the press. It seemed like he was prepared to be friendly.

"In return the French press hasn't been negative about him really since his comeback – everything has been covered fairly. Maybe in the past the French press has been unfair with him, but after he announced his comeback it was fair. Also there was the issue of his cancer campaign, which was quite well reported. Among the French public I felt that many people didn't want to see him back at the Tour de France. But you can't say that reaction is because of the press; the French press never said 'the devil is back' or anything like that. The French press was not negative at all."

2001: It Just Gets Easier...

With Roberto Heras, Armstrong's US Postal team-mate 2001-2003

Although it may not have been the most important thing on Lance Armstrong's mind, the 2001 edition of the Tour de France offered him the chance to join the previous American record holder – Greg LeMond – with three overall titles. Still, there were times during the intervening year between races when Armstrong's appearance at the 2001 race looked to be in doubt. Armstrong publicly suggested that he might decide not to defend his Tour crown come July if the French press continued to publish negative articles about him. Armstrong was especially riled by an investigation by the French prosecutor's office into the US Postal team's possible use of the substance Actovegin. The investigation had been initiated after a report by a French television crew who had rifled through US Postal rubbish bags at the 2000 Tour de France.

In the end the situation was resolved, but Armstrong's preparation for the race was a little different to normal years, opting to ride the Tour of Switzerland rather than the Dauphiné Libéré in the run-up to July. Then immediately after the Tour of Switzerland, which he won, he left by helicopter to train at altitude in Saint Moritz until the Tuesday before the start of the Tour de France.

Also new were some of the faces Armstrong had hired to help him among the US Postal ranks for 2001, with the most important addition to his troops being Jose Luis 'Chechu' Rubiera and the reigning Vuelta a Espana champion, Roberto Heras. Heras had been one of the riders to cause Armstrong trouble in the mountain stages of his previous two Tour wins, and he was hired to help US Postal control the climbs. He was also one of the first examples of Armstrong's newfound philosophy that the US Postal team should be made up of riders that could challenge for overall victory in their own right – by hiring them himself Armstrong would not only have the very best helpers available, he would also have one less challenger.

"During the 2000 season Lance saw me at the Tour de France and wanted me in his team, so I decided to join US Postal," Heras remembers. "I had just won my first Vuelta a Espana, and I came fifth at the 2000 Tour de France, so nobody in Spain – none of the papers or the journalists – could understand why I would decide to ride for somebody else. It was a difficult decision, but looking back on it today I can say it was the right decision because those three years with Lance and US Postal were the best of my career.

"The team was a good organisation, and there was a different mentality because at US Postal the Tour is the main objective, but in the beginning of the season everybody is quite relaxed. The pressure only starts building in May, two or three months before the Tour. Johan Bruyneel and Lance decide who is going to be in the Tour squad in December of the year before, and it's very important for the riders to know that. So for the nine riders who are going to compete at the Tour, the planning of their season is very easy until April or May.

"Another important reason why I went to US Postal is the training camps they hold in the Alps and the Pyrenees to prepare for the Tour. Nobody prepares for the Tour like US Postal, like Johan and Lance. We were preparing for the Tour six months before the race started.

"And I had no problem riding against Joseba Beloki and my old team at Kelme. It was simply my job, and my job in US Postal was similar to the job I did before at Kelme. I was there just to help our team leader, Lance, win the Tour. But after the Tour it meant I could be the team leader for the Vuelta, which was great for me."

Armstrong's anticipated main rival again in 2001, Jan Ullrich, had been coerced into competing at the Giro d'Italia by his Telekom team so that the big German would be lean and mean in plenty of time for the Tour. Seemingly it had worked, with Ullrich appearing at the Grand Départ in Dunkirk looking close to his racing weight. Ullrich was in good spirits having been crowned German national champion and also being the reigning Olympic champion after winning the road race in Sydney in September 2000.

"Before the Tour I personally thought nobody would be a threat to Lance, because he gave the team a feeling of great confidence," Heras says. "But we were always looking at Ullrich because Ullrich and his Telekom team were always the biggest dangers for us. Ullrich was always dangerous. Beloki was dangerous also, but we didn't think he was as much of a threat as Ullrich."

While Armstrong had been busy hiring riders like Heras and Rubiera, team Telekom had been reinforcing its own ranks in the off-season. Much to Armstrong's displeasure it had succeeded in attracting an important defector from US Postal, Armstrong's mountain domestique and long-time friend Kevin Livingston. But whatever threat Ullrich and his team may have posed, Heras does not remember being unduly worried: "Before the race we all felt very confident about Lance's chances to win because Lance was so strong. He was always so strong at training camps. Also, all the riders who would make up the Tour squad worked together at training camps and at races, so that just helped grow confidence."

Unlike in 2000, the 2001 Tour featured a genuine prologue. The conditions for the 8.2-kilometre challenge around the seafront streets of Dunkirk were dreary, with heavy clouds overhead, but the threat of rain held off. Following his impressive debut the previous year, David Millar of Cofidis was seen as a possible early wearer of the yellow jersey, but a rear-wheel puncture put paid to his chances.

One of the earlier stars of the prologue had been Armstrong's Norwegian team-mate Steffen Kjaergaard who had gone all-out to half distance, laying down a marker for Armstrong to follow later. But as the big names – Festina's Christophe Moreau, Ullrich and Armstrong – began their rides the result sheet was headed by ONCE's Igor Gonzales de Galdeano with a time of 9-23.

Moreau battled his way around the course, in and out of the saddle, tongue dangling out of his open mouth in his trademark style, and he was greeted with rapturous applause from all the home fans. At the halfway mark he was just one second behind Kjaergaard's time. Into the finishing straight Moreau hugged the left-hand barriers, smoothly rocking his bike, trying to coax more speed out of it. As he approached the line he bared his teeth for one final effort and claimed a time of 9-20, three seconds faster than Gonzalez de Galdeano and the new provisional leader.

Ullrich may have looked in good form, and he may have been wearing the bands of the German national time trial champion, but at the halfway mark he was five seconds down on Kjaergaard's time and ranked only 23rd. As he appeared in the finishing straight he looked like a massive ocean liner, sailing smoothly onwards, with all his efforts going into forward momentum. Crossing the line he recorded a time of 9-27, seven seconds behind Moreau.

Armstrong, sporting a custom-made Giro aero helmet with 'Lance' painted down the middle and wearing the yellow jersey he had won the year before, was the last man off. From the start ramp he didn't disappoint, beating down on the pedals and sprinting along the opening stretch. At the halfway point, and with the distant rumble of thunder ominously suggesting it could ruin his day, he was two seconds behind Kjaergaard's benchmark. Gradually, his legs appearing to whirr at twice the speed of the slow gear-grinding Ullrich, the reigning champ clawed back time. Into the long final straight it still looked all to fight for. Out of the saddle, Armstrong made a last effort for the line. But it was not quite enough. He finished in third place at 9-24.

Proving the international flavour of the Tour it was a Frenchman, Christophe Moreau, wearing the yellow jersey; a Spaniard, Gonzalez de Galdeano, was second three seconds behind; an American, Armstrong, was third, four seconds behind; and a German, Ullrich was fourth, seven seconds in arrears.

Stage one ended in a bunch sprint while stage two offered the day's victor an unusual prize: a £15,000 Antwerp diamond. Rabobank's Marc Wauters outwitted his 15 other breakaway companions to take the stage, the overall lead, and the jewellery. Due to the break there were big changes overall with Wauters in yellow from Crédit Agricole's Stuart O'Grady by 12 seconds and Domo's Servais Knaven in third at 27 seconds. Moreau was down in fourth also at 27 seconds, Armstrong was 11th at 31 seconds and Ullrich was 12th at 34 seconds.

Stage three remained in Belgium and featured a two-kilometre uphill finish. Team Telekom set the pace as the field headed for the finale, with Jan Ullrich taking a position three from the front trying to lead out Erik Zabel, while Armstrong rode just behind. Zabel took the stage win and in what amounted to an early head-to-head clash of the overall favourites Armstrong beat Ullrich, to finish 10th and 13th respectively. Overall O'Grady took the race lead with Wauters having a difficult day, but the time gaps between the favourites remained static.

Stage four headed back into France from Hoy to Verdun, and brought back some interesting memories for one member of the peloton. The Tour de France had only ever visited Verdun once before, and that was in 1993, when a 21-year-old by the name of Lance Armstrong, in his first ever Tour, took an amazing stage win. But this time it was CSC's French legend Laurent Jalabert who won, with no major changes to the overall standings.

The next day, stage five, was the 67-kilometre team time trial from Verdun to Bar le Duc. Under black clouds and on slippery roads it would be an ultimate test of a squad's power and skill. The US Postal team had started the stage challenge not quite as near the last of the starters as they would have wanted, although they were able to target the result of Ullrich's Telekom team who began before them. The Telekom squad looked surprisingly weak and came across the line with the bare minimum five riders needed to record a time. Their figure of 1-23-22 was three seconds slower than the then stage leaders, Rabobank.

But before US Postal could start worrying about beating anybody, with 18 kilometres of the course still left to ride they suffered a disaster.

"I remember being behind Christian Vande Velde," Heras says. "The white line in the middle of the road was wet and Vande Velde's wheel slipped on it, and he crashed. I was close behind him so when he crashed I crashed as well. After that we got up but the team had raced on. Then I could hear Lance on the team radio saying: 'Wait, wait. Wait for Robbie and Vande Velde.' It was a brave decision for Lance, and after the stage I went to him to say: 'Thank you, it was a great honour that a rider like you waited for me.'"

In truth Armstrong was probably more interested in waiting for the powerful time triallist Vande Velde to rejoin than Heras.

Meanwhile, at the finish line teams were coming home with good times. The Spanish Kelme squad, more normally known for the quality of its mountain stage riders, had set some impressive figures at the time-checks and finished with the new best time: 1-23-10. Then US Postal entered the finishing area. Armstrong led from the front, his face a mixture of anger and determination. Big George Hincapie – one of the powerful engines of the US Postal outfit – controlled the body of the squad, while the other team members made their way gingerly round the final corners. They set the provisional leading time at 1-22-58, but looking at the time-checks coming in from teams out on the course it wouldn't last long.

In fact it didn't even last beyond the next team's arrival. The Spanish ONCE team crossed the line at 1-22-03, 55 seconds quicker than US Postal. Then Moreau's Festina team appeared with a time of 1-22-26, 32 seconds quicker than US Postal. And all the time Crédit Agricole, the last team to start the time trial, seemed to be going quicker still. As they entered Bar le Duc yellow jersey Stuart O'Grady brought up the rear, urging his team-mates to the finish. They crossed the line at 1-21-32, not only cementing O'Grady's hold on the yellow jersey but also putting more of their men into the top three overall – Jens Voigt second at 26 seconds, and Bobby Julich third at 27 seconds.

With ONCE and Festina also setting better results, US Postal's time was good only for fourth on the day, leaving Armstrong in 15th place overall at 1-53. Telekom's pretty poor display put them seventh in the team time trial challenge, resulting in Ullrich dropping to 19th at 2-20. But Beloki's ONCE squad's impressive display of team power had raised him to fifth overall at 1-07.

Despite the relatively poor showing, Heras remembers the team wasn't too upset that evening: "The team wasn't unhappy because we crashed. When you start a team time trial and it's raining like that these things can happen. It was just an accident. The team was a little unhappy because we didn't win the stage, but it wasn't so bad because we didn't lose that much time."

Stage six finished in a sprint then stage seven, being held on Bastille Day, saw Laurent Jalabert become the hero of France again to take the win. Just behind him Jens Voigt took second, and stole the yellow jersey from his Crédit Agricole team-mate O'Grady, who finished with the main bunch almost four and a half minutes later. Of the favourites, Beloki was sixth at 5-10, Moreau was ninth at 5-20, Armstrong was 15th at 5-56 and Ullrich was 19th at 6-23.

Stage eight, 222.5 kilometres from Colmar to Pontarlier, was another terribly wet day in what had already been a particularly poor Tour weather-wise. Erik Dekker took the win while O'Grady resumed the overall race lead by being in a group of chasers two and a half minutes later. Rather surprisingly the main field had allowed the break to get a 35-minute gap, meaning changes on the overall standings. O'Grady was back in yellow, in second was Bonjour's François Simon at 4-32 and in third was Rabobank's Bram de Groot at 21-26. But among the overall favourites Beloki was 14th, now 34-33 minutes behind O'Grady, Moreau was 17th at 34-43, Armstrong was 24th at 35-19 and Ullrich was 27th at 35-46.

Despite the massive time gap between Armstrong and the yellow jersey, Heras says there was no feeling of panic: "When O'Grady and the other riders were in that break that got so far ahead we weren't concerned. Thirty-five minutes is a lot of time, but we knew that none of the riders in the break were dangerous to Lance on the general classification. Before the mountains we were always confident that the race was going well."

Stage nine took the race into the foothills of the Alps and saw another breakaway with Fassa Bortolo's Serguei Ivanov escaping to take the win. There were no major changes to the overall standings.

The first true day in the hills, stage 10, took on a number of tough climbs, in fact, three hors catégorie climbs: the Col de la Madeleine, the Col du Glandon, finishing with an uphill slog on perhaps the most famous mountain in cycling: Alpe d'Huez. But more important than the hills were the games Armstrong was about to play along the 209-kilometre route. When the group of favourites reached the Col de la Madeleine, Armstrong was only just hanging onto its coattails and grimacing unlike cycling fans had ever seen so early into a stage, while at the front of the group Ullrich's Telekom squad pushed the pace. Leading the stage was Laurent Roux of the Jean Delatour team, on a solo break, who was still six minutes ahead when the star names reached the bottom of the climb to Alpe d'Huez. With instructions coming up from the Telekom team management, who had also seen Armstrong in apparent difficulty, Ullrich's squad put everybody they had on the front in an all-out attempt to cause Armstrong as much pain as possible.

As attacks came from all sides, Armstrong moved up to sit on the wheel of Ullrich. Then suddenly Armstrong's mountain lieutenant 'Chechu' Rubiera burst through the pack with Armstrong following in his wake. Ullrich was in trouble, but he just managed to hang onto the two US Postal riders' wheels. He and the rest of the Telekom team discovered that Armstrong's problems so far this day had been nothing more than an elaborate ruse.

Heras explains what happened: "Our team's planning of the stage was that Viatcheslav Ekimov would go to the front and pull the peloton for the first 100 kilometres – Ekimov alone – until the Madeleine. Then the team would really increase the speed on the climb of the Madeleine. But after Ekimov finished his work we saw the Telekom team come to the front and take over the pace setting, increasing the speed on the Madeleine. Our planning changed completely, and Lance decided to pretend he was in trouble. It was Lance's decision entirely to do that, nobody else had thought about that."

And it worked a treat. With Ullrich now just managing to match the pace on the slopes of Alpe d'Huez, Armstrong turned round to face the German. It was a scene that has become one of the iconic moments in Armstrong's - and cycling's – history. Armstrong gave Ullrich 'The Look'. He bent his head round to look directly into Ullrich's eyes, took a long hard stare for two or three seconds, then faced forward again and was gone, sprinting up the Alpe. Armstrong had been playing possum.

Armstrong danced his way up the climb, never sitting in the saddle, rocking his bike double-time. Roux was still leading the stage by over four minutes when the American made his attack, but the distance was simply swallowed up. At six kilometres to go, with a corridor of American flags fluttering in the breeze, Armstrong could see Roux. He spun up to him, alongside him, and with absolutely no recognition for the man who had heroically spent the day ahead of the field, disappeared off into the distance. Down the slope Beloki, Ullrich and Moreau struggled on together, now 1-40 behind.

Armstrong battled through the heavy crowd, then entered the relative respite of the barriered section of the climb. His mouth gaping, his legs still revolving at around 95rpm, he sailed onwards and upwards. Then into the last kilometre he changed into the bigger gears, and sprinted round the corners and road furniture before the climb to the line. Finally Armstrong could raise his hands, punch the air and take the win. Ullrich, who had only just gone under the last kilometre banner, trundled onwards with pure power and a face displaying abject pain, to finish 1-59 behind Armstrong. Beloki arrived 10 seconds later and Moreau came in 2-30 behind Armstrong.

Overall Armstrong wasn't in yellow, that went to François Simon who had put in a great ride to limit his losses and finish 29th, but the American was up to fourth overall, 20-07 behind Simon. Second was the Kazakh rider, Andrei Kivilev of Cofidis, at 11-54, while the day's earlier yellow jersey O'Grady was third at 18-10. Behind Armstrong the race was also hotting up: Beloki was fifth at 21-42,

Moreau was sixth at 22-21, and Ullrich was seventh at 22-41.

Afterwards Armstrong explained how the day had unfolded: "In the team meeting this morning we had a plan to ride to win and fortunately Telekom helped us. They basically made the race so I was able to sit back with Chechu and Roberto and wait for the final climb. I decided to give Ullrich a look, see how he was, and give a little surge and see what happened."

If stage 10 was slowly brought to the boil, stage 11 would be a fight from the very outset, with the 2001 Tour's first individual time trial. And just to add a little more piquancy, this was a mountain time trial, starting in Grenoble and covering 32 kilometres to the 1,730m summit of Chamrousse.

Although one of the peloton's best mountain riders, Heras had no interest in showing the full range of his climbing ability today, partly because he was still suffering from a knee injury that had been caused in the team time trial crash, and partly because his job simply wasn't to win anything himself.

"At the individual time trials it depends on your situation how you approach it," Heras says. "One year I was eighth on GC so I rode for myself at the time trial, but normally I wouldn't be so high up the overall standings so I would go easy. That's what I did here in 2001, because I could help the team more in the following days. The team was committed to working for Lance in the general classification, and anyway my knee was still very sore. Before the crash I felt very good but during the week after the crash I felt very bad and it wasn't until the Pyrenees that it felt a little better."

Of the overall favourites Ullrich set off first, followed by Moreau, Beloki, then Armstrong. Initially it looked like Ullrich was going well, but it was nothing compared to Armstrong. Despite having started wearing a full head fairing, by the time Armstrong hit the real slopes his head was bare, and he was gaining almost a second per kilometre on the German. At the first checkpoint, 13.5 kilometres into the race, Armstrong was leading the split times by 11 seconds to Ullrich. By the 21.5-kilometre checkpoint he was an astounding 47 seconds quicker than Ullrich, and 1-20 quicker than Beloki. But by the third checkpoint, 28.3 kilometres into the course, Armstrong had started to slow. The time difference between him and Ullrich was down to 42 seconds as the American – as he had tended to do in all his Tour de France time trials – began to pay for a fast start.

Ullrich ground his way on to the finish and as the road levelled off near the line the big German for once almost seemed to step up that slow pedalling motion to something a little nearer the fast-spinning technique of Armstrong. His mouth open wide, a nasal band stretched taut across his nose, Ullrich never got out of the saddle, but he came his closest yet to sprinting in this year's mountain stages. And his time was the fastest yet: 1-08-27. Moreau arrived next at 1-10-27, then came Beloki with 1-09-02.

And then came Armstrong. With his hi-tech skinsuit unzipped to his abdomen, and his crucifix dangling round his neck, it looked like he was dressed for anything other than a top-level time trial. But the gradient had ensured this was less about drag factors and aero technology and more about basic, pure cycling endurance. The Texan's eyes were hidden behind dark glasses, but his mouth told the story, teeth bared as he bobbed up and down to the line to beat Ullrich's time by a round minute: 1-07-27. Overall Simon was still in yellow, now 11-01 ahead of Kivilev in second. Armstrong was up to third at 13-07, Beloki was fourth at 16-17, Ullrich was fifth at 16-41 and Moreau, now slowly dropping away from the fight for the lead, was sixth at 18-21.

Finally, the riders had a rest day before beginning their assault on the Pyrenees. The good news was that their next rest day was only three stages away, the bad news was that those three stages could each quite easily be the toughest of this year's Tour. According to Heras the US Postal team had a very simple plan for this second range of mountains: "The plan when we hit the Pyrenees was to put the pressure on the climbs against Lance's foes, and to try to conserve energy."

The pressure was soon too much for one of Lance's rivals when Christophe Moreau simply climbed off his bike and abandoned. But the US Postal leader had plenty of other things to worry about on stage 12. In the insufferable heat the competitors had to face one third-category climb, two second-category hills and one first-category challenge on the way to the first-category summit finish at Ax les Thermes.

By the final climb Armstrong and Ullrich were matching each other. It was apparent that Ullrich felt this Tour may be coming back towards him, and even took to the front to lift the pace. Armstrong flung off his US Postal cap in a sign that he meant business and settled into the German's slipstream, while the second-placed rider overall, Kivilev, kept a watching brief on the American's wheel. Armstrong took over pace-setting duties and together he and Ullrich started mopping up riders who lay ahead of them on the route. Leading on the road were Italian one-day specialist Paolo Bettini of Mapei, Euskaltel's David Etxebarria and Kelme's Felix Cardenas. After riding together as a group Cardenas attacked and disappeared up the hill alone.

With Ullrich setting the pace, he and Armstrong were joined from behind by Euskaltel's Roberto Laiseka, who quickly jumped away – to no reaction from Ullrich or Armstrong – and joined up with his team-mate Etxebarria. Armstrong lifted the pace, but Ullrich – despite being in obvious pain – managed to remain on his back wheel. Eventually Etxebarria dropped back but Laiseka carried on to chase Cardenas.

Then came the important attack. Armstrong didn't just raise the pace, he sent it into the stratosphere; he didn't just sway his bike from side to side, he sent it rocking like a fishing boat in a gale. Ullrich had no answer, his face twisted into a hideous grimace, while Armstrong's eyes, no longer hidden by sunglasses, were fixed on the neutral service car ahead which marked the position of Laiseka. With each pedal stroke he edged ever nearer. Cardenas was too far in the lead to be challenged and he took the line first, while Laiseka survived in second place, 13 seconds behind Cardenas but just two seconds ahead of Armstrong. More important than the stage positions was the fact that the Texan had gained yet more time – 23 seconds – on Ullrich, and a lot more on his other rivals.

Overall Simon had held onto the yellow jersey but his lead was down to 8-42 over Kivilev. Armstrong was still third but now by only 9-10, Beloki was in fourth at 13-14, and Ullrich was breathing down his neck in fifth just a second behind at 13-15.

Stage 13 was another massive trek in the mountains, taking the riders from Foix to Pla d'Adet and going over some famous mountains: the Col du Portet d'Aspet, the Col de Menté, the Col du Portillon, the Col de Peyresourde, the Col de Val Louron Azet before the highest climb of the day up to the finish at Saint

Lary Soulan. It was always bound to be a tough stage, probably the hardest of the Tour, but for Armstrong it was a day that also held additional significance, as it would pass the memorial to Fabio Casartelli, Armstrong's Motorola team-mate who died on the Portet d'Aspet at the 1995 Tour.

Laurent Jalabert, having quite an impressive Tour, started off the aggression with a lone attack early on the stage but it was Ullrich, putting in a big effort on the Col de Peyresourde, that was the first to mix things up among the favourites. Ullrich's Telekom team had already sent Kevin Livingston up the road with the plan being that Ullrich would at some point join him, and the pink duo could then work together. Just in front of Livingston was a small group containing another Telekom rider, Alexandre Vinokourov. In contrast, all of Armstrong's US Postal helpers were long gone, unable to keep up with the pace.

Armstrong and Beloki were prepared for Ullrich's attacks and jumped on his wheel, but the rest of the group splintered away in shattered fragments. Soon Beloki was also in trouble as Ullrich, at his most aggressive and for once out of the saddle, pummeled the climb with pedal strokes of pure power. Armstrong, as expected, bounced in the German's wake, and they crossed the Peyresourde's summit together.

On the descent there was a moment of high drama as Ullrich lost his line through a high-speed corner, surged through the tall grass at the side of a crash barrier and disappeared from view. Livingston stopped to help as his team leader clambered back up the slope, seemingly uninjured, although his German champion's jersey bore the scars of a roll in the bushes. Armstrong, who had been following Ullrich, was gone and out of sight but the US Postal leader sportingly, and sensibly, sat up to wait. Ullrich's crash had allowed Beloki and Kivilev to catch up and join Armstrong, so the Texan had little choice but to ride with them, perhaps not as slowly as he would have liked, while Livingston and Ullrich went hell for leather trying to catch up behind. By the bottom of the descent Armstrong, Ullrich, Kivilev, Beloki and Livingston were all together.

With the race heading towards the final climb to Saint Lary Soulan on the Pla d'Adet, Jalabert was still out in front 1-25 ahead of Mapei's Stefano Garzelli and 1-45 ahead of Ullrich, Armstrong and now his US Postal team-mate Heras who had caught up, while Beloki dangled just behind them. The Armstrong trio caught up with Garzelli as they negotiated the twisting, turning road cut into the mountainside. Heras pushed on as hard and as far as he could in the service of his leader, but eventually he could do no more.

"My knee was getting better, and I did as much as I could," Heras says. Armstrong went to take over pace-setting duties but in that same instant Ullrich attacked again, head down, legs churning.

They were just 1-13 behind Jalabert on the road, and over seven minutes ahead of François Simon, the man who still held the yellow jersey, and who had been 9-10 in front of Armstrong at the start of the day. Despite Ullrich putting in repeated attempts to lift the pace and get an advantage on Armstrong it was the American who came to the front and launched out of the saddle, making a gap. Armstrong didn't sprint, he just lifted the tempo and was gone. Within moments he was alongside Jalabert, who bravely lifted his own pace to try and match Armstrong's, but then Armstrong sprang onwards alone. Ullrich refused to give in completely and pushed his body's diesel engine harder and harder, his mouth gulping air as he also caught and passed Jalabert.

With three kilometres to go the time difference between Armstrong and Ullrich was up to 38 seconds, but for once the gap to Ullrich wasn't really what Armstrong was interested in, he was more concerned with gaining the 9-10 to take yellow from Simon. After a short flat Armstrong hit the last two-kilometre climb to the finish, never altering that high cadence, still popping out of the saddle as he rode between walls of rabid bike fans. Into the final kilometre and the time difference between him and Ullrich was over 50 seconds. Finally Armstrong zipped up his jersey, pointed two fingers to the sky – in memory of Casartelli – punched the air and took one of his greatest victories.

Behind Armstrong, Ullrich pushed on, fighting to increase his advantage over Joseba Beloki and aiming to secure second place overall. He arrived a minute down. Beloki crossed the line 46 seconds later and Kivilev finished 10th, 4-02 down on the winner. François Simon eventually appeared at the summit 13-20 after Armstrong. The yellow jersey was now in the hands of the American, and it looked unlikely to be leaving him. Overall Armstrong led the race by 3-54 to

Kivilev in second, Simon was third at 4-31, Ullrich was fourth at 5-13, and Beloki was fifth at 6-02.

"It is emotional because I have never passed the Fabio Casartelli memorial in the Tour de France," Armstrong said afterwards. "This was the first time that I rode by it. The first reaction you have is that it is a terrible descent, it's the worst descent that we ever do. You can see how there was a crash there. When I passed it today I just said to myself quietly: 'OK there's only one winner today, there may be a breakaway, they may have 10 minutes, but I'm going to win this today.'"

Looking back on the stage now Heras concurs with his team leader's thoughts. "Normally when Lance won a stage we could see how he was riding, and how confident he was. Barring an accident or illness, for me I was always sure he'd win the Tour and this stage showed how strong he was."

The final stage in the mountains for the 2001 Tour arrived with the promise of a following rest day for the souls still riding, but before they could relax they would have to negotiate 141.5 kilometres to the summit finish at Luz Ardiden, and climb the highest mountain of the entire Tour, the 2,115m Col du Tourmalet en route.

As the race began the final climb of Luz Ardiden Ullrich had his team-mate Giuseppe Guerini leading the group of favourites, while Armstrong sat just behind with one of his own lieutenants, Heras. Up ahead a three-man breakaway containing Fassa Bortolo's Wladimir Belli, Lotto's Mario Aerts and Cofidis's David Moncoutié surged their way through the dense crowd that lined the climb. Among the group of favourites Euskaltel's Roberto Laiseka attacked, pleasing many of the Spanish fans who had crossed just three miles over the border to watch the race, while neither Ullrich nor Armstrong cared to react. In the same group, not too far behind, Andrei Kivilev lurked ready to spoil what most people thought were the expected results.

Laiseka flew his way up the climb, while at the front Belli broke away from his two companions. Laiseka caught and passed Aerts and Moncoutié, and set about looking for Belli, quickly catching the Italian before again sprinting off alone. Back in the yellow jersey group there was little dramatic action, despite Ullrich and Guerini desperately trying to lift the pace to drop Kivilev. At four and a half kilometres to go Laiseka had 1-20 over the chasing Armstrong and Ullrich group, with Belli still somewhere in no man's land in between.

Finally, with Kivilev and Beloki disappearing off the back, the group of overall favourites had been whittled down to just Ullrich, Armstrong and a pace-setting Heras.

"That stage to Luz Ardiden was a great day for me," Heras says. "I felt great and I could really help Lance put pressure on Ullrich. My job was to help Lance, and if I could even stay with Lance until the last kilometre of the climb that would be the best thing. For me it was nice, it was a pleasure the times when I could dictate the pace. That day, staying with Lance all the way to the finish, was probably my best memory of the Tour."

As Laiseka entered the barriered part of the course with just two kilometres to go he enjoyed a 42-second lead over Belli, with Armstrong, Ullrich and Heras 1-13 down. Laiseka wound his way round the final few corners while, behind, Ullrich's pride refused to submit and he launched one last desperate attack. Armstrong followed and then let the German grind out the pace for them both. Laiseka took the line, kissing the air and crossing himself. Belli rode in second, 54 seconds later, and at 1-08 Ullrich led Armstrong in for third. The American did not contest the time bonus that came with the third placing and which Ullrich needed to secure second place in the overall classification. The two great Tour combatants gave each other a subtle, touching hand hold as they crossed the line – foes on the road, but friends in sport.

Overall Armstrong still led the race but Ullrich had managed to usurp Kivilev, just, for second place. The German was 5-05 behind Armstrong, while Kivilev was only 5-13 down. That eight-second gap between second and third overall was, incidentally, exactly the time bonus Ullrich had received for third place on the stage. Fourth was Beloki at 6-33 while Simon was slowly falling down the rankings, in fifth at 10-54.

After a rest day in the city of Pau the riders turned towards Paris. The US Postal plan for these final days of the Tour was the same as it always had been in Armstrong's previous two overall victories. "In the last week, it depends on the stages, but normally you see breaks go away," Heras says. "A lot of the teams are down to five or six riders, everybody is tired, and you just control the race. For Lance we just had to control the first few kilometres until the breakaway had gone, and then just get him to the finish line safely."

Stages 15, 16 and 17 all saw breakaways take the spoils, although stage 16 featured some drama with a mass pile-up involving Jan Ullrich. Ullrich was fine to continue and there were no major changes to the overall standings.

Stage 18 was the last individual time trial, and the last realistic chance for the race to see significant changes in the general classification. It was a flat 61-kilometre course from Montluçon to Saint Amand Montrond and, as expected, Armstrong was dominant, setting records at all the time-checks en route. Ullrich seemed to be having some problems, whether with his kit or his body, and could only manage to record the second best time at the finish, 1-15-55, which was 15 seconds slower than the benchmark of 1-15-40 set by ONCE's Igor Gonzalez de Galdeano earlier in the day. Within a couple of minutes Ullrich was down to the third best time of the day as Armstrong cemented his superiority in the 2001 Tour de France by winning the final time trial with a figure of 1-14-16, recording an average speed of 49.28kph.

Overall Armstrong had extended his lead over Ullrich to 6-44 while Beloki had managed to leapfrog Kivilev into third place at 9-05. It meant that barring unforeseen circumstances the final podium in Paris would be a carbon copy of that seen in the 2000 Tour de France.

"I think it's important not only to win the Tour but, if you're in a position to win and you're in the yellow jersey, in my opinion it's important that the yellow jersey show up at the last time trial and prove that he's the best, and prove that he deserves to win the Tour," Armstrong said.

Stage 19 ended in a bunch sprint and then it was to Paris and the final stage. The US Postal squad had the honour of leading the field into the French capital, before a seven-man break escaped on the Champs-Elysées. Despite a last ditch effort by Telekom's Alexandre Vinokourov to stay away on the final lap, the peloton just managed to bring the race all together and Lampre's Jan Svorada took the stage. Armstrong rolled in 70th, under clear Parisian skies, with his bright yellow jersey gleaming.

"That last stage, finishing on the Champs-Elysées, was a really nice moment, it was a special moment," Heras remembers. "Any rider who reaches the Champs-Elysées knows it is a special moment, for everybody, not just the winners. There are so many people watching the race, everyone is happy. We had a party that night after the stage. We had dinner with the sponsors and many people had flown in from the USA, from Europe, from all over the world. Before the dinner we had a little get-together with just the nine riders and their wives, and Johan and the staff. And Lance said thank you to us, he said it was a pleasure riding with us. It was a special moment for the riders and our families."

While Armstrong left France to start thinking about Tour victory number four, for Heras there were more immediate concerns: "In the Pyrenees I felt a little better but by the time we reached Paris my knee was hurting again, it was inflamed and very bad. I went home and spent a week off my bike waiting for it to recover. The doctors looked at it and told me not to touch the bike, it would be dangerous because I had an infection there and they wanted me to get better so they could see if I could race the Vuelta."

Heras did end up racing the Vuelta but there would be no fairytale finish to his year as he only managed to finish fourth in Spain. He would have to wait two more years, until 2003, to secure his home Grand Tour win in US Postal colours.

After the 2005 Vuelta Heras was banned from competition after failing a test for EPO and has not returned to professional cycling.

The Road to 1999

With Eddie Borysewicz, Armstrong's Subaru-Montgomery team boss 1990-1992;
Sean Yates, Armstrong's Motorola team-mate 1992-1996; and Dr Scott Shapiro,
the neurosurgeon that removed Armstrong's brain tumours in 1996

When people speak of Lance Armstrong's story the word 'fairytale' never seems to be too far away, but his story began in less than idyllic circumstances. Lance Edward Gunderson was born on September 18th, 1971 to Linda Mooneyham and Eddie Gunderson, two 17-year-olds from Texas, neither of whom were ready for marriage, even less so children. By the time their son had turned two the couple had split and, to this day, Lance maintains that he has no interest in meeting his biological father, saying he thinks of him simply as the "DNA donor".

With Eddie gone, Linda took on a range of part-time jobs to support her small family and a couple of years later she remarried, to Terry Armstrong, a travelling salesman. Terry legally adopted Lance when he was around five years old, giving him the Armstrong surname.

The young Lance had an initial taste of life in the saddle with his first bike given to him by his maternal grandfather – the only father figure he was particularly close to – and he also competed in junior BMX events. But he found his natural calling at the age of 13 when he spotted an advert in a local bike shop for a junior triathlon competition. He won his first event, and then he spread his gaze further afield, competing and winning junior triathlons across Texas. Although Armstrong's sporting career was taking off, life at home was splintering, and after 10 years of marriage, Terry and Linda Armstrong split up and then divorced.

In 1987, at the age of just 15, Armstrong entered the President's Triathlon in Lake Lavon, Texas, and despite most of the competitors being adults Armstrong finished 32nd. He began to earn good prize money on the triathlon circuit, and he also had the chance to concentrate on his cycling, entering Tuesday evening criteriums near his home in Plano, Texas. Meanwhile, at his swimming club, Armstrong was being lined up as a prospective national team member and even future Olympian in the pool. It was quickly clear that he was a natural athlete, and a physical test at Dallas's Cooper Clinic when Armstrong was 16 showed his VO2 max – the measure of his oxygen-using ability – was massive. It was also discovered that his body simply made less lactic acid than most other people's, so he could compete for longer and faster before feeling fatigue.

During his final school year, in 1989, Armstrong had his first taste of international sport, being invited to Colorado Springs to train with the US national junior cycling team and be part of the squad that would go to race the Junior World Championships in Moscow. Then, after graduating, while many of his friends went on to university, Armstrong decided to follow his cycling career and moved to Austin to keep on racing.

Earlier in 1989 American cycling had seen the creation of a new elite super-team, Suburu-Montgomery. Not only did Subaru-Montgomery have money behind it – it was partly financed by tycoon Thom Weisel of Montgomery Securities, who would later be the driving force behind the US Postal team – but it was also managed by Eddie Borysewicz. Better known as Eddie B, he is one of the legends of American cycling: a Polish immigrant who came to the United States in the late Seventies and completely rewrote the training manual for American cyclists with his Eastern European preparation techniques.

Not all of the training techniques Eddie B brought with him were particularly pleasant, and it was Borysewicz's knowledge of blood doping – which at the time wasn't specifically outlawed by sports governing bodies – that helped the US national team claim nine medals at the 1984 Olympic Games. But that period was well behind him when Armstrong became one of his riders and by 1989 Borysewicz had left his role as the US national coach, deciding instead to create an elite amateur squad with some of the best American riders.

"I first heard about Lance when my friend Mike Fraser, who was the vice-president of the United States Cycling Federation, said to me: 'Eddie, I know you are always looking for young guys to develop. There is some animal in Texas you should look at.' And he was talking about Lance," Borysewicz says.

"So I contacted Lance and we set up a meeting after some local race down in Austin, Texas. It was just like any typical meeting I would have with any young guy, and Lance's mother was there too. I had watched the race, and I thought he was really very aggressive, he was very powerful. He was so young, but he was a very powerful man who didn't yet know much about cycling. Lance's mum was very nice, but they didn't have a lot of money. I remember Lance rode a small bike, which is why his back is still not really perfect.

"I talked to him, and I talked to his mum. I remember asking him what kind of sickness he had had in the past, because it was important for me to know how healthy he was, and he told me nothing. I said: 'OK, fine, nothing major, but you must have had the flu?' 'No,' he said. 'OK, what about headache?' I asked. Again he said: 'No.' So I looked at his mum and she said: 'No, no, he is very healthy, he is never sick.' That was a positive surprise for me. He was also very enthusiastic, he wanted to be a bike rider."

The Subaru-Montgomery team operated as an amateur squad in 1990 – with all of its riders except Armstrong becoming classed as professionals in 1991 – but Borysewicz still offered Armstrong an allowance. Despite the fact that Armstrong has since become a multi-millionaire businessman, Borysewicz remembers the talk he had with Armstrong about money was a very humble affair back then. "Lance told me he was a triathlete, and he had managed to earn some money, so I told him I was going to pay him $12,000. He was very shy after hearing this and he said he wasn't worth this $12,000. I said to him: 'You might not be worth it, but your body is worth it, and you need to put the bread on the table.'

"I told him to go speak to his friends, I was sure his cycling friends would know of me and my team, so I got a call from him after a week or two saying he'd like to join the team. I think I then asked him for a blood test, and he did everything I asked. After a few days he said he was ready to come. We had a team house with a few riders, like Mike McCarthy and other good guys, in California. So I sent Lance a ticket and he came out to California and stayed with us. That was in the off-season, in October or November 1989, and that began our relationship. He was very coachable, very nice, very positive. He just wanted to be a good bike rider."

Perhaps more in keeping with the Lance Armstrong the public knows today was his attitude on the bike. The plan was for Armstrong to learn the role of a domestique first and then progress towards becoming a team leader, but that approach together with Borysewicz's goal not to rush Armstrong's physical development was often a sticking point. "He has an extremely competitive character, and it was the same when he was with us. He doesn't have the mindset to be a domestique, which was probably part of the problem we had with him at times because I was trying to develop him slowly. But he wanted to be a winner," Borysewicz says.

And a winner, or at least a leading rider, he quickly became. Borysewicz recalls the successes: "I remember some good races for Lance, like when he went to the World Amateur Championship in Tokyo in Japan, he was just outside the top-10 in his first year at the Worlds. He still had some weaknesses, like tactics and experience. He wasn't a leader at Subaru-Montgomery because we had guys there better than him. But the year after we signed him we could fully control his preparation in the off-season and then he had his very successful year. He was supposed to be just a developer, but he was very happy about winning the Settimana Bergamasca race in 1991 because it was a very big deal."

That win at the Settimana Bergamasca – a prestigious European stage race – was the first for an American rider. Unfortunately, though, it probably also marked the beginning of the end of Armstrong's relationship with the Subaru-Montgomery squad. When Armstrong first signed with Subaru-Montgomery he had also been approached by Chris Carmichael to be a member of the US national squad. So Armstrong rode as an amateur for Borysewicz and Subaru-Montgomery team in domestic US events, but he rode for Carmichael as part of the US national team at races abroad. At the Settimana Bergamasca both teams were competing and Armstrong was riding for the US squad, in conflict with his trade team, which caused significant problems.

Borysewicz remembers the race well: "We had a bit of stress at the 1991 Settimana Bergamasca. I don't like to talk about that much, because it's in the past. Lance really wanted to win this race, and I could understand that, and Carmichael pushed him to do that. But we had Nate Reiss in the Subaru-Montgomery team who could win the race, and I wanted everybody to help him do that. But Chris Carmichael was against it. Even though we still saw Lance as a Subaru-Montgomery rider, in that particular race he was riding for the US national team, where Carmichael was the boss.

"I know Carmichael hired Czech riders and Russian riders to try to help Lance win the race, but those guys blew up and the situation was very dangerous for Lance. So Carmichael then came to us to ask for help. People might have thought I would be upset, but I was different. I told our young team: 'Gentlemen, I respect your feelings, but this is one of our guys and we have to do it.' And they really did work for him and Lance won the race. There was a little bit of bad feeling because after Lance won that race and came back to the United States he said nothing. He didn't say thank you, and our guys were a bit upset. There was a bit of a problem between the other guys and him. But for a young guy in that situation that was pretty normal. For me it was fine, I wasn't upset."

Even to this day there is still the residue of bad feeling between Borysewicz and Carmichael, with both of them claiming to be 'the man who discovered Lance Armstrong' all those years ago. Borysewicz's animosity towards Carmichael may be partly attributable to the fact it was Carmichael who introduced Armstrong to Jim Ochowicz, the boss of the Motorola squad, and hence took Armstrong away from Subaru-Montgomery into the realms of the professional peloton for the 1992 season. Borysewicz says that's not the case: "Chris Carmichael helped arrange Lance a good deal with a move to Motorola, and so he went to Motorola because they offered him big money.

"I wasn't mad that he went to Motorola because it was just money. I was more sad that he went to Stuttgart, to the 1991 World Championship, and he just quit in the middle of the race. Then at the 1992 Olympic Games he wasn't in the top 10. But then straight after the Olympics he turned pro and within a year everything changed, so I think he probably turned pro at the perfect time."

Borysewicz and Armstrong's career would cross paths again, six years later, when another team Borysewicz had started up with help from Thom Weisel, this time called US Postal, found a post-cancer Armstrong without a deal. "I always believed he would be a very, very good rider. Of course everybody, including me, was a bit surprised by his results after cancer," Borysewicz says. "I even left the US Postal team because – even though I like Lance and I wanted to have Lance on our team – I didn't want to build the US Postal team around Lance, so I had a disagreement with the sponsor and I left. But Lance did a miracle, and miracles don't happen very often."

Despite his relationship with Armstrong seemingly ending a little sourly on two occasions, Borysewicz is at pains to make his feelings clear: "I love cycling and I love Lance. We sometimes had different opinions about his development and other things, but it was a great privilege for me to work with him, and I am very happy that I found him and started him on his career. I will never forget his words after he won the 1993 World Championship in Oslo. I went up to him and said congratulations, and he replied: 'Thank you, I could never have been here without you.' That paid me back for everything."

Before there was any talk of World Championship wins, though, Armstrong had to join his first professional squad, Motorola, where he would spend five seasons riding as an aggressive one-day specialist. Throughout those five years he formed a close bond with veteran British rider Sean Yates. Yates had started his career in 1982 with the Peugeot team, and by the time Armstrong entered the sport he had spent a decade at the peak of professional cycling. Within the Motorola squad Yates was something of the sergeant major: the firm old hand there to get the younger riders in order.

"The first time I met and talked to Lance he was riding for Subaru-Montgomery in the DuPont Tour and I was riding for Motorola, that was in 1991," Yates remembers. "We were actually in a race-winning breakaway together in Richmond, Virginia: me, Lance and three or four others. He was cool – I remember talking to him. The next time I saw him was at the beginning of 1992 at the Motorola training camp. He signed with Motorola in 1991 but he rode with Subaru-Montgomery as an amateur until the Barcelona Olympics in 1992, then turned pro. Even so, he came to the camp and trained with us in Santa Rosa, which incidentally is where the Astana team held their training camp at the start of 2009 – so 18 years after Lance was first at a training camp in Santa Rosa he was back there again.

"At that first camp, for some reason Lance and I seemed to get on well and we did some long rides, just me and him. He wasn't so good at descending, he was OK but we had some terrible tyres, the road-holding was appalling, and for Lance trying to learn with these tyres was the ultimate test really. I remember going down these hills in Santa Rosa, in the wet, and trying to teach Lance how to descend."

Even though they had hit it off, Yates still had to pull rank with the precocious

Armstrong on occasion. "I remember one ride, I think it was just me and him, we stopped at a general store out in the country where there were a load of rednecks. There was somebody who was a bit slow or not quite all there working behind the counter, and Lance was chuckling about her for some reason. I must have not been too impressed that he was taking the mickey out of this person because I just turned round to him and said: 'We'll see who is bloody laughing when you turn pro, boy.' Those were my exact words. Obviously I never knew he was going to win seven Tours de France and everything else, but that's a story he repeats to this day.

"I was a bit of a tyrant, or that was my reputation because of the way I talked to individuals, especially young guys. The impression I gave out to the young riders was that they had better toe the line or they would be history," Yates says.

At the time Armstrong was not seen as a potential Grand Tour winner, if anything his outright strength and aggression was perfectly suited to the one-day Classics, and that was where he started his Motorola career. The first top-level professional race he competed in was the Clasica San Sebastian. For Armstrong – a man who had been regularly ruling the roost in domestic American events – the pace of competition came as quite a shock, and he finished plum last. But things quickly picked up. He was sent to some races in Spain, where he won a stage at the Vuelta a Galicia, and then he returned to the Classics arena, finishing an impressive second at the 1992 Championship of Zurich. To end the season he raced in Italy, where he was joined by Yates.

"I didn't see Lance at any of his first races but then he went to three races in Italy culminating at the Tour of Lombardy, which is where I saw him again because I was racing there. I shared a room with him then. We ended up being room-mates a lot. I would say between 80 and 90 per cent of the time we were at the same races we would share a room. I don't know why that was the case other than we got on well, and normally you were put in a room with someone you got on well with."

Come the start of the 1993 season Armstrong was very much an integral part of the Motorola team, and he was expected to be a major force in the early-season one-day races. "In the Classics in his first full year, we stayed in a room at the Holiday Inn in Ghent, and that was a three-week stint," Yates remembers.

"Lance was going to all the big races, like the Tour of Flanders, and he was getting pummeled. That year, his first year in Belgium, he was expected to be up there among the big-hitters in the Classics. I remember sitting down with him after coming back from a race and he said: 'If I don't start performing in these races I'm just going to pack it in and go to university.' I said: 'Christ! You can't just roll up and expect to be beating guys like Johan Museeuw and Andrei Tchmil who have been doing it donkey's years. This is as tough as it gets.'

"But in a typical year I never did the hilly Classics with Lance, I only did up to Paris-Roubaix, then I had a break, and then we would go to the DuPont Tour. Lance won that race a couple of times, although he finished second in 1993, and I did a lot of the work riding on the front for him there."

Armstrong's natural ability came to the fore perhaps sooner than anyone expected. Over the course of the season he became the first cyclist to win a million-dollar prize, completing an American triple – the Thrift Drug Classic, the Kmart Classic and the US Pro Championships – to secure the unique cash reward. Then, at his very first Tour de France, in his first full year as a neo-pro, the young Texan made his mark with an aggressive stage win.

"I remember Lance at the Tour de France in 1993 particularly because he won the US Pro Championships and he was wearing the US national jersey when he won his first stage," Yates recalls. "I was rooming with him at that Tour. He wasn't nervous but he was excited I guess. I remember on stage seven Motorola had Max Sciandri and Alvaro Mejia in the break, but Bjarne Riis of the Ariostea team won by beating them both. I remember Lance was really angry that our boys had lost the stage, and it had finished in the Reims area, so hearing that Riis had got bottles of champagne and all these other prizes for winning the stage annoyed Lance so much he went out and won the next day.

"I remember on stage eight a breakaway went from the start and we had to ride our nuts off to catch it – it was like a team time trial for about 20 kilometres. Then we came to a climb and I remember getting Lance right on my wheel, taking him to the bottom of this climb in a good position, and then he went away in a breakaway and won the stage."

Just a year after turning professional, Armstrong repaid the Motorola's team faith in him with an amazing Tour de France stage win. It is a great achievement to win a stage of the Tour at any point of your life, but to do it at the age of 21, in your first participation in the race, and wearing your national champion's jersey, is almost beyond a dream. Under clear, bright skies Armstrong was part of a break with Raul Alcala, Ronan Pensec, Dominique Arnould, Giancarlo Perini and Stephen Roche that had just managed to reach the town of Verdun ahead of the fast-closing main field. While Roche faded off the back the five other combatants competed in a winner-takes-all battle for the line, with Armstrong powering around the left-hand side and punching the air as he took victory.

Curiously, Yates remembers Armstrong got a military seal of approval for the stage win: "That day we had a five-star general from the US Army visiting the team and he was sitting in the Motorola race car. He came with a chauffeur in a bulletproof Mercedes that weighed about six tonnes and had glass two inches thick, but during the stage he sat with 'Och' [Motorola boss Jim Ochowicz] in our team car. I remember Och was delighted because Lance won the stage, and the general was happy because he had had a fantastic day out."

At still such a young age it was unlikely Armstrong was ever going to be able to do much more in the 1993 Tour than perhaps take another stage win, and he quit the race after stage 11. "It was his first Tour and he just felt he had had enough," Yates remembers. "I think his girlfriend was there and he just left the race. He was pretty big and muscular then, similar to the way he was after returning to cycling in late 2008, after retirement. His body is such that he only has to look at a weight bar and he puts on muscle."

Although he didn't reach Paris it was still an impressive showing from the young American, but even greater things were just around the corner. Two months later, in September, the 1993 World Championships were held in Norway, and Armstrong sealed his amazing season by beating some of the greatest riders of the day in a straight fight. Before the race began, pundits were talking about whether the Italian Gianni Bugno would be able to take his third world title in a row, or if the reigning Tour de France and Giro d'Italia victor Miguel Indurain would be able to seal the 'big three' and add the World Championship to his season's haul. Despite his growing reputation as a one-day specialist, very few people would have had 21-year-old Lance Armstrong down as a favourite.

The course, 14 laps of an 18.4-kilometre circuit which snaked through the tight, greasy streets of down-town Oslo, during almost constant rain, was a nightmare. It was in marked contrast to the World Amateur Championships that had been held on the same roads in glorious sunshine the day before and where a 19-year-old German called Jan Ullrich had announced his presence to the cycling world by taking the title. Neither Ullrich nor Armstrong knew it at the time, but their names would continue to be spoken of in the same breath for most of their careers.

Having been lubricated by heavy rainfall, almost all the corners on the course were potential crash sites. In fact, even the straights witnessed tumbles as riders lost control of their bikes on the white road markings. Italian favourite Moreno Argentin slid out of the race; Raul Alcala, who had pipped Armstrong to the overall title at the Tour DuPont, crashed over the barriers onto the adjoining tram track; even Armstrong took a tumble on at least two occasions.

Despite a constant stream of speculative attacks it wasn't until Danish star Bjarne Riis's effort on lap 12 that cracks started to appear. By the end of lap 13 a strong breakaway group featuring Indurain, Armstrong, Riis, Claudio Chiappucci, Dag-Otto Lauritzen, Frans Maassen, Gerard Rué, Andrei Tchmil and Olaf Ludwig had managed to get away from the peloton.

As the final lap began Lauritzen and Maassen attacked and were quickly joined by Ludwig, but the trio failed to secure a big gap. Lauritzen attacked again while Armstrong made the bridge to Maassen just behind. Armstrong and Maassen worked together to bring back Lauritzen, and they were also joined from behind by Rué. The quartet didn't work together for long before Armstrong launched himself off the front on the main climb of the circuit, the Ekeberg.

It was a brave and confident attack, and by the time the race returned to Oslo's docklands Armstrong had built up a gap of 20 seconds, while the group behind seemed unable to organise themselves into an effective chase. Armstrong's body, a heavy-set, muscular machine pumping pure power through the pedals, cut through the rain. He held his nerve, and his lead, to the finish line, punching the air despite the heavy downpour. Indurain took the sprint for second.

At the age of 21 Armstrong became the youngest professional world cycling champion in history, but perhaps more interesting was his behaviour after the race. The winner of the championship was due to meet King Harald of Sweden, but Armstrong refused to do so unless his mother – who had accompanied him to the race – could also attend. It made for an uncomfortable scene as security officials decided what to do, but Armstrong got his way, his mother was allowed in, and a quite incredible 1993 season finished on a royal high.

Yates didn't compete at the 1993 World Championships, but he was watching the race keenly on television: "Obviously Lance was a fantastic talent and he proved it when he won the World Championships in Oslo. I didn't race those Worlds, in fact I was staying in Dag-Otto Lauritzen's house who lived in Grimstad, about 300 kilometres away. Dag-Otto was planning a big party which was going to be his last criterium, his last race, after the Worlds. So I came over for Dag-Otto's big final party, but Dag-Otto ended up flying in the Worlds and came in sixth, and he decided to race on for another year. And then Lance went and won the thing. It was quite a race."

After the excitement of 1993, the 1994 season could never quite live up to the heights of his first full year among the pro peloton. Even so, Armstrong claimed victories at the Thrift Drug Classic and stages of the DuPont Tour, and he took notable runner-up spots in Liège-Bastogne-Liège, the Clasica San Sebastian and at the Dupont Tour overall. He ended the season 25th in the world rankings.

Armstrong may have been a truly modern cyclist but Yates remembers him being fascinated by stories of bygone racing days. "I shared a lot of time in hotel rooms with Lance and he liked me to tell him all these stories about way back when, about my career and what happened in past years," Yates says.

"I remember he was always on the case with his money, even in his first year. I didn't have a laptop until way beyond when I retired, but Lance had a laptop even back in the mid-'90s and he'd go online to look at his stocks and shares. When his shares were up he'd say, 'I'm going to have a good day tomorrow.' I also remember he'd ring up his coach, Chris Carmichael. They'd chat and Lance would email him his SRM files showing his power output for Carmichael to look over. He was really new-school and I was old-school – I had never used a computer, or a power meter, or had a coach or anything like that. I think that was all slightly amusing for him."

And the work that Yates did for Armstrong didn't stop when the race was over. "I remember I used to wash his clothes for him," Yates says. "In those days we had to wash our own clothes. What we would do was get to the hotel, strip off, and there would be a cup of washing powder in your room. You'd dump your clothes in the sink, wash them, rinse them, and we had a centrifugal spinner in one of the masseurs' rooms, and we'd dump them in there to get the water out. Then we'd hang them up to dry. I would do all that for Lance. For me it was just two minutes' work and I was happy to do it, and I knew he didn't like doing it."

The 1995 season was another step up the ladder, and it saw Armstrong win the Clasica San Sebastian, the DuPont Tour overall with three stage victories, a stage of Paris-Nice and another stage of the Tour de France, but that final achievement only came in the most tragic of circumstances. On stage 15 to Cauterets, Fabio Casartelli, the 24-year-old reigning Olympic road race champion and a member of the Motorola team, crashed on the descent of the Col du Portet d'Aspet, fatally striking his head on the kerb. The experience affected many in the team deeply, none more so than Armstrong, whose initial thought was to abandon the race. The day after Casartelli's accident, in a mark of respect, the race neutralised the stage and allowed the Motorola team to lead the rest of the peloton. Casartelli's bike, wrapped in black ribbon and standing alone on top of the Motorola team car, followed the riders along the day's course.

Yates remembers the episode well: "When Casartelli died I wasn't actually still on the race. I had abandoned two or three days before that. It was a horrendous time really. I had gone back to Nice where I was living and I was watching the race on the television. We saw the crash, and then heard the news when it came through. I remember the next day Lance called me and he was very upset. He was in tears. I can't remember his exact words, but he was saying how very upset he felt. Very upset. It really affected him.

"Then we had Casartelli's funeral, and because I wasn't on the race any more I went to the funeral in Como, Italy. Och flew over with somebody from the Tour de France, and me and another guy from Motorola, Bjorn Stenersen, were two of the pallbearers. It was just a dreadful experience. Fabio had just had a young child with his wife. I remember it all: the funeral, and the church, and the music and the wailing. It was a baking hot day and I just remember being drenched in sweat carrying the coffin for 400 metres to the grave. It was a traumatic time."

Motorola boss Jim Ochowicz let it be known to his team that Casartelli had targeted stage 18 to Limoges for a good ride. With that in his mind Armstrong decided that stage 18 would be his chance to show his own mark of respect to Casartelli. He escaped with a group of six riders and then set off alone, with almost 30 kilometres left to race. Seemingly inspired by the spirit of Casartelli, Armstrong powered to the finish, repeatedly pointing his fingers to the heavens in the closing couple of hundred metres, and won the stage by 33 seconds.

Armstrong's growing ability to put himself in the mix at the world's biggest cycle races meant he was soon seen as Motorola's star rider, and he was enjoying the trappings that his position brought.

"Lance got the flash house, the flash car, and had a bit of the Premiership footballer-type status," Yates remembers. "Back then Lance had been world champ and he was seen as the future of the team. He wasn't the boss of the team, but he was the star of the team. After all, he was an American and we had an American sponsor. There was Andy Hampsten who won the Giro and had won on Alpe d'Huez in the Tour, but he was on his way out. The other American favourite, Davis Phinney, was finished. And then there was Lance, who was able to win all sorts of big races."

Happy at Motorola, the 1996 season was another good one for Armstrong. Although he didn't have a headline-grabbing stage win at the Tour de France he did completely dominate his native Tour DuPont, taking five stages and the overall, and he became the first American to win the Flèche Wallonne Classic. In addition to that Armstrong finished second at another historic Classic, Liège-Bastogne-Liège; second in the Tour of Holland; and second overall in the great early-season stage race Paris-Nice. By the end of the year he was ranked ninth in the world.

Because of this success he was rewarded with a $2.5 million contract with the leading French team, Cofidis. Armstrong's move to a new squad was made all the more necessary because of Ochowicz's inability to find a replacement sponsor for

Motorola. But over the course of the year Armstrong had started to feel increasingly under the weather, and noticed one of his testicles had become swollen – neither symptom, though, was particularly unusual for a professional cyclist. He dropped out of the 2006 Tour after just five days, having developed a sore throat and bronchitis. Then at the Olympic Games in Atlanta – which Armstrong had planned to be the highlight of his season – he managed to finish only sixth in the time trial, and 12th in the road race. Those were not the results he was looking for, and he prepared to rest for the winter.

Yates, himself coming to the end of his racing days with his imminent retirement, remembers thinking something might have been wrong: "The last race Lance rode before he was diagnosed with cancer was with me: we did a two-up time trial in Germany, the Baden Baden Cup, and he wasn't going so well – well, not as well as he should have been going. The race was in Freiburg but we flew out of Basle, and on the way to the airport he fell asleep in the back of the car. Lance never, ever fell asleep in the car after a race, he was always a livewire. That day he did, though, and I thought that was most unusual. Then a few weeks afterwards Jim Ochowicz phoned me up and said Lance had been diagnosed with cancer. He must have had it pretty bad when we did that race, which explains why he didn't perform so well. But with Lance being such an animal he was still able to ride a half-decent time trial even while infested with cancer.

"As it happened Motorola's sponsorship ended, Lance got cancer, and I retired all at the same time. Och was trying to find a new sponsor, and I was going to become a directeur sportif on the team. But Och couldn't find a sponsor so Lance couldn't continue with the team, and so he signed with Cofidis. But if Och had found a sponsor Lance would have gone back to him."

While Armstrong underwent treatment for his cancer, Yates disappeared into retirement and, looking back at his career, he says he may have retired a lot earlier had it not been for the inspiration that Armstrong provided: "Lance was my mate and I really got on well with him. I was someone who rode for the leader and Lance gave me an incentive to ride – I needed someone to ride for. I was going to retire a bit earlier, then Lance wanted me to keep going for another year, then another year. He kept saying: 'You can't retire yet.'"

But Yates's story with Armstrong didn't just end in 1996. In 2005 Armstrong hired his old room-mate as a directeur sportif for his Discovery Channel team, and Yates stayed with the squad even after Armstrong retired from the sport. When Discovery lost its sponsorship in 2007 Yates was briefly out of a job, but then Johan Bruyneel moved to take over the reins at the Astana team and Yates followed him. And when Armstrong returned to cycling in 2009 as a member of the Astana team, it meant the old friends were back in the same set-up again, more than 15 years after they first met.

"Lance is just a normal guy," Yates says before correcting himself. "Well he's not a normal guy: he's survived cancer, he's raised millions and millions for charity, he's hobnobbed with presidents and dated film stars and pop stars, and he's made millions. But when he's in a room having a team meeting and he's taking the mickey out of me and my English accent, it's just like it was back then. He's just Lance, but the public can't get a feeling of what he is really like because he can't be himself in the public eye.

"He's my hero to a certain extent. And like before I would wash his clothes, now if he asks for something when we're at a hotel or somewhere I'll run upstairs and get it for him. Not because I think I've got to do it because it's Lance, but because I want everything to be right for him."

On Monday October 7th, 1996 things definitely weren't right for Armstrong. He held a press conference to tell the world some important news. "On Wednesday October 2nd I was diagnosed with testicular cancer. Prior to seeing my doctor last week I had been experiencing pain and swelling in one of my testicles and I coughed up some blood. On Thursday October 3rd I underwent surgery at Saint David's Hospital here in Austin to have the malignant testicle removed and the surgery was successful. A CAT scan was performed the same day. The CAT scan revealed that the condition has also spread to my abdomen."

Answering questions from journalists, Armstrong admitted the discovery had affected him terribly: "I have never cried a lot, but in the last week I cry all the time, and that helps, I think."

The previous couple of weeks had been tough. On September 18th Armstrong celebrated his 25th birthday. A couple of days later he had a party with friends and then went out to watch a music concert but during the course of the evening he was struck by a headache so bad he had to leave early. The next morning the headache had gone but his vision was blurred. A couple of days later Armstrong coughed up blood. He called a friend and doctor, Rick Parker, to check him over, but by then Armstrong had washed away the blood he had coughed up into the sink. Parker invited Armstrong to dinner the following week. He went but found it almost impossible to sit down, such was the pain coming from his right testicle.

The following morning, Wednesday October 2nd, Armstrong's testicle had swollen to the size of an orange and he was unable to sit in the saddle during his training ride. He called Parker again, who scheduled an appointment for him that afternoon with urologist Dr Jim Reeves. After an examination, and then a chest x-ray, the diagnosis was shocking. Armstrong had testicular cancer which had spread – as the x-rays showed – to his lungs.

What happened next was a whirlwind. At seven o'clock the next morning, Thursday October 3rd, Armstrong had surgery to remove his right testicle. The surgery went well, but blood tests showed that his cancer was very far advanced and spreading rapidly. Armstrong was released from hospital the next day, Friday October 4th. Having been told that there was a chance treatment could leave him infertile, Armstrong travelled to bank sperm on Saturday October 5th. On the morning of Monday October 7th Armstrong held that press conference, then later that afternoon he began his first course of chemotherapy. Finally in his week from hell, on Thursday October 10th doctors made the discovery that the cancer had spread to his brain. And those weren't his only problems: because he had just signed a new contract with the Cofidis team, Armstrong also discovered he had no health insurance.

Although his cancer treatment began with his doctors in Austin, Armstrong decided to look around for the best possible care. He switched his treatment to the testicular-cancer specialists at Indiana University Medical Centre, who worked under the guidance of Dr Larry Einhorn, the world's leading expert in testicular cancer treatment. Dr Craig Nichols would act as Armstrong's consultant, while neurosurgeon Dr Scott Shapiro was tasked with removing the tumours from Armstrong's brain.

Shapiro remembers his first meeting with Armstrong well: "It was a Saturday morning [October 19th] and I had been called the night before by my good friend Craig Nichols asking if I would sit down and look at the x-ray films and discuss the case. So I walked into a room where Lance was with his mommy, there was another gentleman there – I don't remember who he was, but I'm sure he must have been one of Lance's coaches or agents or something. I looked at the films, the images, and told Lance what I would do, and we exchanged some conversation. Obviously he was very scared, probably a little brash. Anybody in his kind of position as an elite sportsman tends to have a big ego and is a little cocky. But I reassured him that I knew what I was doing and that we would take good care of him."

On Friday October 25th Armstrong underwent brain surgery. "Lance had metastatic testicular cancer and he had at least six lesions in his lung and two in his brain, one on each side," Shapiro says. "Traditionally in the old days we wouldn't operate on more than one brain metastases but in the modern era, especially with image guidance, we do operate. So to me it was a straightforward case from a neurosurgical perspective.

"I saw Lance on the morning of surgery. He was very nervous. I remember seeing the staff wheel him to the front desk area, and I remember he closed his eyes and you could see he was very nervous. But our senior nurse at that time was a very sweet person and she had a calming effect on him."

In later years Armstrong would say his recovery from cancer was a miracle because if he had been diagnosed with the disease 20 years earlier he would almost certainly have died. One large part of that miracle was the technological advancements that helped Shapiro operate on Armstrong's brain with such accuracy.

"Lance had had an MRI scan and we took the digital information from that and put it into a computer in the operating room," Shapiro says. "He was put asleep under general anaesthetic and we positioned his head in a three-point fixational structure that holds it very steady, and then we could attach a device to that which allows us to navigate [around the brain]. Then we registered our data points so that we had accuracy, and we marked where the two tumours were. One was on the occipital lobe and one was pretty much in the motor strip on the left side. We marked little flaps over those areas and took the tumours out.

"I'm always appropriately concerned that somebody's brain can be affected by surgery. For the tumour that was in the motor strip we used not only navigational aids but also cortical stimulation to define the motor strip, and I actually went into a sulcus – a depression or fissure in the brain – where the tumour came to the surface, and then I shelled it out so we didn't hurt his brain. Everything went OK so we didn't hurt him."

The surgery was successful. "You look at the tumours under the microscope as soon as they are removed, there's no question about that," Shapiro says. "There were some cells and some necrosis, so it was good to take it out. You don't know whether the cells are alive or dead unless you plate them and grow them out, but it was a good thing to get those two metastases out of his brain. And it's always our hope that there aren't any more.

"I always make rounds right after surgery, and I visited Lance again later that night and the next morning and until he went home. He was exceptionally relieved after surgery. He woke up pretty quickly, he was glad to be alive and could talk and move everything. I think it was a big relief to get over that hurdle, but he didn't get much rest because they started chemotherapy right away."

Traditional testicular cancer treatment, and the course Armstrong had originally been following in Austin, would have left his lungs in such a deteriorated state that he would never have been able to race a bike again. But the course that the doctors at Indiana University proposed following – called VIP, which combines vinblastine or etoposide, ifosfamide and cisplatin – meant Armstrong might be able to resume his cycling career once cured.

"I have worked with Dr Larry Einhorn for a long time and he is the leading expert in the world on chemotherapy for testicular cancer. So we knew we didn't have a 100 per cent chance of cure with Lance, but we had a 50 per cent chance roughly and he responded to the treatment and the rest is history," Shapiro says.

"Chemotherapy is pretty scientific. The regimen that was used on Lance avoided bliomicen – which is very pulmonary toxic – and used another agent that is equally effective. This other agent doesn't hurt the lungs, but it makes you more ill with nausea and vomiting, and it makes your white blood cell count go lower, which makes you more susceptible to infection. So Lance's doctors used that to try and preserve his lungs. In the years since Lance's treatment the regimen he followed has become more common. But at the time for Lance, that was 13 years ago, they were still investigating whether that regimen was as effective in terms of long-term survival outcome."

With the surgery's success things had started to turn a corner for Armstrong, and finally he was starting to hear some good news. First came the discovery that all of Armstrong's personal sponsors – Nike, Giro, Oakley and Milton-Bradley – were committed to supporting him despite his predicament. Oakley went one step further and had Armstrong covered by its employee health care policy, meaning he no longer had to worry about how he was going to fund his treatment. The second piece of good news was even more important. Armstrong remained in hospital having chemotherapy for another six days, but tests taken during that time showed the cancer was reacting to the drugs.

In the space of three months Armstrong underwent four cycles of chemotherapy, and he chose to have his remaining courses at the medical centre in Indianapolis rather than nearer his Austin home. Ironically, during this time Armstrong was treated with the drug EPO – the same drug some cyclists were using illegally to improve their performance – to boost his red blood cell count, which had dropped dangerously low as a side effect of the chemotherapy. The cumulative affect of his chemotherapy began to take its toll on his body, and to some extent his spirit.

Shapiro kept in contact with Armstrong while he was having the rest of his treatment: "I periodically checked on him while he was in the hospital having chemotherapy, not every day though, once a week or something like that." But he refutes the idea that Armstrong's status as a world-class athlete was the main reason he overcame cancer. "It's always better to deal with an all-round healthy, robust patient than a heavy-smoking, emphysematous, diabetic patient. So the fact that Lance was a top-level athlete did have an impact on how he responded to the rest of his treatment. But just because you are very healthy and athletic doesn't mean you are going to beat cancer every time. It simply lessened the likelihood of attending complications, like pneumonia."

In medical terms things were going very well. On December 13th Armstrong had his last experience of chemotherapy and all the signs were that he would overcome his disease. As the weeks passed by, and with his blood being regularly tested, the results eventually showed that Armstrong's body was cancer-free. Armstrong had survived, although he was also aware that he was only in remission, and staying free from the disease over the following 12 months would be the biggest sign of maintaining long-term health.

Armstrong may have seen off the disease but resuming his sporting career was another matter entirely. In early 1997 he flew to France for a press conference with the Cofidis team, and he even resumed a training programme. But with his body still recovering from the effects of chemotherapy, cycling any great distance left Armstrong feeling unnaturally fatigued and susceptible to passing germs. In the end, at Dr Nichols' recommendation, Armstrong decided to forget about the 1997 season.

By the late summer Armstrong's coach, Chris Carmichael, was suggesting he should start thinking about racing again. Along with his own doubts and fears – Armstrong was worried that straining his body by racing would allow the cancer to return – there were also practical concerns to consider: Armstrong had a five-year disability policy that was helping support him financially, but if he returned to racing it would be declared void. If he resumed life as a professional cyclist again and then quit, he would be left with no income.

Armstrong decided to give it a go, but there were some obvious problems. The first was that his body had changed dramatically, and he had lost over a stone in weight during his cancer treatment. The second problem cropped up when Cofidis called Bill Stapleton over to a meeting in France, and announced they were terminating Armstrong's contract. Stapleton urged them to change their minds, which they did to some extent, but the deal they ended up offering Armstrong was derisory. Undeterred, Stapleton decided to tout Armstrong's services around the teams that were attending the Interbike cycle show in California.

Armstrong held a press conference saying he was back and ready to race, but it resulted in very little response from any of the world's top squads. Only eventually did the fledgling US Postal squad suggest they might be interested in Armstrong, and the rest, as they say, is history.

Looking back now Shapiro says Armstrong's cancer had a big effect on why he turned into a Grand Tour favourite. "Before Lance got sick with cancer he was somewhat of an undisciplined athlete. He was gifted but he didn't necessarily control his diet, so he was probably overweight for an endurance athlete. But he lost all his weight from his treatment. And when he felt good enough to get back on the bike he was faster because he was skinnier. He learned to control his diet after cancer. I also think before cancer he drank a lot of beer," Shapiro chuckles.

Not surprisingly considering the intimate, if brief, relationship they had, Armstrong and Shapiro have remained in contact: "We see each other once every three or four years and have email contact. I went to see a couple of the Tours de France that he won. I went to Paris and sat in the presidential box with Lance's family, and it was cool. I went also to his house a couple of years ago when he had a 10-year celebration of the start of his foundation – it's a nice house."

2002: ...And Easier

With Jose Luis 'Chechu' Rubiera, Armstrong's US Postal/Discovery Channel
team-mate 2001-2005

The 2002 edition of the Tour de France began with a foreign Grand Départ in Luxembourg. Other aspects of the race were rather more familiar, though, with Lance Armstrong looking in the type of form to win the race again and join Jacques Anquetil, Eddy Merckx and Miguel Indurain in the exclusive club of four-time, consecutive Tour winners.

But there were some good riders ready to stand in his way. The 2000 and 2001 third-placed rider, ONCE's Joseba Beloki was back, as was the previous year's best rider under-25, Kelme's Oscar Sevilla, and French hero Christophe Moreau, who was now with Crédit Agricole. Another one to watch would be Kelme's Santiago Botero. Crucially, though, Armstrong's strongest rival over the last two years, and the man he feared most, Jan Ullrich, would not be riding, having injured his knee.

As seemed to happen from time to time in Ullrich's career, when it rained it poured. In the weeks before the Tour the German was caught by an out of competition dope test, having taken a pill at a nightclub that turned out to contain amphetamines. Although it was taken in a recreational context, the episode didn't impress his Telekom team, particularly as it came only weeks after Ullrich had had his driving licence revoked for drink-driving. Ullrich was banned from competition for six months, and the Telekom team would go on to end its association with him later in the year.

In contrast, Armstrong had had some blissful developments in his private life over the last year, reinforcing his family with a set of twin girls, Isabelle and Grace, born on November 20th, 2001. But in his professional life, US Postal's overbearing philosophy – its single-minded dedication to Armstrong – had caused unhappiness among some of its top riders. Most importantly, Tyler Hamilton had left to captain the CSC team and Levi Leipheimer had moved to lead the Rabobank squad having repeatedly failed in his attempts to be part of the US Postal Tour squad.

One of the riders who would be riding for US Postal again was Jose Luis 'Chechu' Rubiera, a mountain specialist who was brought to the team in 2001. Although Rubiera was developing a reputation as being one of the greatest climbers in the peloton, he was happy to take on a supporting role to Armstrong.

"I'm not sure I could have been a team leader anywhere else," Rubiera says. "I was in the Kelme team until 2000, and I knew that I could win some stages but I was pretty far from being a team leader able to win one of the big tours. I got some offers at the end of the 2000 season and the offer from US Postal was really good. I knew that for the Tour I had to work for Lance Armstrong, but in so many other races I was free to do something for myself, so it was perfect for me."

Rubiera says the loss of Hamilton and Leipheimer were not the most important changes to the squad in 2002. "The biggest difference was that Floyd Landis came into the team. He was a fantastic 'gregario' – a fantastic team worker. The rest of the team was more or less the same with George Hincapie and Pavel Padrnos and Viatcheslav Ekimov and all those great guys who would work on the flat parts of the race. For sure we lost guys like Hamilton and Levi, but the team didn't feel any different, and in the mountains we had Roberto Heras, who was guaranteed to be there helping Lance."

Before the Tour Armstrong gave his thoughts about the race ahead: "I think this will be the hardest of the last four Tours. I think we will see depth in teams, depth in the field that we haven't seen before."

But within US Postal, Rubiera says nobody was really too concerned about any of Armstrong's possible rivals: "He was so strong I don't think Lance was really scared of anyone. Ullrich was always the only one who was able to be close to him. Even though Ullrich was a great, great rider he always looked to me to have some problems to get ready for the Tour, he was often too fat. But in 2002 there was no Ullrich, only Beloki. Lance knew Beloki was a good rival but he also knew he was much stronger than Beloki in both the hills and the time trials."

Armstrong's preparation for the 2002 Tour went to plan with him winning the Dauphiné Libéré, where new boy Landis finished second. For Rubiera, what sticks in his mind most about the months before the Tour were the training camps the US Postal riders went on.

"I had the chance to go with Lance to a few training camps – every year we would go to the Pyrenees and the Alps for a few days to check the stages – and it was a hard job to do that because normally we used to ride the whole stage," Rubiera remembers. "Some days we were training for up to eight hours, just checking the stages. We were riding easy but it was still really hard because at the end of the day you got to the hotel completely tired. And with Lance especially it was not easy because he was so strong.

"I remember twice going on training camps with him at altitude in Tenerife. I was completely flat after that. Lance is so strong, and I was trying to do the same training as him, but my body couldn't cope with it. Often people think the man who trains the most and the hardest is the one who rides the fastest, but you have to have a body that can assimilate that training. You can train as long as you want, and as hard as you want, but if your body won't take it you will just kill yourself. So I went with Lance to Tenerife, and we were really strict with the food and the training, and when we came back he was flying and I was completely dead. It was a bad experience for me but I could see the potential in Lance's body and how naturally strong he is."

The prologue of the 2002 Tour de France pitted the riders against each other on a tight, damp and occasionally cobbled course seven kilometres around the streets of Luxembourg City. The first main challenger to post a significant time was Santiago Botero, covering the route in 9-12, before Lampre's Raimondas Rumsas went top with 9-11. Despite the stage being a prologue, and Armstrong therefore being allowed to wear a yellow skinsuit, the reigning champ decided to start the race in the blue of his US Postal colours. Rolling down the start ramp, Armstrong slowly pushed round an obviously big gear to bring himself up to speed. Soon, though, his legs were whirling.

At the finish line CSC's Laurent Jalabert had produced a stunning performance to sit at the top of the time sheet with 9-10. But Armstrong was out on the course and looking determined. His body was bobbing from side to side, trying to summon every extra watt of power to drive him forward. The time-checks were showing that he could yet pip Jalabert for the Tour's first yellow jersey.

In the last part of the final straight he rose out of the saddle to sprint, his brow furrowed as he looked towards the line. Armstrong took the win by two seconds from Jalabert, with Rumsas at three seconds, Botero at four seconds and Cofidis's David Millar fifth at five seconds. Beloki had also put in a good prologue and finished ninth, just 12 seconds behind Armstrong.

The prologue win inspired massive morale inside the already confident US Postal team. "With Lance it was so easy," Rubiera says. "We had to work a lot, but we rarely had doubts about him. Sometimes we would have doubts about the team and about whether we could control the race, or stay with him in the last part of the mountains stages, but I was pretty sure he would always be there. So when I saw the prologue, and I saw he could win it straight away, I did start to think that if there are no crashes or injuries he should be the winner. In fact, what surprises me most looking back at Lance's career is that even after many years at the Tour he had so few injuries. So many great riders have problems with their knees or back or whatever, but you never saw Lance complaining or getting sick. The fact he was never tired was amazing."

The first road stage of the 2002 Tour was a 192.5-kilometre loop through Luxembourg, and although it featured a few categorised climbs it finished with a last-minute attack by Lampre's Rubens Bertogliati, who also took control of the yellow jersey. Stage two headed into Germany and ended in a bunch sprint, as did stage three, which returned to France. So by the start of stage four's team time trial Telekom's German fastman Erik Zabel was in the yellow jersey, eight seconds ahead of Lotto's Robbie McEwen, with Bertogliati in third 14 seconds back. Jalabert was fourth and Armstrong fifth, both at 17 seconds, with Beloki 14th, 30 seconds off yellow.

The 2002 Tour team time trial covered 67.5 kilometres and took the nine-man squads from Epernay to Château Thierry. Heading west, the riders expected strong headwinds, and there was also a mean climb around halfway into the stage. Certainly the US Postal team was looking for a good performance, but once all the main teams had left the start it was the CSC team that was posting the best results at the time-checks, hoping to get Jalabert in yellow. Their target was the time set by the Spanish ONCE squad, 1-19-49, a figure that could not be bettered by Armstrong's US Postal train, who posted a time of 1-20-05, 16 seconds slower. Despite their early speed the last squad with the potential to win the stage, CSC, could only finish third with a time of 1-20-35. It meant that ONCE's Igor Gonzalez de Galdeano was in yellow with Beloki second at four seconds and Armstrong third at seven seconds.

"We tried our best to win the team time trial," Rubiera says. "We were upset because afterwards we realised that we had gone too slow on the first part of the stage. We lost a lot of time in the first 10 kilometres. Then we made up time, and made up more time, but the stage wasn't long enough for us to beat ONCE. So we felt we could have won the stage but it was our fault for going too easy at the start – Johan was telling us this, so I don't know exactly why it happened. The team time trial is something that is really nice for the riders, all the team goes on the podium to celebrate the victory. It's also something special for the sponsors to have the winners of the team time trial, but that year we just missed out."

Stages five, six, seven and eight were largely flat affairs and Rubiera's role during this stage of the Tour was simply to hang back and wait for the mountains. "I was supposed to really help Lance on the hard stages in the Pyrenees and the Alps. In the first week the guys working from the team would be George Hincapie and Viatcheslav Ekimov and Pavel Padrnos. The first week is always such a mess because there are so many crashes, so it's important that those guys ride at the front with Lance to keep him out of trouble. I don't feel able to do the job that those guys do, they ride at the front pulling at 50kph with Lance on their wheel. I would normally be with Roberto Heras, trying to help the team as much as we could, but most of the time just trying to survive for the second and third week in the mountains."

However, despite US Postal's best-laid plans, even Rubiera was required to assist Armstrong on stage seven. With less than three kilometres to go, just as the peloton caught a group of breakaways, a crash claimed Laurent Jalabert, US Postal climbing domestique Roberto Heras and the biggest name of all, Lance Armstrong. A bodyguard group of all of US Postal's riders dropped behind in a desperate attempt to bring Armstrong back to the main pack.

"I remember that the whole team stopped to wait for Lance, and two or three kilometres from the finish line there was a small climb," Rubiera says. "So we waited for him at the bottom of the climb, but he came like a train. We tried to pull for him, but he was coming so fast we couldn't do anything. He passed all the guys that were waiting for him, he was going much, much faster than us. So we had waited for nothing. The most important thing, though, was that he didn't have any injuries or bigger problems after the crash."

The crash meant Armstrong lost 27 seconds on the rest of the field, dropping him to eighth overall, 34 seconds behind yellow jersey Gonzalez de Galdeano. Beloki was still second at four seconds while his ONCE team-mate Jorg Jaksche was now third at 12 seconds. Stage eight passed with no changes to the top of the overall standings.

For Armstrong it was perhaps a relief to reach stage nine's individual time trial. At least now his destiny was in his own hands as he prepared to take on the 52-kilometre course from Lanester to Lorient, the last 17 kilometres of which would be exposed to the sea breeze along the Brittany coast.

The early marker time was set by Mapei's Hungarian rider Laszlo Bodrogi at 1-02-44, with the prologue's surprise star, Raimondas Rumsas failing to beat it by less than half a second. Of the big names it was Kelme's Santiago Botero who was setting the time-checks alight. The previous year's Tour King of the Mountains had shown a nifty turn of pace on the race against the clock and arrived at the finish with a time of 1-02-19, 25 seconds quicker than Bodrogi and an average speed just over 50kph. Meanwhile, in the start house, Armstrong was preparing to head down the ramp. Gently puffing his checks in and out, the officials counted down the time, and the US Postal leader was away. Some minutes later the man wearing the all-yellow skinsuit, Igor Gonzalez de Galdeano, no mean time triallist himself, slowly revolved his pedals up to speed along the opening straight, hoping to hang on to his prized jersey.

At the time-checks Armstrong was down on Botero's time. By the finishing straight, with his teeth bared and his legs pumping, it became obvious Armstrong would not be winning the stage. Botero's time came and went and the American was yet to reach the line. He recorded a time of 1-02-30, 11 seconds slower than Botero but good enough for second. Behind him Gonzalez be Galdeano was fighting all the way to the finish and came in at 1-02-38 – fourth on the day, he would still be in yellow come the morning. Overall Gonzalez de Galdeano led from Armstrong who was 26 seconds back. Beloki had also put in a decent time trial and was now third at 1-23, while Botero lay fifth at 1-55.

Rubiera says that within the US Postal team there was little concern that

Armstrong had been beaten in the time trial. "We were surprised about the victory by Botero because he was really strong. But at the same time Botero is a guy who is able to do his best and then his worst from day to day. We were laughing about the fact that Botero is a big rider, a great rider, but some days he is super good and some days he is super bad. We would say Botero was either 'on' or 'off', and in that time trial Botero was definitely 'on'. We knew that on another day Botero would probably blow up and lose many minutes. So there were no big concerns about that."

The following day was a rest day, then stage 10 featured a reasonably flat route to Pau in the shadow of the Pyrenees. A four-man break escaped the field so there were no important changes on the overall standings.

Then the riders headed into the Pyrenees, and into the real battle for the Tour de France title. Stage 11 covered 158 kilometres to La Mongie, but only featured two climbs, first the hors catégorie Col d'Aubisque and then finished two-thirds of the way up the first-category Col du Tourmalet. And just to prove a year really isn't that long in cycling, Laurent Jalabert resumed his approach to the Pyrenees in the same way he had left the mountain range in the 2002 Tour: with another lone break. Only a few days earlier Jalabert, one of just three riders to have won both the green jersey and King of the Mountains titles, had announced his retirement from racing at the end of the season, but he wanted to prove he could still ride with style. He attacked with a group of breakaways just 13 kilometres into the stage, then attacked again to crest the Col d'Aubisque alone. With 10 kilometres to go, as the race reached the base of the Tourmalet, Jalabert was in front by over three minutes, but back in the main field the US Postal squad was marshalling proceedings and upping the tempo.

With the last six kilometres of the stage at a punishing gradient of one-in-10, gradually the pace-setting US Postal boys reached their limits. Viatcheslav Ekimov fell away from the front to make way for George Hincapie, then Rubiera took over the tempo, while behind the rest of the group splintered behind. Beloki and Gonzalez de Galdeano lingered not too far away from Armstrong's rear wheel, but Moreau and Euskaltel climber Haimar Zubeldia were among those who did drop away. CSC's new signing, Tyler Hamilton, also couldn't keep up, and even multiple King of the Mountains winner Richard Virenque was facing difficulty.

Finally all Armstrong's Christmases came at once: Botero suffered a puncture and then the yellow jersey, Gonzalez de Galdeano, could not maintain the pace.

From being a large group at the base of the climb Armstrong's mountain lieutenants had produced a tempo that whittled it down to just a dozen or so riders. Under the five-kilometres-to-go banner Roberto Heras took over from Rubiera at the front and lifted the pace again – with only Armstrong and ONCE's Beloki able to follow. At the 2001 Tour it had often been Rubiera who accompanied Armstrong on the crucial final pace-setting leg up the last climb, but in 2002 it seemed that role had been taken on by Heras.

"We used to talk about who would be the last US Postal rider left with Lance," Rubiera says. "At every race you know what condition your team-mates are in, you ask them how they feel, and you have to be honest with them about how you feel. We normally decided in the bus before the start of the race what order the team was going to ride. Every day we talked with the team directeur and we planned the tactics for the stage. At the 2002 Tour we all saw that Roberto was the best, so we saved him for the final stint."

Meanwhile the gap to Jalabert, now grinding his way up the climb, was soon under a minute. Armstrong, as cool as ever, spoke every now and then into his team radio back to Johan Bruyneel, with Heras setting the tempo just in front, and Beloki sitting in his wheel tracks. Eventually Jalabert was swallowed up by the Armstrong group, then bravely matched its pace, but was soon unable to ride at any speed other than his own.

With Heras leading, Armstrong bobbing in and out of the saddle, and Beloki bringing up the rear, the trio stayed together all the way to the final kilometre. It appeared that Armstrong was simply biding his time. He looked over to Beloki, then paused to let him go second in the line, putting himself in the ideal position to launch a winning attack. Wise to what was happening, and not willing to simply roll over, Beloki kept his eyes on Armstrong. With only a couple of hundred metres to go Armstrong sprang and Beloki tried but failed to follow.

Armstrong took the victory with a single small punch of the air. Then came Beloki seven seconds later, and Heras another six seconds behind him. As he had done in all three of his Tour wins, Armstrong yet again made his mark on the first mountain stage of the race, and this time he did the double: he won the stage and took back control of the yellow jersey. Overall Armstrong led the race by 1-12 to Beloki. The morning's yellow jersey, Gonzalez de Galdeano was third at 1-48, Rumsas was fourth at 3-32 and Botero was fifth at 4-13.

Looking back, Rubiera is pretty happy with how he worked that day: "I remember I was feeling pretty good on that stage and I was trying to do a good tempo to try and drop as many riders as I could, to do what we call a 'big selection'. I remember Roberto Heras was there and Lance tried to let him win, but it was really difficult because Beloki was there as well and he was going really fast. It was too complicated for Lance to let Roberto win. It was a difficult decision for Lance, but he wanted to be sure that somebody from the team won the stage. Beloki was much faster than Roberto so Lance had to win the stage himself.

"We knew that Lance could stay in yellow all the way to the finish from then on. When you went with Lance to the Tour you knew that sooner or later he would get in the yellow jersey if everything went well. Sometimes you found yourself wishing he would take the yellow jersey later – in the last week – because that would be easier for us, because then the responsibility for controlling the race would be shared with other teams. Sometimes that is impossible because you have to take advantage of other riders' weaknesses. But the perfect thing is to take the yellow jersey in the last few days because that way you don't make the team do extra work."

If Armstrong couldn't gift the win to Heras he at least gave him due respect in interviews after the stage. "I have to say honestly that I didn't have the legs to attack today. It was Roberto who made the difference," Armstrong said. "He made the pace and all I had to do was follow... The team just started pulling at the bottom of the Aubisque and everybody was great today."

But that first stage in the Pyrenees was a stroll in the park compared to stage 12, which featured five categorised climbs and finished at an altitude of almost 1,800m at Plateau de Beille. Still, there was one thing stage 12 had in common with its predecessor, and that was Laurent Jalabert. The French hero broke away on his own again, and was later joined by Alessio's Laurent Dufaux and ONCE's Isidro Nozal. With 14 kilometres to go the trio had a lead of around two minutes on the yellow jersey group, which was again being pulled along by the twin US

Postal climbing talents of Rubiera and Heras.

The Armstrong pack was gradually whittled down by the pace being set by Rubiera, and it was also rapidly closing in on the leading trio. Sensing that he would be caught close to the finish for the second day running Jalabert attacked and left his two companions. But he was just putting off the inevitable and soon enough he experienced the sensation of Armstrong and attendants cruising up to his rear wheel and going past. That said, US Postal weren't having it entirely their own way, and Beloki, again riding in Armstrong's shadow, had two of his ONCE team-mates – Marcos Serrano and Igor Gonzalez de Galdeano – to support him among the select leading group of barely a dozen riders.

With less than nine kilometres left to race Rubiera and Armstrong popped out of their saddles at the front, raising the tempo in unison. "We usually talked in the stage about how we were feeling, how the stage was going," Rubiera says. "Normally Lance was always going well so he would just tell me that he wanted a bigger tempo on the climbs, he wanted a big selection, and I would do my best to eliminate as many guys as possible. If Lance wanted to attack he normally told me: 'For the next 500 metres go full gas and then I attack.'

"So that was normally what we did, especially on the last climb of a stage. I would pull him along at a fast tempo until the last five of six kilometres of each stage, or even further if I could do it for longer. Then, when he could see I was really tired, Lance would tell me, 'Now do a bloc [all-out] for the next 200 metres or 500 metres.' And then he would do his final attack."

Rubiera worked until he could do no more and pulled to one side, allowing Heras to take his place at the front. The accelerations were too much for Serrano, who fell away at the back, then Gonzalez de Galdeano was gone, and almost in a carbon copy of the previous day's stage the leading group was down to three men: Heras, Armstrong and Beloki. Armstrong made his way past Heras with the deftest of speed increases and bobbed up the road. Heras watched his leader pass and gain a gap while Beloki simply couldn't do anything to respond. Try as he might, the ONCE leader was unable to make any inroads on Armstrong's small lead, and Heras comfortably sat on his wheel watching his every move.

With five kilometres to go Armstrong's lead was around 15 seconds and Beloki seemed to have sensibly decided to limit his losses and follow his own pace up the climb. Heras, sensing his rival was suffering, gave Beloki an extra drain on his morale and attacked. He sprinted up the road with the aim of rejoining Armstrong. But Beloki hadn't crumbled entirely. Being unable to catch up with Armstrong and wary of acting as a target that could inadvertently help Beloki's efforts, Heras sat up and resumed his position on Beloki's wheel. Armstrong now had a lead of 40 seconds, and he looked untroubled, spinning easier and quicker as the gradient started to level out.

Back down the hill Rubiera's thoughts were already on other things. "Once I had done my job I would think about the next day," Rubiera says. "I knew my job was finished and Lance and the team were really happy with me. I could have kept pushing for a place in the top 10 on the stage, or for a better position on the overall standings, but the next day I had to work a lot again, and I preferred to do my job than finish in the top 10 on one stage. The important thing was the team and the victory for Lance. I remember once we were not too far behind in the team competition and I said to Lance: 'Hey Lance, if I keep going maybe we could win the team classification.' He said to me: 'Don't worry about that. There is only one classification which interests us and that is the overall classification. So do your job and then take it easy for the next day.'"

Armstrong's thoughts were more in the present as he passed under the final kilometre banner with 59 seconds' lead. His yellow jersey open to his sternum, his crucifix swaying in tandem with the rocking of his bike, he took no time to savour the moment of a stage win: time, more time, was all he sought. As the line approached he gave a two-handed punch to the air, but it had all the hallmarks of somebody keeping up tradition rather than a truly emotional outburst. Heras and Beloki arrived together, but it was Heras who had the energy to sprint to take second place, 1-04 back. Only seven seconds after them saw the arrival of Botero and Gonzalez de Galdeano. Overall Armstrong led Beloki by 2-28, Gonzalez de Galdeano was third at 3-19, Rumsas was fourth at 5-15 and Botero was fifth at 5-44. Heras's exploits in the service of his leader had lifted him to seventh overall, 8-01 behind Armstrong.

Stage 13 was something of a recuperation day for the riders, featuring three early minor climbs, but being flat thereafter, apart from a tough final ascent to the finish. Britain's David Millar of Cofidis took the stage win from a five-man breakaway group, 10 minutes ahead of the peloton. The top of the overall classification saw no changes.

Mont Ventoux – the scene of perhaps Lance Armstrong's greatest sporting regret, 'the one that got away', when he gifted a stage to Marco Pantani back in the 2000 edition of the Tour – would be the finale of stage 14. Speaking before the Tour Armstrong made it clear he would not repeat his actions from 2000: "If I get there in a good position and I have an opportunity to win again, will I take it? Absolutely. Would I ever give it away again? No, never."

The Ventoux is a hell of a climb, but it was also the only climb on stage 14. However, there was the small matter of 200 kilometres under scorching skies before the riders even reached it. As the race hit the lower slopes of the Ventoux two men – Ag2r's Alexandre Botcharov and five-time King of the Mountains winner Richard Virenque of the Domo-Farm Frites team – were leading the yellow jersey group by five minutes. As the pair pushed on through the lower, forested part of the climb, and with Botcharov looking tired, Virenque attacked. Back in the overall leaders' pack Armstrong was surrounded by a rapidly decreasing group of riders. Eventually he was accompanied by just Beloki, his ONCE team-mate Jose Azevedo, overall fourth place Rumsas and the impressive young Italian Ivan Basso of Fassa Bortolo. With nine kilometres to go Virenque was more than four minutes ahead of Armstrong and company.

As Virenque ploughed on at the front Beloki attacked among his group. Armstrong reacted immediately and, almost in a show of spite, rode straight past the Spaniard to counterattack. He gapped the ONCE rider straight away and disappeared up the road. With his team radio earphone placed firmly in his ears, looking and acting for all the world like some kind of robo-rider, Armstrong hunted down Virenque. Under the five-kilometre banner he was 3-43 behind the Frenchman. There was a mixed reaction from those standing on the sides of the Ventoux. While Virenque – a proven drugs cheat – was being cheered on, many of the crowd simply stood quietly or even booed as Armstrong passed them, although one fan draped in the stars and stripes did sprint alongside him for brief company. Not that Armstrong cared – his eyes were fixed unflinchingly on the road ahead. Virenque moved forward in obvious pain, but as he passed under the last-kilometre flag Armstrong was still another kilometre behind.

Virenque ended up taking the stage and Botcharov held on for second. Armstrong may have missed out on the day's honours by 2-20, but he had increased his lead on all his yellow jersey rivals. Rumsas came in fifth at 3-36, followed by Basso just a couple of seconds later, and Beloki arrived in eighth place at 4-05. Overall Armstrong was now 4-21 ahead of Beloki, Rumsas had moved up to third at 6-39 and Gonzalez de Galdeano was slipping down the placings in fourth at 8-36.

"The Ventoux stage was really fast," Rubiera remembers. "Normally the stage to the Ventoux is really explosive. You get to the bottom of the climb and, because you haven't done any other long hard climbs that day, you arrive at the climb with legs like if you have had an easy day, pushing big, big gears. Then suddenly, bam! Mont Ventoux is almost 10 per cent average in the first part. I remember that stage was really fast. I don't remember Lance saying he wanted to win that day particularly, but we tried to do the same job as always: make a selection and leave him with just a few rivals to beat."

The following day, stage 15, was the longest of the 2002 Tour and headed 226.5 kilometres to the summit of Les Deux Alpes, featuring six categorised climbs en route. A seven-man break that included Santiago Botero had escaped the field and led the yellow jersey group by nine minutes when they reached the final climb. Botero – who, despite winning the time trial at Lorient, had had an 'off' day on the Ventoux and finished a quarter of an hour behind Armstrong – attacked, splintering the lead pack, and set off up the hill alone. But back in the Armstrong group things were being controlled by ONCE's climbing domestiques who were eager to preserve Beloki's second place overall.

Nobody was going to catch Botero for the stage win, but Beloki, determined to salvage some pride, attacked the Armstrong group in the last kilometre. Despite initially reacting slowly to the move, Armstrong was quickly on the Spaniard's wheel and they crossed the line together, with Rumsas just ahead. The results caused no major changes to the general classification, with the exception being that Botero moved up to seventh overall, 11-31 behind Armstrong.

"That was a strong attack from Beloki at the end," Armstrong said afterwards. "I didn't expect that and I didn't know he was attacking until they told me on the radio... It's important that you jump on those attacks immediately, not necessarily to show them who's boss, but certainly to let them know that you're not going to let them go."

If stage 15 was the longest of the Tour, stage 16 was, on paper at least, the hardest. It took in three big-name, big-altitude hors catégorie mountain passes: the Col du Galibier, the Col de la Madeleine, and finished with a final climb to La Plagne. As with the day before a small group escaped the main field and by the final climb one rider was leading the race, this time Dutchman Michael Boogerd of Rabobank. With five kilometres to go Team CSC's climbing specialist Carlos Sastre was in second place on the road giving chase around three minutes back, while Armstrong's group of favourites, which was being propelled at a vicious pace by Rubiera and Heras, was another minute behind Sastre.

As the climb continued Sastre slowly managed to pull Boogerd back, but in the yellow jersey group Armstrong, in a show of wanton dominance, attacked. There was no reason to do it, no gap overall to close, no real challenge to quell, Armstrong simply wanted to win again and show who was the best. The others could do nothing to react. Within two kilometres he had joined Sastre, but with Boogerd just a kilometre from the finish the Dutchman looked assured of glory, and he duly took it. Armstrong allowed Sastre to take second place, patting the exhausted Spaniard on the back, 1-25 after Boogerd. Beloki and Rumsas appeared together 37 seconds later. Overall the gap between Armstrong and Beloki was now 5-06, Rumsas was third at 7-24 and ONCE's Jose Azevedo had leapfrogged Gonzalez de Galdeano into fifth at 12-08.

Asked why Armstrong decided to attack on that stage, when he already had the yellow firmly in his grasp, Rubiera just laughs. "He attacked because he is Lance Armstrong and he is so powerful. He doesn't just try to stay with the group, like Miguel Indurain used to do. He is aggressive and he knew he could win. Boogerd was in the breakaway and he wasn't far away, and I remember that we had some talk with Johan, because Johan was also talking to the directeur from Rabobank.

They were trying to do a deal with us, to let Boogerd win the stage and then they would help us control the race the next day. For us that was perfect, but for sure Lance also wanted to show who was the strongest."

Soon it was goodbye hills. The last day of racing in the Alps was stage 17, which featured four significant climbs, but with no summit finale, and with Armstrong so well established in the yellow jersey, it was a three-man breakaway that led the way to the finish. Tacconi's Dario Frigo took the win, but with Santiago Botero finishing 1-38 ahead of the yellow jersey group he moved up to fourth overall at 10-59. There were no changes among the overall podium places.

Stage 18 was a rolling course with Crédit Agricole's Thor Hushovd victorious from a three-man break. And then it was on to stage 19, the final individual time trial and the last chance for Lance Armstrong to prove how much he deserved the yellow jersey. As in previous years he went into the day determined to seal the Tour with one last victory. The route covered 50 kilometres from Regnie Durette to Mâcon and, in what had already been a sunny Tour de France, it would be run under warm, clear skies.

At the first checkpoint it was Rumsas setting the pace with Armstrong going through in second place, 17 seconds behind. At the second checkpoint Armstrong had turned up the wick and was beating Rumsas's time by seven seconds. Rumsas was going all-out in a bid to leapfrog over Beloki into second overall and his time of 1-04-43 was provisionally top of the leaderboard. Beloki appeared at the line next, finishing in 1-06-01 and holding onto his second place overall by a full minute. Then Armstrong put the final cherry on his quite amazing 2002 Tour by winning the stage with a time of 1-03-50, just less than a minute quicker than Rumsas. Overall, barring an accident, the positions were set: Armstrong led Beloki by 7-17, Rumsas was third at 8-17, Botero was fourth at 13-10, and Gonzalez de Galdeano held on to his well-deserved fifth place at 13-54.

Finally there was the cue for the Armstrong's team-mates to start enjoying themselves. "The day before the last, and especially when we knew the overall was decided, we would go down to the hotel bar and have some beers together," Rubiera says. "Normally some guys even stopped asking for their massages. After so many days working hard you just want to change your mind and start enjoying the race. We used to celebrate in Paris with the official victory, but at the same time, whenever we really thought the race was decided we also used to celebrate with some drinks at the hotel."

The final stage, featuring the traditional swansong on the Champs-Elysées in Paris, ended in a bunch sprint, but not before Raimondas Rumsas – one could perhaps say looking rocket-fuelled – had tried to mount a lone breakaway. In the end it was green jersey Robbie McEwen of Lotto who took victory and sealed the points classification. Armstrong, though, had dominated his fourth Tour, finishing with an advantage of 7-17 on Beloki, and 8-17 on Rumsas.

It was a great moment for Rubiera. "To be in Paris, on the Champs-Elysées, with so many people around, especially all the American supporters, that's amazing, it's something fantastic. To be around Lance on the last stage, showing we were a strong team that could defend the yellow jersey right up to the finish, is something I will remember for always."

Rubiera also had plenty to celebrate personally. He had finished 22nd overall, 16 places higher than his result in 2001, and something that seems amazing for somebody whose whole Tour was dedicated to working for another rider. "I can tell you, I can really promise you, I don't know where I finished on the general classification in any Tour de France that I did with Lance," Rubiera says. "The important thing for me was to do a great job, to do team work. The rest, the GC, I don't really care. I would prefer to be the last one on GC and have Lance say: 'OK you may have been last but thanks very much for your help.' That would be much better for me than being maybe 10th overall and having my team-mates and directeur and Lance thinking: 'He didn't do much for the team.'"

But the story of the 2002 Tour wasn't quite over. The surprise star of the race, Raimondas Rumsas, was about to hit the news again. While he was having his moment of glory on the final Tour podium Rumsas's wife, Edita, was being stopped by police on the border between France and Italy. She was found to have a cocktail of 37 different performance-enhancing substances in her car and, although she claimed it was for her mother-in-law, the police found that rather hard to believe. Preferring his personal liberty over his wife's welfare Rumsas decided not to hang around to speak to French police, so Edita ended up in jail for 68 days before being released on bail. Rumsas went on to fail a dope test at the 2003 Giro d'Italia – where he had finished sixth overall – and was banned for a year.

Rubiera says that among the peloton there was no suspicion about Rumsas: "Nobody thought that was an especially odd result. We knew Rumsas and we knew that he was a good rider and every good rider, if he is in the best condition of his life, can do something amazing. We never thought about doping or anything with Rumsas. We just thought he was in amazing shape."

Rubiera, though, had a much brighter future ahead of him and would become one of the firmest fixtures in the US Postal and Discovery Channel Tour de France teams, accompanying Armstrong to five overall victories. Incredibly, in those same years, he also became one of the few actively racing professional cyclists to pursue an academic career.

"It took me a while," Rubiera says. "To study chemical engineering in Spain takes three years in university but I did it in almost 10 years. I did it step-by-step. Every year I tried to do a little more, but I had to take it slowly because I could only do it in the winter, especially as I could only do exams in February. But it was just a matter of not quitting. It's not a matter of being clever, I don't think I am clever at all, but I tried hard and every year I tried to organise my winter schedule so I could go to classes and prepare for the modules."

In 2008 Rubiera moved to the Astana team as part of Johan Bruyneel's new regime, and in 2009 he ended up once again riding alongside his old team leader, Lance Armstrong.

Americans in Paris

With Jim Ochowicz, 7-Eleven and Motorola team boss 1980-1996
and close friend of Armstrong

For the best part of 80 years the Tour de France missed one vital ingredient that stopped it from being branded a truly globally important sporting event: American competitors. French riders have been a factor in their national Tour since its inception; in 1909 François Faber from Luxembourg took the title; Odile Defraye was the first Belgian to win the race in the 1912; then in 1924 Ottavio Bottechia became the first Italian to win the Tour. In the following decades riders from Switzerland, Spain and Holland all made their mark by claiming the biggest prize in cycling, and even the relatively pedal-shy Brits had a concerted stab at the Tour with a small invasion of their best riders in the 1950s and '60s. But one nationality missing not just from the winner's rostrum but from the entire Tour peloton was the USA.

The roots of change started to grow in the late 1970s when cycling began to see new interest in North America and several talented young riders took the giant step of travelling to Europe to try their luck among the stars of the pro peloton. Leading this handful of hopefuls were riders like Jonathan Boyer, Mike Neel and a certain son of California, Greg LeMond. LeMond in particular had made his mark by winning bronze, silver and gold medals at the 1979 junior World Championships, including a spectacular ride to claim the road race title.

All of these American torchbearers had to simply try their luck, hoping they could find a place in a European-based team, but back home in the US others had bigger ideas. The main guiding force was former Olympic cyclist and speed-skater Jim Ochowicz who, in 1980, had a dream of creating a true American-based professional cycling team, with American riders and American sponsors. Within a year Ochowicz's idea had become a reality of sorts with sponsorship from Schwinn Bicycles and the large convenience-store chain 7-Eleven. In 1982 Schwinn dropped its sponsorship of the team, so 7-Eleven moved to become the single title sponsor of the squad.

While the 7-Eleven team initially competed solely in American events, over in Europe in 1982 Boyer had become the first American rider to compete at the Tour de France, riding for the very French Renault-Elf team of that year's race winner Bernard Hinault. Boyer finished a highly creditable 23rd overall. Much like Lance Armstrong would do 20 years later with his Spanish mountain domestiques, Hinault had a knack for spotting talented riders and especially saw the potential in American cyclists, so he also succeeded in signing LeMond to Renault-Elf.

LeMond went on to claim second place at the 1982 World Championship and then became the first American to win the world title, in 1983, while still only 22 years old. At such a tender age LeMond's Renault-Elf team had held him back from competing at three-week stage races but in 1984 he rode his first Tour de France, finishing an impressive third overall and claiming the white jersey for best young rider.

While LeMond was in the headlines in Europe, back in the US other events were capturing the public's attention. At the 1984 Los Angeles Olympics, under the guidance of head coach Eddie Borysewicz, the United States team had dominated the cycling events, claiming nine medals in all, four of which were golds. Some months later the lustre of the US team's achievements was lost, however, when it was revealed that some of the team had blood doped, or rather blood boosted. Blood boosting had not been specifically outlawed by the International Olympic Committee at the time and it was believed to be a widely-used procedure among Eastern bloc athletes.

But with cycling riding the crest of a wave in the US public's consciousness, Ochowicz decided to take his steadily growing and improving 7-Eleven team over to compete among the professional peloton in Europe. They had an impressive start, although their presence in the European peloton was as much a learning experience for the established pro riders as it was for the Americans.

"European-based American cyclists didn't really exist when we showed up, so there wasn't really anything to compare us to," Ochowicz says. "There were a couple of Americans who raced professionally, Mike Neel and Jonathan Boyer, but one was in Italy, one was in France, so their presence wasn't really big enough to say: 'This is USA cycling making its mark.' Really they were just two good bike racers who were trying to be professionals. They found their niche but it wasn't necessarily American cycling in the scope that 7-Eleven achieved and Motorola, and others thereafter. When 7-Eleven first came to Europe it was a shock or a surprise to see an American team racing. But there was very little fanfare, and very little opinion about us."

Some people might think a whole new team, from a whole new country would have created a fair amount of 'novelty factor' interest and perhaps have caused some bemused looks among the other nationalities, but Ochowicz says that wasn't really the case. "We stopped being a novelty real quick because we won the Trofeo Laigueglia in the first three weeks we raced in Europe. So even though the other riders didn't necessarily know who we were, they found out real quick.

"People don't see each other as threats out there in the pro peloton, but the European riders were seeing a side of America, a country that is well respected in a lot of different ways around the world, and it was coming to Europe for the first time racing as a team. Our presence was creating some new energy, some new direction – instead of the same old faces and countries winning races something different was happening. The sport was changing and it felt like a new era. The first time we went to Europe was 1985, the spring of 1985, and we won the Trofeo Laigueglia then we went to the Giro d'Italia and we won two stages there."

Greg LeMond was also racing at the 1985 Giro, finishing third overall, and was steadily climbing higher up the professional cycling tree. LeMond had been signed again by Hinault to join his new La Vie Claire squad for 1985 and came dangerously close to eclipsing his legendary team leader at that year's Tour de France. Hinault spent most of the Tour suffering from injury and it was only team orders that kept the 24-year-old LeMond from taking his yellow jersey. At the end of the Tour Hinault was just 1-42 ahead of his American team-mate.

It all combined to mean that the following year, 1986, would be when American cycling really broke into the world of big-time bike racing. LeMond was promised full support from Hinault in his bid to win the 1986 Tour de France. Whether Hinault helped or hindered LeMond's challenge that year is another book in itself, but the outcome was that Greg LeMond became the first American to win the Tour de France. And with Ochowicz succeeding in securing a place in the Tour peloton for his 7-Eleven boys, the race saw for the first time a truly American professional cycling team among its number.

"What Greg LeMond was doing was different to what we were doing," Ochowicz says. "We were building a team and he was on his own project, and I think those two factors – 7-Eleven and LeMond – should be viewed differently. The continuation of what we did is still evolving today in American cycling, and being the first American team at the Tour de France was a big deal. That's not to take anything away from what Greg did because winning the Tour is huge, but that was something he did alone.

"I think the French public were happy to see an American team in the peloton and I think that certainly at the Tour de France there is a bit of nationalism that goes on. You even see it today, you get large crowds of Dutch and Danes on the course, and Americans, that cheer on their athletes and their teams. And I think the Tour organisers were also really pleased to see an American team in their race because it was a sign of the globalisation of the sport. I think that we helped jump-start that a bit with a large corporation like 7-Eleven rather than a small sausage factory sponsoring our cycling team."

Ochowicz and 7-Eleven became fixtures in the European peloton and probably their finest moment came in 1988 when Andy Hampsten won the Giro d'Italia, although 7-Eleven also had some fine episodes at the Tour. In 1991 the squad changed sponsorship and became known as the Motorola cycling team, and in 1992 Ochowicz signed a young Texan to the squad, Lance Armstrong. Armstrong's first Tour was in 1993 when, as Sean Yates recalled earlier, he also took his debut Tour stage victory.

"By the time Lance joined the Motorola team we had set out our marker, we were well known and very much respected in the peloton as an organisation," Ochowicz says. "The Tour de France was a huge learning curve for Lance and his career. He had started in 1993, that was his first full rookie year as a pro, so everything he did from then on was a surprise for himself and for us as an organisation. We were trying to develop his skills and talents and assist him with a long-term career in pro cycling.

"But I think the Tour suited him well. It is a big media event and he does well with the media – he always has done and he still does today – and I think that it was a big plus for him to get into our Tour team. He wanted to race against the best of the best, and that's where they are at the Tour. That's the one event all year where the best riders compete, whether they are sprinters, or climbers, or time triallists. They all want to go and show their stuff at the Tour. So Lance wanted to go and do the same thing, and we allowed that to happen, but with some asterisks around that – we didn't want him to go the full distance."

Armstrong circa 1993 was young and strong, but he needed nurturing. Ochowicz knew, though, that he was talented enough to win a Tour stage and despite being just 21 years old, everybody in the Motorola camp was prepared to help him achieve it. "I guess the stage win was just another part of the surprise package that you get with Lance," Ochowicz says. "He was very capable and very determined and extremely motivated. It wasn't surprising for us to see him take that stage win because the whole team rode for him that day. And that was pretty surprising when you look at the people who were on that team, but they put it all on the line for him because they believed in him, and he came through. It was a great day.

"When Lance came to us he was straight out of the amateur ranks so he had a kind of transition into the pro peloton, and with that there's a lot of things that are going on all at one time: the speed of racing is higher, the group of riders is better as a whole, and the distances are much longer. So he had to make those adjustments quickly to settle into that race scene."

Of course Armstrong back then wasn't a favourite for the overall Tour title, but just winning a stage at the Tour was extremely important for any American rider. "The American public knows the Tour by name, but they might not know what Paris-Roubaix is," Ochowicz says. "The Tour is the biggest deal, and the best riders want to compete there, and Lance was in that space. We as a team were in that space where the Tour was very important to us, for everybody in the organisation and our sponsors."

Despite the continued success of Motorola, by 1996 the sponsorship money had dried up and Ochowicz was unable to find a replacement. He withdrew from the professional peloton but continued to coach the US road race teams at World

Championships up until 2003, and was coach of the US road race teams at the 2000 and 2004 Olympics. Ochowicz was inducted into the US Bicycling Hall of Fame in 1996 and has also been president of USA Cycling. More importantly for Armstrong fans, Ochowicz is still a close friend of his former charge and has often been found supporting the Texan at the Tour de France.

"I think Lance holds the Tour in the same esteem as he always has because it's a race that took him a long time to understand. When he did figure it out it has been, for him, a big part of his life – you can't win seven Tours de France without it being a huge part of your life. And the story around his cancer and how that episode of his life is interconnected with his ability to then become a Tour contender is pretty amazing. So I think he still believes the Tour is the big race, and he made it clear after announcing his comeback that he wanted to go back to the Tour to race again."

Ochowicz also believes the relationship between Armstrong and the race organisers, the press, and the French fans isn't necessarily how it has been perceived. "I would say the French public have always been quite positive towards Lance. The Tours I have seen him in, and at the races in France where he has competed, he has always had good support from spectators. And not just spectators, people in general seem to appreciate him, whether it's out training, or at hotels, or wherever.

"The Tour organisation has its own way of managing its event and not everybody agrees with that, but that's fine because everybody should have their own opinion, particularly those who compete, whether they are athletes or teams or whoever. So the Tour continues to evolve, there's new management there with people who weren't there when Lance finished in 2005.

"But ultimately I think that Lance respects the race and he certainly respects the organisation for what they are doing with the Tour."

2003: Taken To The Brink

With Victor Hugo Pena, Armstrong's US Postal team-mate 2001-2004

For a man who had been making and breaking records from the moment he first hopped onto the saddle, the 2003 Tour de France would be special, even by Lance Armstrong's standards. Firstly, it was the centenary edition: one hundred years had past since Maurice Garin won the first race across France. Even more significant for Armstrong personally was the fact that a win at the 2003 Tour would place him alongside Jacques Anquetil, Eddy Merckx, Bernard Hinault and Miguel Indurain in the group of men who have won the race five times.

After the dominance of 2002 it looked like a done deal for Armstrong and he was back with a largely unchanged US Postal team. One of Armstrong's team-mates, the Colombian Victor Hugo Pena, would be riding his third Tour with US Postal.

"Probably my first Tour de France in 2001 was too much for me," Pena says now. "I probably wasn't experienced enough to be in that team but they gave me the opportunity and in 2003 I was doing really well. I learned a lot, I did everything I could do, and 2003 was a dream for me.

"While I was at US Postal the preparation was more or less the same every year. There were 12 or 13 guys who would be the potential Tour de France riders, and most of those guys would do the same races earlier in the year. Johan Bruyneel and Lance would look for the best guys, especially at the Dauphiné Libéré, which is the best race to see how strong the guys are. In 2003 I was doing really well at the training camps; I won a tough mountain stage at the Tour of Murcia; at the Tour of the Algarve I was second; and in the Dauphiné I was working hard for Lance all the time, so I ended up being in the Tour team."

In terms of rivals, Joseba Beloki would be back, but Armstrong was far more concerned with the reemergence of Jan Ullrich. Even by the notoriously unpredictable Ullrich's standards he had had a rocky year since missing the 2002 Tour. After the drink-driving and drug misdemeanors of 2002 Ullrich and his long-suffering Telekom squad finally decided to go their separate ways. Ullrich signed with the relatively little-known Coast team, only to find, four months into the season, the squad suspended for a lack of funds. The legendary Bianchi bike firm – which had been supplying Coast with team bikes and was secretly paying Ullrich's three-million euro annual wage – decided to step into the breach and take over complete sponsorship of the squad.

It wasn't the best platform from which to launch a Tour challenge, and Ullrich's results in the first half of the 2003 season were rather up and down. In April, though, Armstrong said: "Ullrich is in better shape than I have ever seen him before."

"Lance was always thinking about Ullrich, he was always crazy about Ullrich," Pena says. "The only guy who he thought could beat him was Ullrich because he knew he was strong and a real talent. Lance always respected Beloki and other rivals, but he always said: 'If I do everything OK I can win the Tour. It won't be easy but I have a big chance of winning. But if Ullrich is in his best condition then I don't know – I will have to fight."

Armstrong's approval aside, there was one ray of sunshine in Ullrich's life. Just two days before the start of the 2003 Tour, Ullrich and his long-term girlfriend Gaby Weiss welcomed the arrival of a daughter, Sarah, into the world. In Armstrong's personal life, though, things weren't anywhere near as happy. The Tour champ and his wife of four and a half years, Kristin, had issued a press release in February 2003 stating that they were to separate. While they had reconciled and were still officially married at the time the Tour started in July, for a man who publicly professed to be as committed to his family as he was his sport, life behind the scenes must have been tough.

In terms of cycling, Armstrong's run-up to the Tour featured his usual preparation race, the Dauphiné Libéré, which the Texan won for the second year in succession despite Euskaltel's climbing star Iban Mayo looking on particularly good form. But it wasn't all plain sailing at the Dauphiné, Armstrong was involved in a nasty crash and suffered a deep cut on his elbow which required stitching. But it didn't worry Pena.

"Lance always looked good," Pena says. "Johan used to say: 'The only guy who is sure to do the Tour is Lance. As for the other guys I just need to choose the best eight riders.' Lance always had July on his mind. At the end of October 2002 we went to do training in Austin, Texas. And that year there was a duathlon in Austin: five miles running, 20 miles mountain biking, and then five miles running. Lance saw this on the news and he saw that some very strong guys were coming to do this event. So he said: 'I'd like to beat those guys.' Lance competed and he beat them, and that was in November. So while other guys in Europe were resting or taking it easy, Lance was thinking about the Tour de France even in November."

But despite the committed training mindset, Armstrong wasn't superhuman and one thing nobody realised, not even his team-mates, was that as the Tour began Armstrong was suffering from a particularly nasty dose of diarrhoea.

With the 2003 Tour being such a special anniversary the race organisers decided the route should both start and finish in the French capital, and visit the stage-finish towns from 1903 along the way. The prologue time trial began in the shadow of the Eiffel Tower and darted around some of the most iconic landmarks in Paris before ending up back at the Eiffel Tower gardens. As the overall favourites began to prepare for their attempts at the 6.5-kilometre course it was Spaniard Haimar Zubeldia of the Basque Euskaltel squad who led the time sheets with a result of 7-28.

"Before the Tour started we were confident," Pena remembers. "We always thought about the Tour on a day-by-day basis. After every day we spoke about the good things or bad things, or where we could improve. Before the prologue we were checking our bikes, or on the turbo-trainers, because we knew we had to show that we were a strong team. If Lance was to win the prologue but the next rider from our team came in 40th or 50th then it would show we weren't a strong team. So we all wanted to ride strongly in the prologue.

"I actually had Lance behind me in the team car as I did my ride in the prologue. He had had no time to view the prologue course so he was in the car with Johan following me. For me that was OK because in those years we were really good friends and it was a normal relationship between cyclists. People always think that in the US Postal squad we were always working and Lance was the boss, but for us it was no problem." Having Armstrong behind him certainly didn't affect

Pena, who recorded a time of 7-32, which proved good enough for fifth.

Of the big guns it was Jan Ullrich, riding in the evocative, historic celeste colours of Team Bianchi, who sent his warning out to Armstrong. The German registered a time of 7-28 and matched Zubeldia at the top of the leaderboard. Perhaps more important than the time was Ullrich's appearance. He looked lean, powerful and determined. It appeared that he was starting at a higher level than in his previous challenges with Armstrong.

But Ullrich's reign at the top didn't last long and soon his time was bettered by FDJeux's time trial specialist Bradley McGee. The Australian, a former world track pursuit champion, set a new marker of 7-26. Meanwhile, at the halfway checkpoint, another time trial king, David Millar, had recorded a figure five seconds faster than McGee. Also out on the course was Armstrong's old mountain lieutenant Tyler Hamilton, wearing the white and red of the CSC team and now seen as an overall challenger.

Armstrong himself was the last rider to set off down the start ramp, resplendent in the vibrant yellow jersey he had earned at the previous year's race. Quickly Armstrong was out of the saddle, punishing the pedals as he brought the big gear he was churning up to speed. He burst up the opening straight, between press photographers lying prone on the road, and was in full flight by the time he entered the barriered, crowd-flocked roads of the stage proper.

At the finish Hamilton was wringing every last ounce of power from his legs, to record a time of 1-32, putting him provisionally fifth. For Millar, though, there was abject disaster. The Scot, who had been flying around the course, saw the chain slip off his bike's gear cogs with just the final corner to negotiate. Leaning down from the saddle, Millar managed to hook the chain back on, but it cost precious seconds. He sprinted to the finish with just the faintest chance he could still unseat McGee. As Millar crossed the line the official clock ticked 7-26.24, but it wasn't enough: McGee's time had been 7-26.16. The Scot had missed out by just eight hundredths of a second.

Eventually Armstrong found himself alone on the course, legs pistoning, his upper body gently rocking. But into the final straight it was apparent this year the American would not be starting with quite the dominance of the past. He rolled over the line in 7-33, only good enough for seventh place. Overall things were more interesting than perhaps expected. McGee held the yellow jersey by a fraction of a second from David Millar. Zubeldia was third at two seconds, Ullrich was fourth also at two seconds, Pena was fifth at six seconds, Hamilton was sixth also at six seconds, and Armstrong was seventh seven seconds down. Beloki had done a solid time trial to finish ninth, nine seconds behind. Could this be the closest of Armstrong's Tour challenges yet?

"After the prologue Lance came up to me and said: 'Man, you were fucking fast, I don't know how you did it,'" Pena says. "But he knew already I was fast at time trials. At races like Circuit de la Sarthe Lance would come something like ninth in the time trial and I would be 10th, so he knew it was close between us. After that prologue I was already dreaming about the team time trial. There was a big possibility there for me to take the yellow jersey, but there were three stages to go before then, and I knew anything could happen."

As is the custom, the first week of the 2003 Tour was largely made for the sprinters. Stage one ended in a small bunch finish but only after a mass crash near the front of the pack in the final kilometre delayed all but 20 or so of the riders. Most of the big names were either near or behind the accident when it happened and although none of the riders would lose time because the accident happened in the final kilometre, the big question was: were any of them injured?

Riders started to cross the line in dribs and drabs. Ullrich had been delayed in the accident, but wasn't injured. Tyler Hamilton had fallen badly onto his left side and was in terrible pain. And Levi Leipheimer, leading the Rabobank squad, was so badly injured in the crash that he had to abandon the race.

Armstrong had also gone down, despite being surrounded by US Postal riders, with his bike so badly damaged that he had to finish the stage on team-mate Chechu Rubiera's machine. Worryingly, he was also complaining of back pain after the stage.

"I was right next to Lance when the crash happened," Pena says. "The tension was high among the sprinters. But crashes like that always happen in the first week of the Grand Tours. I was close to Lance but the crash happened in the final kilometre, so as long as he didn't crash badly there was nothing to worry about in terms of time." As it happened, the overall standings saw little change.

Despite being in obvious pain, Hamilton took to the start for stage two. An x-ray taken the previous evening showed that he had fractured his collarbone in two places and he would spend the rest of the Tour having nightly examinations to check he wasn't doing long-term damage to his body. The stage itself ended in a bunch gallop – thankfully one that passed without incident. Stage three also ended in a sprint, and again there was a crash, although it only involved one rider, Gerolsteiner's Rene Haselbacher. There were no major changes to the overall classification.

Stage four was the 69-kilometre team time trial, and with the US Postal team yet to win the event at the Tour all eyes were on them to propel Armstrong back up the leaderboard. Interestingly, whatever happened, Armstrong wouldn't take the yellow jersey here because after the prologue Pena was still higher up the general classification than his team boss.

"The night before the team time trial, when I saw I was in the right position to take yellow, I just thought: 'OK, we've got to win the team time trial,'" Pena remembers.

Of the favourites' teams it was the CSC squad of Tyler Hamilton that completed the course first, but their time of 1-20-12 was unable to topple the previous best, set by iBanesto.com at 1-19-32. Then the ONCE team, winners of the 2002 team time trial and who had been setting records at time-checks along the course, arrived at the finish in 1-18-57, putting them comfortably at the head of the timesheet.

Out on the course, Ullrich's Bianchi squad looked to be delivering their team leader a solid performance, but US Postal were going faster still. Ullrich's team arrived at the finish to record a very respectable 1-19-10 for provisional second place, but that looked likely to soon drop to third. All nine US Postal riders kept the concentration high until the line, then George Hincapie and Viatcheslav Ekimov allowed themselves brief moments of celebration, each raising one arm in the air. Hincapie could see on the finish line's clock that they had smashed ONCE's figure by half a minute with a time of 1-18-27. US Postal had scored their first Tour de France team trial win, and Victor Hugo Pena would be the first ever Colombian to wear the yellow jersey. Perhaps more importantly, Lance Armstrong now had an edge on his rivals.

"I think the team time trial was a perfect day," Pena says. "We were pulling so hard and I think everyone was doing a really good job. For the last five kilometres I was thinking: 'I will be in yellow, so please don't crash.' I was nervous, I didn't want anything to go wrong. When we got to the finish Lance congratulated me a lot. He is a guy who is always reading the news, and he was looking at the news in Colombia. Probably in those days he didn't know how big cycling was in Colombia, but then he started to see all the Colombian newspapers had my face on the front page and he said: 'Man, cycling is really big in your country.' He told me he was really happy for my country and he said he hoped I would enjoy wearing the yellow jersey. But I never even considered I could win the Tour because my job was just to work for Lance. That was the deal from the minute I signed my contract with Johan."

After the race Armstrong explained his particular obsession with the team time trial event: "We felt we have not ridden our best in the team time trial for the last few years so to win is a real satisfying feeling. I remember back in 1994 Motorola lost the TTT in Calais by three seconds to MG. The TTT was always Jim Ochowicz's event, his passion. Och always wanted to win it, even though Motorola was never the best team on paper. So it's really good to finally win a stage like this. The desire to win was carried over to US Postal, so I'm sending this win out to Och."

The overall classification had seen a massive shake-up. Pena now led the race by a single second from Armstrong, and other US Postal riders made up the top eight places. Beloki was the nearest of Armstrong's rivals in ninth, 33 seconds behind the yellow jersey, with Ullrich 12th, 39 seconds down. Hamilton, who was still soldiering on, lay 39th at 1-45.

Stages five and six were both flat and allowed Fassa Bortolo's Alessandro Petacchi to rack up his third and fourth stage victories in this Tour. Among the favourites there were no changes on the overall standings.

On stage seven, the 2003 Tour de France finally hit the hills and took in five categorised climbs. Importantly, though, the day finished downhill, which suggested that any time gains would be less significant than if the day were to finish on a summit. And if the previous four years were anything to go by, Armstrong would stake his first claim to the overall title here.

In fact, on a scorchingly hot day, things didn't quite go as expected. First the race witnessed a spate of abandons, then, among the overall favourites something odd was happening: Armstrong wasn't attacking. In fact, on the biggest climb of the day – the Col de la Ramaz – it was French hero Richard Virenque of Quick Step who rode away from the big names. Virenque, noted as a demon descender, pushed just as hard on the downhill run-in to Morzine and took the stage to glorious applause. The main group of race favourites arrived 4-06 after Virenque, meaning that he not only had charge of the King of the Mountains competition, he was now firmly seated in the yellow jersey too. Overall there had been a big shake-up. Armstrong was still second, but now he trailed Virenque rather than his team-mate Pena, and the gap was significant at 2-37. Telekom's Rolf Aldag was third at 2-48. Of Armstrong's rivals Beloki had moved up to sixth, 3-09 behind Virenque, Ullrich was ninth at 3-15, and Hamilton was 20th at 4-21.

Letting Virenque escape seemed a strange tactic. It wasn't unusual for Armstrong to let some selected riders get away when it suited him, but only if he thought they were no threat overall. Although Virenque had gained a reputation for escaping simply to hoover up King of the Mountains points and win the polka-dot jersey, he was also once very much seen as an overall favourite, even finishing second in the 1997 Tour de France. So he could be a threat.

For Pena, that first day in the mountains meant he had lost his yellow jersey: "I was dropped on a climb because I was working hard for the team that day. But we weren't worried about Lance's form. We were always confident because the only guys that saw Lance training and doing tests were us. The eight guys in our team were cyclists with long careers and we understood about cycling and tests and watts, rpm and speed. And earlier in the season, when we saw the test results from Lance, we had to say that nobody could be stronger than him."

If the previous day's stage was an introduction to the Alps, stage eight would be nothing short of a full-blooded battle ending on the 21 celebrated hairpin bends of Alpe d'Huez. At the bottom of the Alpe Brioches la Boulangère's Didier Rous and Ag2r's Mikel Astarloza had a lead on the group of favourites by two and a half minutes. But some sort of normality had resumed among the big names and it was, as expected, five of the blue stormtroopers from US

Postal who were setting the punishing tempo.

Suddenly, within the first kilometre of the climb, Armstrong's men exploded. Heras and Rubiera sprinted at the front of the group, raising the speed to an unsustainable level in an attempt to destroy the pack that had gathered behind them. Virenque disappeared off the back but T-Mobile's Alexandre Vinokourov, Crédit Agricole's Christophe Moreau and CSC's Hamilton all stuck to the wheels of the US Postal boys, who were clearing a path through the 500,000-strong crowd that lined the road. What was not clear initially, was the position of Ullrich and Beloki.

As the climb developed Beloki reappeared in the Armstrong group and then staged an audacious attack, gapping Armstrong and the American's sole remaining helper, Heras. With no reaction from the two US Postal riders, Beloki quickly caught Rous and Astarloza, whose advantage had been gradually whittled down in any case, and set off alone up the hill. Armstrong and Heras seemed content to have Hamilton and two Euskaltel riders, Iban Mayo and Roberto Laiseka, for company, but Beloki was building a lead. With Heras unable to raise the pace any further Armstrong took over duties at the front, sprinting up the slope out of the saddle. Heras fell away, but the other three riders stuck with Armstrong.

At the front Beloki danced in and out of the saddle, pushing a lone furrow onwards, and gained an advantage of 12 seconds. But eventually Armstrong and his three companions had ridden themselves back up to his side. In a classic example of cycling tactics, as soon as the catch was made, Mayo decided to attack, instantly distancing the quartet of Armstrong, Beloki, Hamilton and Laiseka. Before the 2003 Tour began the talk among race pundits wasn't that there was a single powerful challenger to Armstrong's crown, but if all his rivals worked together, then a combined attack could reap rewards. On the slopes of Alpe d'Huez the crowd was seeing this approach in action; first Beloki attacked, then Mayo was gone, then Beloki tried again, then even Hamilton attempted to break free, and then again Beloki attacked. Armstrong leapt across the road to cover the moves by Beloki and Hamilton, but Mayo was left to go. More worryingly for Armstrong, riders were catching his group from behind.

While it meant he was rejoined and reinforced by Heras, it also meant

Armstrong faced more threats from other rivals. One such rider was Vinokourov, who leapt away and earned a gap. Up front Mayo was replicating some of the form he had produced at the Dauphiné Libéré. With four kilometres left to race he had a lead of 1-24 on Vinokourov, and 1-48 the Armstrong, who was still being challenged by Beloki and Hamilton and had been joined by young Italian Ivan Basso, of Fassa Bortolo.

By the final kilometre banner Mayo's advantage was up to almost two minutes, and he used a portion of it to enjoy celebrating along the final run-in to the line. Vinokourov arrived next at 1-45, and Armstrong led in his group at 2-12. But where was Ullrich? The answer came 1-24 after Armstrong crossed the line. It perhaps wasn't a massive disaster for the German, but Armstrong would be happy that, despite his other troubles, he now had a significant cushion on his most feared rival. With Virenque turning up 9-29 behind Mayo, it meant that Armstrong was back in the yellow jersey, with a lead of 40 seconds on Beloki. Mayo was third at 1-10, Vinokourov fourth at 1-17, Mancebo fifth at 1-37 and Hamilton sixth at 1-52. Ullrich wasn't out of the picture either in eighth place at 2-10. So Armstrong led the race, but his rivals knew that this year there were chinks in his armour.

After the stage a clearly rattled Armstrong admitted things hadn't happened quite as he would have liked: "Yeah that was tough, that's for sure... If it keeps going like that it's going to be a long Tour. But I think the first true, true day in the mountains is sometimes strange and I definitely didn't have it today, but I'll get better."

Stage nine was the annual chance for French riders to have their cameo in the Tour: Bastille Day. The day's route also featured one icon of France – the monstrous hors catégorie Col d'Izoard climb. But like the first day in the Alps it would again finish on the flat, so the chances of seeing a result like Mayo's on Alpe d'Huez looked unlikely.

In fact it wasn't the two big climbs on the day's itinerary – the Col du Lautaret and the Izoard – that saw the most action, rather it was two smaller climbs – the Côte de Saint Apollinaire and the Côte de la Rochette – nearer the finish that witnessed Armstrong under real attack. Again Armstrong looked unable to do little more than be defensive and, as the front riders descended the last hill towards Gap, he found himself without any team-mates in a group that contained Ullrich and Beloki. Up ahead, although only by a matter of seconds, Vinokourov had attacked and was tearing down the slope.

Then came a moment of high drama. With four kilometres left to race, and descending at break-neck speed, group pace-setter Beloki's rear tyre swerved violently. Approaching a right-hand bend, the Spaniard suffered what motorcycle riders would call a 'tank slapper'. He twisted to the right, then corrected himself and twisted to the left, but he could not hold the bike upright, crashing to the broken asphalt in a heap. Only two bike lengths behind him, Armstrong was faced with rapidly reducing options to avoid Beloki and ended up riding to the left, into a field. With the other members of the group remaining on the road and riding round a left-hand hairpin bend, Armstrong continued on his bike through the field, cut across the bend, then dismounted, jumped a ditch, and rejoined the others as they came past. It was a supreme display of Armstrong's state of mind and bike control under intense immediate pressure.

Beloki was not as fortunate as Armstrong. Once he had slid to a standstill at the edge of the road he did not move. He was simply left screaming in pain, watched over by two ONCE team-mates, Jose Azevedo and Jorg Jaksche. With a broken elbow, finger and femur he was out of the Tour de France.

Meanwhile the drama had allowed the stage leader to gain a bigger gap and Vinokourov took the line 36 seconds ahead of the Armstrong group. Overall the Kazakh had jumped up the rankings into second place, just 21 seconds behind Armstrong. Beloki was now out of the race so Mayo was still third at 1-02, iBanesto.com's Francisco Mancebo was fourth at 1-37, Hamilton fifth at 1-52 and Ullrich still sixth at 2-10.

Despite Vinokourov's rise up the overall classification Pena says the team wasn't concerned: "We were never worried about Vinokourov, it was always Ullrich. Journalists and television commentators could say what they liked, but we actually saw these guys on their bikes, every day, and we'd been seeing the same guys racing at other races. We knew what the other guys were doing in winter training, so we knew what to expect."

The next few days saw little action among the favourites. Stage 10 was won by a two-man breakaway with the main field arriving 21 minutes later, then there was a rest day. Stage 11 saw iBanesto.com's Juan-Antonio Flecha beat seven other breakaways while the main bunch arrived 42 seconds later. There were no major changes to the overall standings.

During the flat stages Pena knew exactly what his role was: "Normally my job was to pull the bunch for the first 100 kilometres. At the beginning I would jump on the breaks, and after the break was gone I would be pulling at the front of the peloton with people like Viatcheslav Ekimov, or Pavel Padrnos, or riders like that. One of the things I always missed at the Tour de France was not being there at the end of stages on the climbs. I was a better climber than George Hincapie in those days but I was never there at the end of climbs. It wasn't my decision – at the team meetings Johan would always say who the first guys to pull the bunch would be, and I was always one of them. So that was probably the only thing that I missed during my years with Lance."

Pena couldn't do anything for Armstrong on stage 12 because it was the 2003 Tour's first individual time trial. Going into the 47-kilometre test, normally Armstrong's domain, the Texan was in the yellow jersey, but only just, and with his under-par displays so far his rivals were fancying their chances.

Of the big names Ullrich was the first one to take to the road and he looked in sparkling form. At the second checkpoint, at 33.5 kilometres, the German registered a time 1-52 quicker than the previous best, that set by Euskaltel's Haimar Zubeldia. Behind Ullrich his former team-mate Alexandre Vinokourov was also riding well. But after Ullrich's scintillating pace most eyes were on Armstrong, and at the 33.5-kilometre checkpoint it was apparent the Texan had no answer for the German. He went through with a time 39 seconds slower than Ullrich's – it was a gap he couldn't hope to close in the 14 kilometres that remained. Ullrich kept churning his massive gear as he approached the finish, gritting his teeth, to record a time of 58-32, more than two and a half minutes clear of the previous best.

Vinokourov finished his ride in a time of 1-00-38 to go second with only Armstrong left able to push him down to third. To the outside world Armstrong's body was working like a model of efficiency as always, but the time sheets were saying otherwise, and due to the effects of diarrhoea his body was severely dehydrated. As he rounded the last bend into the final straight he was already more than a minute down on Ullrich. He crossed the line at 1-00-08, good enough only for second.

The result saw Ullrich leap into second place overall, 34 seconds behind Armstrong, who had just retained the race lead. Vinokourov was third at 51 seconds and Hamilton was fourth at 2-59. After the stage Ullrich was obviously pleased with himself as he spoke to the press: "Victory is always sweet."

For Armstrong, Pena and the rest of the US Postal team life wasn't quite so sweet. "I was shocked when Lance couldn't win that first individual time trial," Pena says. "We all said something must have been wrong. Especially when Johan told him Ullrich was beating him, Lance's morale really went down. Then we found out Lance had very bad diarrhoea. I remember we didn't see Lance the night after the time trial or even the next morning. Then before stage 13 he came to us and said: 'Guys, I'm sorry, I couldn't do it. I don't what happened to me but I feel really odd. I'm sorry guys.' To me it felt very strange that a guy like him would be saying sorry to someone like me. I said: 'No man, don't worry.' But he looked like he felt a bit ashamed or something."

Stage 13 was the beginning of the 2003 Tour's visit to the Pyrenees and it promised fireworks with two first-category climbs in short order, first the Port de Pailhères and then the summit finish at Plateau de Bonascre.

As the race reached the Bonascre a three-man breakaway featuring US Postal's Rubiera, CSC's Carlos Sastre and iBanesto.com's Juan Miguel Mercado led the way, while the group of overall favourites lay 2-05 behind. In that bunch US Postal's Heras and Manuel Beltran set the pace, turning up the wick as they hit the lower slopes. Beltran managed to mount one last great change in pace, causing the group to splinter, but it had little effect on Ullrich, who cruised up to ride alongside Armstrong. And just behind Armstrong the other favourites followed his tempo without problem.

At the front Sastre had attacked and was pushing on alone, but back among the men fighting for the yellow jersey there were developments. Hamilton could take no more and slipped back, leaving Armstrong's group down to just seven riders: Armstrong, Ullrich, Vinokourov, Mayo, Zubeldia, CSC's Ivan Basso and Crédit Agricole's Christophe Moreau. Into the last four kilometres Zubeldia attacked, Ullrich chased him immediately, then Vinokourov, Armstrong and Basso managed to tag along. Among these five riders Ullrich took over pace-setting duties, looking cool and calm. Zubeldia attacked again, and again he was matched. Then Vinokourov went with a concerted attack. Showing immense power, Ullrich steamed onto his wheel and in the process opened up the faintest of gaps on Armstrong. That was enough and Armstrong's resolve seemed to evaporate. Zubeldia made his way past, then Basso, and the yellow jersey was left at the back of the group, desperately trying to hold on.

Incidental to the real action, Sastre pushed alone to the win. But Ullrich had soon caught and passed the previous second-placed rider on the stage, Mercado, and the time bonus the German could now win might be enough to take the yellow jersey from Armstrong. Ullrich weaved through the streets, almost clipping the barriers trying to take as much time from Armstrong as possible. He crossed the line in second place, 1-01 after Sastre, with a resurgent Zubeldia on his wheel. But Armstrong had succeeded in rallying his efforts and arrived after only seven seconds. Vinokourov finished fifth, 10 seconds later.

Again the overall standings had seen some changes. Armstrong now led Ullrich by just 15 seconds and Vinokourov was third at 1-01. After Vinokourov the other challengers were starting to slip away: Zubeldia in fourth was 4-16 back; Hamilton in fifth was 4-25 back; and Mayo in sixth was 5-20 away from the yellow jersey.

The second day in the Pyrenees, stage 14 to Loudenvielle was expected to be a real killer with six first or second-category climbs en route. Richard Virenque, already in the polka-dot jersey of the King of the Mountains, was out looking to wrap up the title and was part of an early 17-man break that escaped the main field. By the last climb, the Col de Peyresourde, the leading group had been whittled down to just three men: Virenque, Saeco's Tour of Italy champion Gilberto Simoni, and Alessio's Laurent Dufaux. About a minute behind them was Brioches la Boulangère's Walter Bénéteau, then came CSC's Andrea Peron, and then at 1-41 came a group of three chasers led by Alexandre Vinokourov.

The yellow jersey group, which comprised just Armstrong, Zubeldia, Basso and Ullrich – who was again looking comfortable and setting the pace on the front – rode about another minute behind them. Over the summit of the Peyresourde, Armstrong took to the front and raised the pace. Ullrich also helped keep the speed high, despite the fact that this descent was where the German famously disappeared over the side of the road back in the 2001 Tour. Slowly the quartet started to catch the Vinokourov group, and with three kilometres left to race the gap was down to around 40 seconds.

At the front Simoni outsprinted Dufaux and Virenque for the stage win. Vinokourov, Mayo and Zampieri arrived 41 seconds later. Vinokourov needed 1-01 on Armstrong to take the race lead, but the yellow jersey group crossed the line just 43 seconds after the Kazakh. Overall it meant that Vinokourov was still third but now just 18 seconds behind Armstrong, while Ullrich remained in second place at 15 seconds.

"I felt better," Armstrong said after the stage. "You can't recover from a time trial like that with such severe dehydration in one day... Today I felt better and hopefully tomorrow it's another uptake. Vinokourov is aggressive but I'm worried about Ullrich, not Vino."

Stage 15 included more brutish climbs including the Col d'Aspin, the Col du Tourmalet and ended at the summit of Luz Ardiden. And despite the race's second rest day on the horizon, nobody was planning a slow wind down. By the time the race reached the final climb it was young French hope Sylvain Chavanel of Brioches la Boulangère that led the way, holding a gap of 4-38 from a small group of favourites that included Armstrong, Ullrich, Vinokourov and Mayo. With 10 kilometres to go Mayo attacked and Armstrong, for the first appreciable time this Tour, reacted with venom. He jumped onto the Spaniard's wheel immediately and then attacked as well. It was a classic Armstrong move, but it didn't reap the traditional result and he was unable to shake off either Mayo or Ullrich. The Bianchi rider in particular simply cruised up the climb in Armstrong's wake.

Then disaster happened.

In a Tour that had already been full of drama it was a moment of high anxiety. Armstrong's right-hand brake lever caught the strap of a yellow satchel being held by a young fan at the road's edge. The yellow jersey fell heavily onto his left side, Mayo tumbled over him, and Ullrich had to perform an emergency swerving manoeuvre to stay upright. Mayo was up first and on his way, but Armstrong's chain had come off and it took him a while to sort it out. Chechu Rubiera had waited for him and once it was established that his bike was fine to ride the two sprinted off up the hill.

Up ahead Ullrich, in a display of amazing sportsmanship, had slowed to wait for his American rival. Rubiera and Armstrong caught up with Mayo at the tail end of the Ullrich group, then there was another bizarre moment. Powering up the hill at full speed out of the saddle, Armstrong's foot slipped out of his clip-in pedals and his lower body crashed onto his bike's top tube. Somehow he managed to avoid crashing, but he had to spend a few more precious moments collecting his breath and checking his pedals were not broken.

Once Armstrong had regained the group, he and Rubiera immediately headed past Ullrich and took up pace-setting duties at the front. With normality resumed, and nine kilometres left to the summit, Mayo attacked again, and again Armstrong followed him and counterattacked. Mayo managed to stay on his wheel briefly, but this time Ullrich just couldn't react and trundled on at his own pace. Armstrong, his arm bleeding from the crash, bobbed his way onwards while Ullrich, face snarling, did everything he could to limit the gap.

Armstrong soon had the struggling Chavanel in his sights. In a day of sporting gestures Armstrong produced another, patting the young Frenchman's back as he powered past. Onwards, through deep crowds lining the route, the yellow jersey ploughed. By the two-kilometres-to-go banner the time gap between Armstrong and Ullrich was 45 seconds, but Ullrich – shadowed by Euskaltel riders Mayo and Zubeldia, and then Basso and Moreau – was gradually reducing the difference.

Armstrong bobbed upwards, into the barriered part of the route and under the final kilometre sign, perspiration dripping off his body. Eventually he approached the finish line but there were no victory celebrations. In hazy, misty conditions the American threw his bike forward over the line, more exhausted than perhaps the Tour de France had ever seen him. Forty seconds later Ullrich suffered the ignominy of being ambushed for the second-place time bonus by Mayo. Then came Zubeldia, Moreau, Basso and Hamilton. Vinokourov appeared eighth, 2-07 behind Armstrong and surely ended his bid for the yellow jersey. Overall Armstrong had a much more significant gap over Ullrich – 1-07. Vinokourov was still in third, but was now 2-45 behind.

After the stage Armstrong explained what had happened at the crucial moment: "A spectator had something, probably like a bag, and the handle was just swinging around and it caught onto my handlebar... It scared the hell out of me. It was lucky that the bike wasn't messed up. The only problem is that the chain came off. I put the chain on and there you go."

In fact, Pena remembers, Armstrong's bike was messed up: "At the end, when the mechanic was putting Lance's bike on the roof of the team car he saw the bike was completely broken. The down tube was broken, completely broken, but for some reason the tube stayed in place, probably because Lance has quite a soft pedalling style and doesn't stress his bike too much. I saw what happened on the stage on the television afterwards. When I saw it I said: 'Lance has put on a really big show for the Tour and for its history.' It felt like everything had built up to that crash."

And the excitement didn't end when the stage finished. High on adrenalin, Armstrong was determined to share his joy with his team. "After that stage we were sure Lance could win the Tour," Pena says. "Later we were in the team bus riding to the hotel and Lance was supposed to be going back by helicopter, but then he called us, he called Johan or someone from the team, to ask us where we were. We told him and he said: 'OK, wait for me, I'll tell the pilot of the helicopter to land it and I want to jump in the bus with my guys.' We saw the helicopter landing near us in a big, flat field and we could see him running across the field to us, from the helicopter to the bus. Then he jumped on the bus and he was screaming.

"That day was one of the best days of my life. I remember my brother was there with us on the bus, he came to watch the Tour de France, and afterwards he said: 'Man, there is no-one like Lance.' Lance got on the bus and started screaming and yelling and talking for probably 10 minutes. He was yelling: 'I'm the fucking best. I work 24 hours a day, seven days a week, for this race. I'm the best. No-one can beat me.' It was like he was thinking aloud, talking to nobody in particular, running from the front of the bus to the back of the bus. We were there getting goosebumps. Lance was giving hugs to everyone, telling us we're the best. I don't think any of the other big stars of cycling ever behaved like that."

After the high excitement of the last few stages the riders finally had a rest day and then three flat stages leading up to the last individual time trial. Stage 16, from Pau to Bayonne, was another landmark day of the Tour, with Tyler Hamilton – already seen as the bravest rider of the 2003 edition – completing a 143-kilometre solo break to take the win despite his broken collarbone. The main field arrived 1-55 later. Overall, among the top three there was no change, but Hamilton's audacious break lifted him to sixth overall, 6-37 behind Armstrong.

Pena remembers Hamilton's stage victory was no gift: "That day we were pulling and pulling, and other teams were pulling and pulling, trying to get Hamilton back, but it was only ever little by little and we could never catch him. We were definitely trying to catch him because he was one of the important riders on the general classification. We didn't want him to get too far ahead, but it was really difficult to keep the time gap."

Stage 17 was also won by another lone breakaway, this time Quick Step's Servais Knaven, then stage 18 was taken by iBanesto.com's Pablo Lastras from a small group. The stage also saw a slight change to the overall standings as Ullrich managed to jump Armstrong at the first intermediate sprint of the day and pick up a small time bonus, reducing his deficit to 1-05.

And so to the final battleground: the 49-kilometre largely flat individual time trial from Pornic to Nantes, and its rain-soaked road surface. In terrible conditions it was going to be a question of staying upright first and being quick second. Time trial specialist David Millar came through the rain unscathed to set the early marker with a time of 54-05, but really today all eyes were on just two men. Millar gave his opinion about the conditions the two leaders faced: "It's absolutely an ice-rink in the last 15 kilometres. Lance and Jan shouldn't have to take risks like that."

Pena shared Millar's feelings about the conditions: "That day it was raining and windy like never before. The conditions were really bad. I was doing my time trial without using my aerobars, I was just trying to keep my bike upright with my normal handlebars. When I finished Johan came over and asked how I went. He asked where it was dangerous and what the different corners were like, which wheels to use. Then he started to take opinions from the other guys and he transmitted those ideas to Lance."

Ullrich was off before Armstrong and was quickly powering around the glistening streets like a super tanker. The German set the quickest result at the second time-check, although Armstrong wasn't playing safe either and was going all-out to win the stage. He passed the same point just two seconds down on Ullrich – the Bianchi star would need a much bigger advantage to take yellow.

In an instant it was all rendered immaterial. Ullrich, pushing his machine to the limit, entered a roundabout and saw his front wheel wash away from him. He careened on the slippery asphalt, sparks flying from his rear derailleur as it rubbed along the road, and came to a stop on the kerb. Although he was quickly up and riding again, vital seconds, his nerve – and now surely the Tour – were lost. Armstrong had seemingly been warned about what had happened to his rival and entered the scene of Ullrich's crash with caution.

Ullrich crossed the line with a time of 54-30, 25 seconds slower than Millar and down in third place. Now he had to wait to see if Armstrong would suffer any mishap, but there was no such accident. Armstrong sped onwards on the straights, then slowed to gently take the corners. Finally he sprinted to the finish and allowed himself a smile and a clench of the fist. His time of 54-19 usurped Ullrich in third place, and secured the yellow jersey. Overall Armstrong led Ullrich by 1-16, Vinokourov had fallen away in third, now 4-29 back, and Hamilton, who had completed his astonishing Tour de France by recording the second fastest time in the time trial, was up to fourth at 6-32.

After the stage Armstrong was congratulated by his wife, the model example of wedded bliss despite their problems earlier in the year. He was obviously relieved as he spoke to the press afterwards: "I don't think I've ever been so nervous before a bike race. I was nervous because I didn't have such a big advantage on Jan, and also because of the weather, the difference between winning and losing because of a crash is so fine. After I heard Jan had crashed I basically sat up and said I'm not taking any risks. I'm definitely having a beer tonight. I told the boys last night that if I made it through today we're going to have some beers. Beers are on me."

The final stage saw the US Postal boys wearing a new celebratory grey uniform, but other than that it was the traditional last day in Paris, and thankfully, after the rain of the time trial, the cobbles of the Champs-Elysées were dry. The day ended in a bunch sprint with Jean Delatour's Jean-Patrick Nazon taking the victory. Incredibly, Ullrich actually made some time up on Armstrong with a split in the pack meaning the yellow jersey crossed the line 15 seconds down on the German, but it was too little too late.

"The last day was a great day," Pena remembers. "It was my third time on the Champs-Elysées working for the best team, pulling for the best rider in the world, and my brother was there watching me. I think everyone in the team enjoyed that day, not just Lance. But my three days when I was in the yellow jersey during the Tour were unbelievable for me.

"When we finished in Paris we always had a big meeting with our families and the sponsors and the team. It wasn't really a party, just a nice, long dinner. The president of US Postal would talk, and Johan would talk, Lance would talk. It was a nice moment to enjoy with your friends and your family. Before the dinner Lance had a meeting with us at the hotel in Paris and we spent an hour – just Lance, Johan and us – talking, remembering moments from the Tour, joking around. We'd talk about the funny things that happened," Pena says.

"I remembered on the prologue Johan was talking to us, saying: 'OK guys you are here at the Tour de France again, do your best, avoid crashes, take care with food, be careful, remember that we have a lot to win and a lot to lose.' That day was really hot and the air conditioning on the bus wasn't working so they opened the windows on the top of the bus. At that moment a bird did a shit on Johan's shirt. On the bus there was one Czech guy, three American guys, a Colombian, two Spanish guys, all different nationalities. Everybody started talking about what it means in their countries when something like that happens. I told Johan that in Colombia when a bird shits on your clothing it is good luck. Then another guy said that in his country it is good luck but it also means you are going to have a lot of hard work first. Another one said when that happens it means you are going to get a big prize but it's going to be really hard to get it. Johan said: 'OK, I just hope we're going to win the Tour de France.' Then when we were in Paris, remembering that moment, Johan said: 'For next year I will be sure to keep the bus window shut. I don't want to suffer like that again.'"

The final overall standing stood with Armstrong taking his magical fifth Tour win, placing him among the four other greatest champions of Tour de France history. Ullrich was the runner-up, also for the fifth time, 1-01 behind. Vinokourov was third at 4-14, and Hamilton's amazing Tour finished with him in fourth, 6-17 behind Armstrong.

For Pena, the memories are still vivid: "Getting in the US Postal Tour de France squad was like a dream for me. What more could I ask for? For a Colombian guy whose dream is to do the Tour de France, and to do it with the best team in the world at the time, and to be in the team with the best rider in the world, made me feel really like I was dreaming.

"Working with Lance was great. I always talked with him no problem, I had a really good relationship with him. Too many people don't like Lance and talk badly about him. But Lance gave me the opportunity to dream and to be at the Tour de France, and to know him. For me he was a guy to imitate. In my personal life I am always talking about my time with Lance and what he did. He is a life model, a sporting example."

Lance's Bikes

With Scott Daubert, Trek Bicycle liaison to US Postal and
Discovery Channel teams 2002-2007

Looking back at photographs from old Tours de France it's sometimes hard to believe that the riders in their woolen jerseys, perched on their heavy steel frames, were actually using the most up-to-date equipment they had at the time. In the 21st century you would find it hard to identify even an ounce of steel on a modern road bike, with manufacturers utilising a full range of exotic metals and carbon composites in their products.

All through his career, and especially since his first Tour win in 1999, Lance Armstrong has had a very particular and often demanding approach to his choice of cycling equipment. He has become known as 'Mr One Per Cent', and has placed great store in finding every ounce or watt of advantage in each piece of his kit. The Armstrong philosophy follows the idea that small fractions of advantage add up together to form a big advantage. Some people ascribe this obsession with detail to Armstrong's battle with cancer and how he focused so intently on every aspect of his care – from diet, to choice of chemotherapy course, even to which drugs were being administered to him, when and why.

But even before cancer Armstrong always enjoyed a particularly close relationship with a select group of equipment providers. Many, if not all, of Armstrong's personal sponsors and suppliers stuck with him during his cancer treatment, despite the fact that there was little guarantee he would ever race again. In return he has repaid them with a continuing loyalty, although that doesn't mean he puts up with less-than-perfect kit.

Ironically, the one part of Armstrong's equipment arsenal which is made by a company that did not have strong links with him before cancer is probably the most important part of all: his bike. For his entire post-cancer career, including his 2009 comeback, Armstrong's bikes have been supplied by American manufacturer Trek. Scott Daubert is now Trek's global road bike brand manager, but in his previous role for the company he worked as the liaison between Trek and the US Postal and Discovery Channel teams. Daubert knows better than anyone else what it is like to produce equipment for Lance Armstrong.

"After Lance had cancer I believe there were very few companies, bicycle companies in particular, that felt he was worth much any more," Daubert says. "The director of marketing at Trek at that time was Mary Munroe, and she was contacted by Lance, or somebody on behalf of Lance, and they started talking. Mary really had great vision and she felt that Lance's time hadn't really come around yet, so she somehow talked people at Trek into going out on a limb and supporting him.

"My personal relationship with Lance actually started at the Olympic Games in Atlanta in 1996. I was there as a mountain bike mechanic and all the USA cyclists were all in one big house in Conyers, Georgia, and it happened that Lance and the road guys were passing through one day and we met in the parking lot there. Then I worked with Lance in 1999 at a couple of mountain bike races where he had come in as a guest rider for two or three different events. And then we met again at the Interbike show in Las Vegas that same year."

Although Daubert had had a passing association with Armstrong, it became a lot more direct at the end of 2001. "Lance felt that a better bike would make him a better athlete and perhaps give him better chances. He started working closely with Trek and quickly found that there was more information being passed back and forth than he had time to manage, and Trek didn't really have a way to get information to him and then get feedback on the technical aspect of things. So some talk started about how we needed a position that would help facilitate the passing of information. I think my boss at the time, who was the director of marketing, and Lance must have remembered me from 1999 and I got drafted into that. That was in December 2001, just around Christmas time, and by the first or second week of January 2002 I was in Spain working with Lance, right in the thick of it.

"I would go to as many races as US Postal could stand me at, or as many races as I could tolerate. So I travelled to Europe six or eight times in that first year. I would go to the big Classic races, or I would go to small stage races in France, or I would help with what Trek would be doing at the Tour de France if we had any promotions or anything like that. All of my time with the team would be spent trying to collect information about whichever parts the team was using. We owned just about the entire race bicycle that US Postal was riding at that time – we made the wheels, the components and the frame – so all of those parts had to work in symphony. There's no place where bicycles get abused like they do in the European peloton, so that was the best place to go to get feedback for our equipment."

Although Armstrong is a pretty forthright character, often Daubert had to go looking for opinions. "Sometimes I had to poke a little bit just to get some information. But when Lance did have something to say it was usually spot-on. Often it was what he didn't say that gave us the clue we were going in the right direction. He would say: 'Yeah it's good,' or: 'It's comfortable, I can race this.' But that might be all of the feedback you would get. You wouldn't get the photos or thank you messages or anything that was more concrete and showed more confirmation. Almost no news was good news for some deliveries.

"But we also had parts that wouldn't go any further in development because we just couldn't get them to work right, and in that situation Lance would be quick to say: 'This just isn't measuring up.' Lance is pretty demanding in that he expects near-perfection from the get-go. So when we were trying to develop a product and it showed up only partially baked, sometimes that was tough, that often caused some problems. You are working as hard as you can, and you can only do so much in the laboratory, or only do so much designing something by a computer before you have to hand it over to the human to get that final evaluation. I think that was tough on Lance because he would be riding something that wasn't to his satisfaction, and he'd come back and say: 'You guys have got to do better than this.' And then there's this push and pull where we try to explain that we've done as much as we can and now we needed his help, but he'd want it further along than we could get it."

Ultimately, though, Daubert says Armstrong's approach is all about practicality. "Lance was always professional in that he tells you what the problem is. He doesn't beat about the bush or make you guess. He is direct and to the point, and often that comes across as being really harsh or short, or rude maybe sometimes. But really you have to weed through that emotional part of it and get to the core.

So sometimes you are taken aback by how frank he can be, but his point is: 'This is an issue that's not working for me and I need some help,' or: 'You guys really have got to do better.' The message you had to take from it was: what exactly is he looking for? And not think about how he is presenting the problem."

Like Armstrong himself, Trek's focus on technical developments built up to the Tour de France. But once July came, Daubert saw his job change. "Usually by the time the Tour starts the team is several months into product that they trust. If we had anything new planned, Johan Bruyneel mandated that all of that new product had to be finished with development by the Dauphiné Libéré, in the second week in June. And that's still how we do it today. If we had anything that we were going to introduce for the 2009 Tour then it had to be done and completed come the Dauphiné, or it didn't get to the Tour. It's just so that Johan has a week of racing on it, so he can say: 'This is fine, we can work with it.'

"Then when the Tour started my job was just to be damage control in case something happened. There was an instance in 2002 or 2003 when Mavic was upset that the team was riding Bontrager wheels and not Mavic wheels. There was an alleged patent infringement that Mavic was concerned about, so I was there to help the various lawyers that were working the case, trying to get things sorted out. And once the Tour started I was really almost only there as, say, a conversation piece. If US media was there and they had questions about Lance's bike or the team's equipment, or if they had a Trek-specific question, then I could speak to them."

Occasionally in pro cycling riders will have their own preference of kit suppliers, but for contractual reasons they will rebrand it with stickers from their official equipment sponsors, but Trek takes great pride in ensuring that everything that features the Trek name really is a Trek product. "The only occasion when that wasn't the case was in the very first year that we worked with Lance, in 1999. He rode on a Lightspeed Blade in the time trial events. But that is the one exception to what he has been riding. Anything that was given to him from Trek has been a Trek-made product."

After experiencing such a close result at the 2003 Tour Armstrong brought together all his equipment suppliers to work as one team, named 'Formula One'. "The idea of the 'Formula One' team came from Lance's friend Bart Knaggs,"

Daubert says. "Bart's vision was that all of the people who contribute to what it takes for Lance or the team to win should probably get together and work in concert. Perhaps the helmet could fit better with the eyewear, or the helmet could fit better to the jersey, and so on. I was part of the 'Formula One' team in that the parts Trek was supplying to the team – the wheels, the frames and the handlebars, and how they worked together – was what I was overseeing. I would go to the wind tunnel when we were doing wind tunnel testing, or I would go on a reconnaissance ride with Lance if he was going to look at a certain course using the bike he was hoping to ride, just to videotape the course and get some feedback.

"We worked with Oakley a little bit, and Giro a little bit. There might have been a Shimano representative there too. It was kind of carte blanche as far as the budget went: whatever it took to win the Tour. We'd share ideas, ask what the other guys were working on, and say what we were working on. I never felt uncomfortable that I was giving away secrets, and I don't think I learned anything from anybody else. For instance, we talked about surface textures to help aerodynamics, and I know Giro and Trek were both discussing that at one point. We were just saying: 'Hey, if you put a texture on that, would it make it aerodynamically better?' It was technology we may have talked about within our own companies, but it might have had a better application somewhere else."

One of the biggest tasks Trek and the rest of the 'Formula One' team had to come up with was to create a time trial bike that could rival the one Jan Ullrich used in 2003. "Oh boy, that was a big project," Daubert remembers. "The bike that Ullrich raced was a Walser, a Swiss-made carbon bike, and the main benefit of that bike was that it put the rider's feet very close together, so they were more aerodynamic. We made a bike that followed similar dimensions. We tried to put Lance's feet together, and from the numbers we were getting from testing, on paper it was a huge advantage. It was faster than anything we had designed before.

"However, there comes a point where comfort has to be part of the equation, and if Lance was uncomfortable having his feet 18mm closer together then you can't use it because ultimately Lance is the guy that has got to ride it for an hour and five minutes over 55 kilometres. If he is coming back saying he is not comfortable, therefore he's not making power, therefore he's losing time, you have to reconsider.

"The frustrating part of all that was having to swallow the pill that Lance knew his body better than we did. We had to listen to what he was saying, even though the numbers and data from the wind tunnel were so enticing. Previously we had been just giving up seconds to the Ullrich bike, but with this new bike we were winning back a minute and a half over a 50-kilometre course. So it was a lot of time and Lance recognised that it was significant, it was just that he also knew that his body wasn't able to do it, so we had to take a step back and say: 'OK, we understand, we don't like it, but we understand it.'"

With such an intense focus on one rider, Daubert knows better than anybody just what Armstrong's preferences are when it comes to his bike set-up. Crucially for Lance fans, Daubert also says it is something that can be replicated with off-the-shelf equipment. "I think now Lance's bike set-up has become almost the norm because people have copied little bits of it. It's a little more upright than is traditional, his hand position is higher, he's got his brake hoods rolled back on his handlebars, his hands are pretty high in relation to where his hips are. His pedal cadence and where his saddle sits is obviously unique to Lance and how he rides. But as far as the equipment and what he is using is concerned, aside from paint jobs, he is riding production parts. We have the ability to manufacture custom parts, but we prefer our race teams to ride production parts."

That ability to say the bike you buy from a local bike dealer is exactly the same as the one that won the Tour de France is a marketing goldmine, and it's important to remember the relationship between Armstrong and Trek isn't just about being at the pinnacle of professional sport, it's also about commerce. "Lance helped our business. We made better products because of his name and his ability to help us develop something, so at the bottom line that helped us make money. But behind the scenes, he never asked for anything personally that he wouldn't really use or didn't value. What he was asking for was something that would help him be a better bike racer or help us make a better bike. So there was never really a case of jumping through hoops just because he wanted us to, or going in a certain direction because he thought it would be cool or trendy."

And when Armstrong associated himself with a particular product he didn't just lend his name to it. In the case of Trek's Madone road bike – which is named after the mountain Armstrong used for training – he had a very direct, personal role in its creation. "When we introduced the 2003 Madone model road bike, we introduced it through Lance and he was the one helping us shape that bike to have a certain ride quality," Daubert says. "We went through several iterations before we finally got it to where Lance was saying: 'OK, I am very happy with this.' So he was directly involved with that project. For other projects he may have been on the periphery. For example, if we had a new wheel design we were working on I would get as much information from other team riders as I would from Lance."

Although the Madone has gone on to become a commercial success, its development wasn't plain sailing. "We were struggling with some chainstay dimensions or carbon lay-ups in the chainstays. We learned through our own testing and through working with Lance that how that chainstay is shaped, or what the carbon lay-up schedule is within that chainstay, has a strong bearing on how the whole bike performs. We were struggling with what we wanted to do and how we would actually do it. We could get the right stiffness but then the bike would be too heavy, or we could get the weight down and then the bike didn't ride exactly right. I remember having several pretty in-depth conversations with Lance about what we were trying to do with this bike, because it wasn't working.

"Then there are other things that were purely matters of opinion, where we would be trying to do a design that was unique or interesting-looking and had some design functions, but in Lance's eyes – or even more specifically, in Johan's eyes – the bike was really ugly. The Madone sold pretty well because it was new and different and had a technical benefit to it, but it was far from being traditional, and the traditional part of bikes is what Johan and Lance really liked. So we never really saw eye-to-eye on that particular bike," Daubert says.

"Ultimately, though, we made it to sell bikes, we wanted to get more people on our bikes. But it would have done us no good at all to make something that Lance wouldn't ride, so we had to go to him to ask: 'What are you looking for in a bike? And as we develop it can you ride with us and say what it's doing for you?' Lance has a pretty good sense of touch and he has so many miles in his legs, so he can say what works for him, and you can put some faith in that."

Curiously, despite having Armstrong as its most famous rider, and despite the

Madone – the 'Lance bike' – being such a strong seller, Trek has never released an 'Armstrong' branded range of bikes. "There's been talk over the last 10 years if there should be a Lance line of bikes, the way there is a Trek line of bikes," Daubert says. "We've never gone down that road very far because Lance and the people that own Trek have often got together and looked at the possibilities here, and it always ends up coming up short. So as far as I know there's no plan to ever have a Lance Armstrong line of bikes."

Coming right up to date, Daubert says it's not just the names in the peloton that might have changed in the years that Armstrong has been away from pro cycling, even the 2009 bikes are significantly altered compared to the ones on which he ended the Tour in 2005.

"Lance's Madone 6.9 this year is significantly different in that it has a sloping top tube. In 2003 we introduced a sloping top tube design to Lance, because a lot of our competitors were going to a sloping top tube and being successful in sales. But we were never able to get a sloping top tube bike underneath Lance when he was racing up to 2005 because he just really didn't like the way that it looked, and I think Johan had an opinion there too. Johan had spent some time on sloping top tube bikes when he was racing and he preferred a traditional bike. But Lance's bike now does have a sloping top tube and that doesn't seem to be much of an issue for Lance now. And the carbon technology has advanced again since 2005, so we are able to make the thing lighter and stronger and stiffer all at the same time."

CHAPTER 11

2004: Record Breaker

With Graham Watson, cycle race photographing legend and official photographer
to US Postal, Discovery Channel and Astana teams

In 2004 Lance Armstrong would try to achieve what none of the other great
champions of Tour de France history had been able to do – a sixth overall win.
And he had no intention of making his record-breaking edition anywhere near as
nail-biting as the 2003 race.

Long before the Tour began, the 2003 race was already starting to look like
a freakish one-off. First of all Jan Ullrich was back in the bright cerise of the
T-Mobile squad. The German had claimed that 2003 was just a test year, and
2004 would be his proper shot at beating Armstrong, but his near-success in the
previous year's race seemed to have gone straight to his belly. He had spent the
first half of the season looking particularly portly, although success at his final
Tour warm-up race, the Tour of Switzerland, made some observers think Ullrich
had ridden himself into top form. Other potential rivals for Armstrong included
his former US Postal team-mate Roberto Heras, now the leader at the Liberty
Seguros squad; Ivan Basso, who had moved to CSC; Tyler Hamilton, leader at the
Phonak team; and Iban Mayo, who remained at Euskaltel-Euskadi.

By 2004 photographer Graham Watson had become a good friend of
Armstrong's. "I first met Lance in 1992," Watson says. "Some people – guys like
Phil Anderson and Steve Bauer – had pre-warned me about Lance, they said to
watch out with him because he was a bit special, meaning he was unpredictable
and had a slight attitude I think. But the guy I met was very nice, very correct,
very respectful. He asked a lot about me and my career. I took it that he had seen
my name in a magazine and he wanted to meet me in person, and he was planning
to be around for a long time. I think he was setting up a long working career
together.

"Going into the 2004 Tour people that knew about cycling also knew that
Lance would never be that bad again as he was in 2003 – he'd never let himself

come to the Tour de France with such an unbalanced preparation. He was so angry with himself for almost losing the 2003 Tour that he deliberately came back and trained even harder in 2004 so it wouldn't happen again."

Domestically things were very different but at least now settled for Armstrong. Despite the display of unity at the 2003 Tour, Armstrong and his wife Kristin had divorced in December, and by the time of the 2004 race he was seeing rock star Sheryl Crow. Armstrong and Crow had met at a charity event for children in October 2003, and by the following summer they were very definitely a high-profile item.

"There was a fantastic buzz around the race with Sheryl Crow accompanying Lance and it also played a tremendous role in Lance's wellbeing that year at that Tour," Watson says. "With Sheryl Crow I think there was a genuine love affair. And Sheryl came with an enormous entourage. You don't normally get genuine rock stars at the Tour de France and she was a lovely lady, the perfect companion for him. She was quite a mature woman and by that time she had probably seen almost everything in life, so she was able to carry off this relationship with Lance very well in front of the media."

In Armstrong's professional life things had been a bit more tempestuous and, away from his rivals on the road, there were his rivals in the media. In the days leading up to the start of the Tour the cycling press was talking about just one thing, a new book by David Walsh and Pierre Ballester called *LA Confidentiel*. Walsh, the chief sports writer for the *Sunday Times*, and Ballester, the former chief sports writer for *L'Equipe*, had collated a series of interviews with people who had once been close to Armstrong. Combined, these interviews gave the strong suggestion Armstrong had used performance-enhancing products. Armstrong and his lawyers had done everything they could to ban the book or delay its publication but it was on French bookshop shelves when the Tour started.

"Lance is a very bright guy and he is always looking for internet stories about himself so he knows what to expect," Watson says. "Walsh and him locked horns way back in 1999 and I think since then Lance and his people had a bit of a radar out there so they would know what was coming. What people don't realise is that these things just make Lance more angry, more determined to win. Lance always needs an enemy, and ironically at the 2004 Tour there wasn't really one in terms of rival riders because all the opposition fell by the wayside. But you could say that those books by Walsh and Ballester spurred him on because he knew, in turn, it would hurt them."

In any case, *LA Confidentiel* hadn't scared away prospective sponsors and one piece of good news Armstrong received before the Tour was that the Discovery Channel television company had agreed to replace US Postal as team sponsor at the end of the season. Also, in terms of strengthening the squad, Johan Bruyneel had signed Jose Azevedo, Joseba Beloki's former mountain domestique, to help Armstrong in the hills.

"Johan Bruyneel had had his eye on Azevedo for a few years and he slotted in so well at that team that it worked brilliantly," Watson says. "He was always alongside Lance or leading him along in the mountains. Bruyneel once told me that if there was just one cyclist he could have with Lance on his team for the rest of his life it would be Azevedo, because he was so damn good. I think he was the man that he rated the most highly out of all of his foot soldiers."

The race itself started with a 6.1-kilometre prologue through the streets of the Belgian city of Liège, which included some tricky cobbled stretches. Spain's Oscar Pereiro of Phonak was topping the leaderboard with 7-01 when Fassa Bortolo's Fabian Cancellara proved that all the hype surrounding his time trialling ability was well founded by registering a time of 6-50. It was a mark that would stand all the way until Armstrong rolled down the start ramp. The Tour champ, not wearing a yellow jersey despite being allowed to do so, was quickly up to speed. Ahead of him there was Ullrich, looking smooth and relaxed with the crowd loudly cheering him on, and Tyler Hamilton further ahead.

Hamilton appeared at the finish line with a time of 7-08, then Ullrich smoothly cruised in at 7-07. Finally Armstrong appeared, crossing the line at 6-52, two seconds shy of Cancellara's time but 15 seconds quicker than Ullrich. The American had put pressure and a small time gap on his overall rivals, but it was the 23-year-old Swiss, Cancellara, who would wear the first yellow jersey, in his first ever Tour de France. Armstrong was second at two seconds with Illes Balears's Jose Gutierrez in third at eight seconds. Ullrich was 16th at 17 seconds, Hamilton was 18th at 18 seconds, and Basso was 70th at 29 seconds.

"As a photographer you don't get chance to compare riders' form, you're just taking pictures of guys going very fast," Watson explains. "It's only when you look at the results sheet afterwards that you realise what happened. I remember that day in Liège because a lot of people were saying that Lance could have beaten Cancellara if he had wanted to, and he later admitted that he had backed off. He was beating Ullrich by 20 seconds or something, which in a six-kilometre prologue is massive – and the brain came in behind him and said: 'Relax, let Cancellara win and let his team carry the yellow jersey for a few days.' The damage was done to Ullrich in that opening stage."

Stage one saw a number of riders – including Domina Vacanze's veteran sprint king Mario Cipollini – fall foul of the slippery conditions, but the day finished in a bunch sprint and there were no massive changes overall. Stage two followed a similar format but time bonuses in the first two days' sprints meant Crédit Agricole's Norwegian star Thor Hushovd took over the yellow jersey from Cancellara, while the time gaps between Armstrong and his overall rivals remained constant.

Stage three broke from the traditional idea of Tour de France opening-week stages in that it covered four kilometres of *pavé* – the famous cobbles of Paris-Roubaix. As well as being incredibly uncomfortable to ride over, the cobbles can be lethally slippery, and they offered an extra potential risk to the overall favourites. Ironically the peloton hadn't even reached the cobbles when the stage claimed its first high-profile victim. Iban Mayo hit the floor and shredded his shorts as the riders jockeyed for position in the run-up to the *pavé*. The race effectively split in two, with US Postal protecting Armstrong at the front of the main peloton, and another large group featuring Mayo and Hushovd chasing behind. At the finish Ag2r's Jean-Patrick Nazon took the victory while Armstrong and most of his main rivals finished just behind. Mayo's group arrived almost four minutes after the winner.

"There was a definite sense of nervousness about the *pavé* section," Watson remembers. "You knew people like Lance – with George Hincapie around him – and even Ullrich were going to make the little climbers suffer on the *pavé*. Some people criticised running the Tour de France there but everybody had to ride over the cobbles and Lance and those guys made the most advantage they could over them. There were lots of little crashes leading up to the first cobblestones because everybody was trying to get up to the front, but as far as the Tour in general was concerned it was fantastic to have a phase like that so early in the race where time gaps were already showing up.

"For my job, I prefer to have these unusual things appear in the Tour because it keeps me on my toes and we all need these little challenges. In the 2004 Tour the prologue got everybody fired up because Lance was in good form, and then he couldn't wait to get to the cobblestones. He had to be held back and made not to attack – he let other people attack and he just followed."

Stage four was the team time trial but this year there was a change in the rules. Unlike in previous Tours where the real-time differences between squads at the finish line would be transferred to individuals' times in the overall standings, for the 2004 Tour a new system was in place. This system dictated that the time differences between squads would be a fixed amount depending on what placing the team finished in. So the riders of the squad that came in second would lose 20 seconds in the overall standings to the riders of the winning team. The riders of the team in third would be given a 30-second deficit overall, the fourth-placed team would get a 40-second deficit, and so on.

If the new rules weren't dreary enough, the leaden skies and slippery roads along the 64.5-kilometre course were pretty foreboding. When Armstrong's US Postal squad began as the last team to start the stage, the time to beat was Illes Balears's figure of 1-13-18. Despite being the reigning champions of the Tour team time trial Armstrong's 'Blue Train' didn't start off in a particularly impressive way, notching up only the fifth best time through the first checkpoint and having already shed one of their riders, Benjamin Noval, who couldn't keep up. By the second checkpoint, at 42 kilometres, things had improved for Armstrong's army and they recorded the fastest time yet, 30 seconds quicker than Illes Balears.

At the finish line Jan Ullrich's pink and white T-Mobile squad, led in by German time trial champion Andreas Klöden, bounced over the cobbled street to record the second best time of the day, 1-13-22, only four seconds slower than Illes Balears. Behind T-Mobile, Tyler Hamilton's Phonak team was experiencing a meltdown of sorts and had been reduced to just five riders – the bare minimum needed to register a time. For whatever reason, Phonak's approach – to leave its slower riders behind on the road – seemed to work and the remaining quintet crossed the line with a time of 1-13-10, putting them provisionally top of the leaderboard. Next in were the troops of CSC, who crossed the line 39 seconds slower than Phonak, placing them provisionally fourth.

But out on the course US Postal were storming. At the third time-check they were a massive 1-08 quicker than the previous best time; all they had to do was keep the tempo up and stay safe. As had become custom in the Tour team time trials, US Postal's sergeant major George Hincapie led the squad through the final few corners. With smiles gracing the faces of all remaining eight team members, they crossed the line with a time of 1-12-03. The boys in blue had won the stage, and Armstrong was back in yellow.

Watson remembers the day well: "US Postal went out to kill, they weren't going to take any prisoners. The team time trial is a sacred stage to win for any team, most especially for US Postal because in 2003 – and this is where Lance's psychology comes into play – the team had to help him through the team time trial. They won the stage in 2003 but Lance really, really hated having to be almost carried to the finish. But 2004 was his chance to turn on the gas, get to the front, and show everyone how good he could be. It was another electrifying stage and it further cemented US Postal's control."

Because of the new time rules, Armstrong's advantage over his rivals wasn't the minute plus his team had achieved on the road, but overall the Texan led the race from four of his team-mates. Of his major rivals Hamilton was in eighth place at 36 seconds, Ullrich was 16th at 55 seconds, and Basso was 26th at 1-17.

Stage five saw no improvement in the weather, but the sun was shining – metaphorically speaking at least – on a breakaway group of non-threats who were allowed to get away and they finished with an advantage of 12-33 over the peloton. Cofidis's Stuart O'Grady took the stage win but young Frenchman, Thomas Voeckler of Brioches la Boulangère took control of the leader's jersey. With Voeckler's four breakaway companions also appearing in the top five overall Armstrong was now placed sixth, but the relative time differences among the big names remained the same.

"I remember that was a very wet stage, on rolling terrain with some early crashes on white lines," Watson says. "But I think the break being allowed to go and get a massive lead had been planned beforehand anyway and US Postal achieved what they wanted. It wasn't a remarkable stage for any other reason other than it poured down and a break was allowed to get away.

"Where there is a big breakaway on a stage as a photographer I can do what I want, more or less. What I tend to do is tuck in behind the break, watch their lead grow and obviously take a few pictures of them every now and again. But once they have got three or four minutes' advantage I would use them as a way of taking myself out in the countryside. If you ride behind them and you see a wonderful scenery shot coming up – the scenery is one of the most important aspects in capturing the Tour de France – you just pull over to the side of the road, find your place, and wait for the peloton to come by. Then you go past the peloton and do it all again until the real racing starts."

On stage six the weather had perked up but it didn't stop the crashes and this time it was Armstrong who suffered a problem. With little panic his US Postal team-mates quickly got him back on his feet and with the rest of the peloton. Under the final-kilometre banner there was another big accident which split the field in two. A front portion of 30 or so riders contested the stage win, with young Belgian star Tom Boonen of Quick Step securing his first Tour stage victory. Because the accident happened just within the last kilometre nobody suffered any time handicap, so the overall standings remained as they were.

Stages seven and eight ended in sprints with no effect on the overall classification, then came the first rest day of the 2004 Tour. Although the mountains were looming large, stage nine offered little in the way of quality preparation for them with another sprint finish and no big changes to the overall standings.

Stage 10 headed into the hills, but not the classic slopes of the Pyrenees or Alps, rather it took on the slightly less impressive challenges of the Massif Central. What it lacked in quality it more than made up for in quantity, cresting nine categorised climbs in a monster of a stage. And it was Bastille Day: a perfect chance for a French climber to make his mark and rack up some King of the Mountains points. In fact, it was a day made to measure for Quick Step's Richard Virenque, and the darling of French housewives didn't disappoint, producing a fine breakaway attempt, first alongside Axel Merckx of Lotto-Domo, then setting off on his own. Virenque duly took a very popular victory among the home fans.

The first part of the main bunch, containing Armstrong, Ullrich and the yellow jersey Voeckler, arrived at 5-19 after Virenque. But due to a split in the pack, Hamilton and Heras carelessly lost another seven seconds to Armstrong. Overall Voeckler was still in yellow and there were few changes other than Virenque jumping to fourth. Armstrong was sixth at 9-35, Hamilton 11th at 10-18, Ullrich was 17th at 10-30 and Basso was 20th at 10-52.

Despite featuring five climbs en route, stage 11 headed mainly downhill and saw another French star – Cofidis's David Moncoutié – win the stage. The overall main contenders finished altogether 5-58 later so there were no major changes to the top of the overall standings.

Finally the real battle for the overall title began on stage 12, which crested the Col d'Aspin before climbing up the Tourmalet to a summit finish at La Mongie. Despite Ullrich putting in a tentative attack on the descent of the Col d'Aspin, the overall favourites were all together as they began the final battle up to La Mongie.

It was quickly apparent that Ullrich was suffering on the slopes, so Armstrong, along with team-mate Jose Azevedo, increased the tempo to the maximum. After repeated attacks CSC's Carlos Sastre broke away, then Illes Balears's Francesco Mancebo, and then Ivan Basso split off the front as well. Gradually Armstrong and T-Mobile's Andreas Klöden regrouped with Sastre, Basso and Mancebo, while Klöden's team leader Jan Ullrich, and Tyler Hamilton and Roberto Heras were all dropped from the group.

Eventually Armstrong, ticking over his high cadence, upped the pace at the front with only Basso able to hold his wheel. By the finish line the pair had distanced everybody, and it was the 26-year-old Italian who took the victory, joining an exclusive club of riders who had managed to stay with Lance Armstrong to a summit finish, and then sprint past him to the line.

"That stage to La Mongie was confirmation that US Postal were going to take the Tour de France apart," Watson says. "They had gone crazy until the team time trial and then they backed off completely. All the way down to the Pyrenees you saw Voeckler's team on the front every day, doing all the work, and they were loving it. But as soon as the stage started to La Mongie, US Postal were on the front and the game was over. It was just a question of whether Voeckler lost the jersey that day, or the next day, or the next week. It wasn't a definitive stage by any means, it was just confirmation that Lance was strong and that Basso would probably become his main rival.

"Basso was very interesting. Photographically he is a very attractive person. In those days he wore his white and red CSC jersey, which was very photogenic, and he was very elegant. And he seemed totally intimidated by Lance, which is the most important thing for Lance. You could see it in all the pictures of Basso's face: he is hurting, he is sort of grimacing, he is sweating, but the eyes give away a little fear. Lance had the better of him all the time."

Of the other riders, it was Klöden who arrived next, 20 seconds down on Basso, but potentially inheriting the lead of the T-Mobile team. Then came Mancebo at 24 seconds and Sastre fifth at 33 seconds. Mayo finished in ninth at 1-03, Ullrich was a dismal 20th and lost 2-30 to Armstrong, and Hamilton came in 34th at 3-27. Voeckler put in a supreme effort to finish the stage 41st, losing just 3-59 to Armstrong and keeping hold of the yellow jersey. In the battle for the overall lead, the young Frenchman was now 5-24 ahead of Armstrong, who had risen to second place. Sandy Casar was third at 5-50, Richard Virenque was fourth at 6-20, Klöden fifth at 6-33, and Basso was sixth overall also at 6-33. Ullrich was down in 16th overall at 9-01 and Hamilton was in 20th at 9-46.

On paper, stage 13 looked a strong possibility for Armstrong to take control of the yellow jersey – it was a tough day that climbed seven categorised climbs and finished with the fierce slopes to Plateau de Beille. Before the race ever really warmed up, after just 79 kilometres, the Tour was one favourite lighter with Tyler Hamilton abandoning, claiming a back problem was affecting his ability to climb. Iban Mayo also attempted to give up but he was forced to carry on by the Euskaltel team management.

Armstrong's US Postal troops set the pace for the main pack of overall favourites while CSC's Jens Voigt and the emaciated-looking Dutch climber Michael Rasmussen of the Rabobank team led the stage ahead on the road. Thomas Voeckler, doing another pride-fuelled ride, spent most of the stage yo-yoing off the back of the Armstrong group, but by the time they hit the slopes of the final climb to Plateau de Beille he was well adrift.

Then, as had become customary, it was time for the US Postal boys to turn up the pace, with new signing Jose Azevedo the last of Armstrong's lieutenants to do a stint at the front. His work put Ullrich in trouble, then Rabobank's Levi Leipheimer started to suffer. Gradually Azevedo reduced the group to just himself, Armstrong, Ivan Basso and Gerolsteiner's Georg Totschnig. Soon the quartet caught and passed Voigt, then swallowed up and spat out Rasmussen, and still Azevedo pulled his boss further up the hill, shrinking the leading group to just a trio: Azevedo, Armstrong and Basso.

Under the bright sunlight each competitor was dripping with sweat but eventually Armstrong lit his blue touch paper and exploded. Azevedo was dropped but Basso hung on. Armstrong jumped out of the saddle, raising the pace, but Basso was unshakeable. Together they shared pace-setting duties until the final few hundred metres, when Armstrong made it clear he wasn't planning to repeat yesterday's result. He zipped up his jersey, hung behind Basso's rear wheel, then sprinted around the Italian to the finish line and punched the air. Totschnig arrived at 1-05; Klöden pipped Mancebo to fourth place, both finishing 1-27 behind Armstrong; then Ullrich arrived in sixth place at 2-42.

Voeckler, the new hero of France, arrived in 13th place, 4-42 behind Armstrong. But the clench of his fist and the smile on his face as he crossed the line revealed he had held on to the race lead – just. It meant he would wear the yellow jersey for probably three more days, with the Tour completing a flat stage and then a rest day before hitting the next big mountains of the Alps.

"I think Voeckler surprised US Postal by holding onto yellow for so long – I think they thought he would give up the jersey before he did, but it was another aspect of a very exciting Tour de France," Watson says. "Voeckler got lucky and got in the right break at the right time, and US Postal let him go. But he woke up to his responsibility of wearing yellow, and he rode beyond himself. It was an example of the famed notion that wearing the yellow jersey pushes you to ride so much better than you are normally capable. You don't give up the yellow jersey as easily as some people think, you hold onto it right until the end."

In terms of cold numbers Voeckler was now just 22 seconds ahead of Armstrong. Basso was third at 1-39, Klöden fourth at 3-18, Mancebo fifth at 3-28, and Totschnig rose to sixth overall at 6-08. Armstrong's loyal pace-setter

Azevedo was seventh at 6-43, and Ullrich was a relatively lowly eighth, 7-01 behind the race leader.

Outside observers were wondering if the situation at T-Mobile meant that Ullrich would now ride in support of Klöden, but Watson says the notion of Klöden being a team leader was slightly misplaced: "Klöden is quite unsure of himself and he found himself up ahead almost by accident when Ullrich cracked. Klöden was strong but he went to the 2004 Tour probably expecting Ullrich to be better. I don't think he has much personal ambition, so although he was suddenly being heralded as the future of the Tour de France for Germany, in reality he is too timid a person, and too limited a cyclist, to go that far."

After the excitement of the mountains, stage 14 was a bit of a disappointment as a group of 10 riders was allowed to escape and contest the stage win between themselves. The main peloton arrived more than 14 minutes later. There were no changes to the top of the overall. The next day was a rest day for the riders, giving Thomas Voeckler chance to admire his yellow jerseys. Come the following morning, and the Tour's visit to the Alps, it looked unlikely that he would own the symbolic garment for much longer.

Stage 15 featured seven significant Alpine climbs, although the Tour was now one more pre-race favourite lighter as Iban Mayo finally got his wish to abandon. As the stage developed, a breakaway that included Rasmussen and King of the Mountains leader Virenque led the race from a large elite bunch featuring Armstrong, Basso, Klöden, Mancebo and Ullrich. Voeckler, though, was not part of the pack. On the slopes of the Col de l'Echarasson Rasmussen and Virenque set off on their own at the front, while further back Ullrich did almost the unthinkable and sprinted out of the saddle in a full-blooded attack. Ullrich established a decent gap of around 40 seconds before the US Postal boys found themselves sharing pace-setting duties with Basso's CSC team to haul the German back in.

"I thought Ullrich was just playing for TV with that attack," Watson says. "Ullrich is a natural attacker and he knew what Lance was planning for that day so he had to try something. Ullrich also knew the next day was the Alpe d'Huez time trial and he was petrified of it, so he wanted to at least stir up the race a little bit for TV, just to take a bit of pressure off himself before the time trial. His attack was meaningful and it had a lot of weight because he was still a strong guy, but I also felt the chase wasn't full-on, there was a bit of gamesmanship. At that point Ullrich had lost so much time that he wasn't really a threat – I think US Postal let him stay out longer than they needed to, just to make the attack look exciting"

By the run-in to the finale a bunch of 10 star riders led the way: Sastre, Voigt, Leipheimer, Azevedo, Ullrich, Klöden, Armstrong, Basso, along with the now-caught Rasmussen and Virenque. They swept through the rolling streets of Villard de Lans, with Armstrong curiously taking station at the back of the group, watching his rivals. Then the group left the town to take on the last brutish, if brief, climb in the final two kilometres. Armstrong's lieutenant, Azevedo, took to the front while the others fought for position behind. Sastre and Voigt soon peeled off the back, then Azevedo, then Rasmussen and Virenque. With a kilometre left to race Klöden led Ullrich, Basso, Armstrong and Leipheimer, each one of them preparing for the final battle. The T-Mobile duo of Klöden and Ullrich had the numerical advantage, and Klöden tried to lead out his team leader, but his legs could take little more.

Into the final bends it became a simple three-way sprint finish – Ullrich, against Basso, against Armstrong. Ullrich couldn't match the injection of speed from his rivals, and Basso couldn't match the power, or perhaps the greed, of Armstrong. So it was another stage win for the Texan – his 17th in total over his career – but this was one he obviously wanted, triple-punching the air above the line.

"You don't see much of the lead-up to the finale as a photographer because you are plonked on the finish line about three or four minutes before the race gets there," Watson says. "But when it arrived everybody was full of emotion because we were all still waiting for Lance to unleash his big attack. This was the first day where he put in some speed work and turned round to everybody and said this is the real Lance Armstrong. He did a sprint that he probably hadn't done in his life up to that point. Lance just went ballistic and beat them all, and his victory salute on the line was exuberant to say the least. He couldn't have been happier and there was a lot of strong body language. I remember that victory salute being even more energetic than when he won the World Championship in 1993. It meant an awful lot more to him than people realised for some reason.

"I'm not sure what it is, but you can tell a lot about the riders from what I call their body language. I could tell Lance couldn't wait to unleash his power that day. Although Ullrich had attacked earlier, he looked very self-conscious about it, unsure of himself. I knew Ullrich didn't have it, but he had to attack, whereas Lance that day, his eyes were such that you could tell that he couldn't wait to race."

Basso finished in the same time as Armstrong, Ullrich was third, three seconds back, then Klöden finished fourth at six seconds. Voeckler arrived in 54th place 9-30 behind Armstrong, comfortably relinquishing control of the yellow jersey. Overall Armstrong was where he wanted to be: in the lead. Basso was second at 1-25, Klöden was third at 3-22, Mancebo was fourth at 5-39 and Ullrich was now fifth at 6-54.

"I feel strong, I felt good all day. I don't feel necessarily wasted right now," Armstrong said afterwards. "The time trial is tomorrow evening so there's basically 24 hours of recovery, so we'll see what happens. But Basso is the biggest threat, he's the one who is climbing the best. And you'll see a good time trial from Jan because he's a time trial specialist and it looks like he's coming up."

Stage 16 was the first time ever the Tour de France had held an individual time trial up Alpe d'Huez, and it was probably the one stage that Armstrong feared the most. Not that the slopes of the most famous mountain in cycling held any mystery for the Texan, he had won there before already. What Armstrong really feared was that one of the predicted half-million spectators who lined the sides of the Alpe's 15.5-kilometre ascent would try in some way to attack him. Although few people knew it at the time, Armstrong's team had received threats against their rider, and there was a real possibility that the yellow jersey may have been advised not to participate in the stage, and therefore forfeit the Tour.

Despite being close to the team, Watson knew nothing about the situation: "I was actually quite surprised much later when it was announced that apparently there had been a gendarme travelling with Lance who had a pistol. Every cyclist in the time trial has at least one gendarme as an advance guard, and apparently the one in front of Lance was a bit more than a normal gendarme, he was trained ready to defend somebody. But sometimes around Lance there tends to be a bit of spin and it's hard to know how much of a story is true. This gendarme was travelling ahead of Lance and really the place to defend somebody in that situation is behind, because if somebody had attacked Lance this gendarme would have already gone past them. So I think a little more was made of the threats against Lance than there really was."

As far as the times were concerned, Phonak's Santos Gonzalez had set the marker to beat – 41-52 – when Armstrong took to the start ramp. The Alpe d'Huez time trial was always going to be unlike any other time trial, and that was immediately obvious with the kit Armstrong was riding. Gone were the aero helmets and handlebars of a typical race against the clock, the yellow jersey instead opted for a traditional team cap placed backwards over his head and normal drop handlebars. Today there would be less emphasis on efficiently scything through the air, and more on scything through the mass of people who had converged on the Alpe to watch this spectacle.

Armstrong was soon into his high-tempo style, while up ahead both Basso and Ullrich – who had decided to use aero bars – met with cheers from the roadside. Along the course it was Armstrong's man Jose Azevedo – sitting in sixth overall – who was again setting the pace with the best times at the checkpoints. His reign didn't last for long though as Ullrich, his cheeks crimson with effort, started to beat them. But then came Armstrong, bobbing up and down, who was going faster still.

Onwards up the hill Ullrich continued pushing his massive gear, looking almost comfortable in his pain. Between the great German champion and the yellow jersey the other riders were suffering: Mancebo's overall bid was crumbling, Klöden was just trying to keep his place in the general classification, and Basso was struggling, weaving ever so slightly and gradually being caught by Armstrong.

Ullrich rode into the final two kilometres, the slightly flatter part of the course, and used the opportunity to step up into an even bigger gear and really pick up the pace. His mouth open to its widest, his nose dripping sweat, Ullrich was experiencing a form of redemption and showed the world just what a great rider he was – even if his time-checks were being bettered by Armstrong.

The German exploded onto the home straight, exuding pure aggression and power. His time of 40-42 went top of the leaderboard.

Out on the course Armstrong had caught Basso, the differences in the two pedalling styles fascinatingly apparent. The yellow jersey's high-energy bouncing technique contrasted with the tired, laboured tick-over of Basso. After a few moments together Armstrong raised himself out of the saddle and sprinted away. Nearer the finish Klöden had almost caught Mancebo and recorded an impressive 41-22, just 40 seconds slower than his team-mate Ullrich.

Armstrong swooped around the final few corners, taking every possible advantage, then launched into the home straight. He attacked the line like a man possessed and his time – 39-41 – was a whole 1-01 faster than Ullrich. Finally came the figure of Basso, well beaten by Armstrong but still able to record the eighth fastest time of the day, a 42-04.

"For me it was a very simple day," Watson remembers. "I just went up the mountain to find a place I liked, in the last two kilometres on the climb where the final two or three hairpin bends are, and I just set up shop there for the whole day. It was as plain and bland as photographing a domestic time trial.

"But I think it was the most feared Tour de France stage in any of the years Lance won. It was the most feared by him, and the most feared by possibly everybody: there were just so many people spectating. What I remember most about it was that the faces of the top-10 guys overall showed not just the effort of racing up such a terrible mountain, but also the phobia of having so many people so close to them. Lance gave everything and he won the stage and won it well – really he won the 2004 Tour de France that day – but in his face you can see a fear. I would say he was scared. By 2004 he had achieved a fair bit of stardom around the world and he wasn't such a young man any more, and I think he was scared by the energy coming from the spectators along that climb. I don't think it was something that he wanted to repeat."

Overall the implications were substantial. Armstrong had significantly increased his lead on everyone and, barring an accident, his sixth overall victory looked assured. The gap to Basso in second was now 3-48, Klöden was third at 5-03 and Ullrich was fourth at 7-55. Azevedo had risen to fifth overall, 9-19 behind his US Postal team leader.

Afterwards Armstrong explained his feelings going into the stage: "I wanted it bad. I wanted it because of the history around the mountain and because of the importance to the race... The spectators are always close on the road. That's the way it was in the Pyrenees and when you open the road they're going to get close. Quite frankly I have to say, although I enjoyed my day, I think it is a really bad idea to do a time trial on this mountain. It's not safe. There's too much at stake to have Alpe d'Huez open, to put a million people on the side of it, some of whom have been there for up to a week, and who might have been drinking all day long. If they get a little angry then stuff can happen."

Stage 17 would see the most miles of climbing of any 2004 Tour stage, with three first-category ascents and one hors catégorie climb – the Col de la Madeleine at a height of 2,000m. There may not have been a summit finish and the overall battle may have been seemingly wrapped up, but Richard Virenque was prepared for a busy stage as he attempted to cement his hold on the polka-dot jersey. The Frenchman was beaten to the summit of the Madeleine by Saeco's Gilberto Simoni, but two climbs later he had racked up enough points to be certain of his seventh King of the Mountains title. Virenque and the group he was in eventually got caught by the pack of favourites, and by the time the race reached the outskirts of Le Grand Bornand there were just five men leading the stage: Armstrong, Basso, Klöden, Ullrich and Armstrong's team-mate Floyd Landis.

Despite being a hard mountain stage, Tour spectators would be treated to a rare example of the use of team tactics as the two T-Mobile riders – Klöden and Ullrich – and the two US Postal boys – Armstrong and Landis – tried to out-psych each other in the final kilometre, with Basso a powerless bystander. Landis, who had been dangling off the back, was the first to attack. Ullrich chased hard, while Armstrong marked his wheel. The group reformed under the final kilometre banner, and immediately Klöden burst off the front. Armstrong and Landis failed to respond initially, but Landis took to the front of the group and raised the pace.

Klöden looked assured of the stage victory, but he was tiring. With just 200 metres to go Armstrong decided to turn on the power. Klöden failed to realise just how quickly the yellow jersey was catching him, and on the line it was, incredibly, Armstrong who took yet another stage victory by just a fraction of a second. The American seemed delighted and surprised in equal measure. Behind him Ullrich hung his head. Overall there was little change other than extended time gaps. Armstrong led Basso by 4-09, Klöden was third at 5-11 and Ullrich was fourth at 8-08.

"It was a fantastic finish to the stage," Watson says. "Every day was getting better. That stage was almost a bonus stage but it was very much like Lance's win in Villard de Lans. We saw an almighty victory salute: arms spread, grinning face, mouth wide open. I can remember the image of Lance winning stages at the 2004 Tour in particular because he was winning sorts of stages that he had never won before in his reign at the Tour, he won them in a way that we had never seen him do before, and he took such enjoyment out of winning those stages. I think he couldn't realise how much energy he had. Lance didn't use to win sprints, and that was a flat stage finish so it really was like a sprint, but he found the extra momentum and won it."

A rolling course that featured none of the big hills of the last week, but enough lumps and bumps to be testing greeted the riders on stage 18. As it happened, the action would end up being less about the course and more about the personalities involved, not least the man wearing the yellow jersey. A six-man breakaway had escaped the main bunch and were happily ploughing their own furrow until a small-time Italian rider from the Domina Vacanze team called Filippo Simeoni tried to join them. Simeoni was one of the star witnesses in a doping case against Dr Michele Ferrari, who just happened to be Lance Armstrong's coach and personal friend. Before the Tour Armstrong had called Simeoni a liar in the Italian press and Simeoni was suing him for slander. Now, in full public view, midway through cycling's greatest event, the animosity between the two was being displayed in glorious technicolour.

As soon as he saw Simeoni escape the peloton Armstrong followed him all the way until they bridged with the escape group. The leading pack was all too aware of the fact they had no chance of battling for the stage win while the yellow jersey was among their number, but Armstrong said he would only go back if Simeoni accompanied him. In the end the Italian had to capitulate to peer pressure and drop back to the main bunch. It was not cycling's, or Armstrong's, greatest moment. But it was good news for the break, which survived to contest the victory. There were no major changes to the overall standings.

"That was a strange day because it was the day before the final time trial and traditionally a stage where a break is allowed to go away and nobody chases it because they are more interested in the next day's time trial. It's also a day when the champions let lesser riders win, and prefer to have a day off in effect," Watson says.

"A break had gone, I followed it, then I went back to try to get some shots of the peloton and I saw Lance attack. I thought it was a joke, I thought: 'What is he doing?' And I was the only photographer there because on a day like this most of the photographers would do the start then drive ahead and have a good lunch before the finish. Suddenly I realised that I was seeing Lance attacking, and he really was attacking, he had the full aggressive face on, going after this escape.

"So the peloton tried to chase him, but it couldn't and broke into about three groups trying. Although Lance had effectively won the Tour already, professionally the other riders couldn't just let him ride away from the peloton on a flat stage. When he got to the escape he went to the other riders, and they were pretty astonished to see Lance Armstrong ride up to them, and he said: 'This guy, Simeoni, I don't want him with you and if he stays here the peloton will chase you down.' So for a few minutes they talked about this. There were some quite experienced guys in the break and eventually Simeoni had to say: 'OK guys, I'll drop back to the peloton.'

"Before the peloton caught the two of them Lance seemed to be saying to Simeoni: 'This is the way it works, you bad-mouth me, you don't get chance to escape.' It was one of the few negative things Lance has done in all of his years as a pro. It was very public, there was some TV coverage although it wasn't broadcast live, and he came across as having too much aggression. He had won the Tour, he had won over millions of fans, why not let the guy try to win a stage? Obviously there was some bad blood there which we didn't know about then, but it was a little bit of bully boy tactics and I thought it was a bit silly."

At the finish Simeoni explained to reporters what had gone on: "Armstrong showed what sort of person he is today. To repeat his words on camera would be inappropriate. I prefer to keep them to myself but they were hurtful. Yes it is true that Armstrong asked Cipollini to keep me out of the Tour team. Cipollini did everything to keep me out of the Tour team. I wanted to win that stage to thank Vincenzo Santoni, my team manager, who had faith in me and brought me to the Tour de France... I wanted to get off my bike and give up cycling today. I have to thank my team-mates Michele Scarponi, Francesco Secchiari and Massimiliano Mori, and riders like Paolo Bettini and Salvatore Commesso for their kind words. They showed me that although 90 per cent of the riders are with Armstrong, 10 per cent are with me. That's enough for me."

Armstrong responded: "I just follow the wheels. It's absolutely not true that I asked Cipollini to stop him racing this Tour. How can I ask that team who not to take? I can barely control that on my own team."

The 2004 Tour's final individual time trial appeared on stage 19 and was another chance for one more Armstrong stage win. The overall victory was hardly in any doubt, but the battle for the other podium placings would be hot. At the mid-stage checkpoints Ullrich was setting the fastest times, but only until Armstrong appeared and bettered them. At the line, to rapturous applause, Ullrich recorded the leading time so far: 1-07-50. Next came Klöden, fighting his way to the line, to record a 1-08-16. Basso was working even harder, silently screaming over the final kilometres, and this time holding off the threat of the chasing Armstrong to finish with a time of 1-09-39. It was a brave effort, but it wasn't good enough to hold on to second place overall.

Then came Armstrong. The yellow jersey coolly coasted over the line with a time of 1-06-49, more than a minute quicker than Ullrich, to secure his fifth stage win this Tour. Klöden had moved up to second at 6-38, Basso was third at 6-59, and Ullrich was fourth at 9-09. Amazingly Armstrong's loyal mountain guide Jose Azevedo was still fifth overall at 14-30.

Watson says that final time trial performance was proof that Armstrong was a league above everyone else: "On the penultimate day of the Tour even the best man can have a bad day, but Lance was still full-on, he was still going for it. I believe he would have liked that Tour to have been four weeks long, not just three weeks, because he had a lot more to give, he hadn't spent enough energy, and the time trial just proved it."

The final stage, stage 20, headed from Montereau to Paris and finished with nine laps of the Champs-Elysées. Simeoni tried a hopeful attack once more but in the end Tom Boonen won the sprint and the stage. A slight gap in the bunch meant Armstrong lost 19 seconds to his rivals but it didn't matter. The final overall placings had Armstrong in yellow by 6-19 to Klöden, Basso was third at 6-40, and Ullrich was fourth at 8-50.

Armstrong had become the first rider ever to win six Tours de France. But was six enough?

For Watson, the answer was an emphatic no. "I was lucky in the years before, especially in 1999 when I was much closer to him and the team because there were no other photographers around them. We were having a drink one night – Lance, me, and a few of his people – and somebody asked if he could win two Tours. I didn't say it, because I knew he could win two or three or four. But I think I said something about he had to win at least three, and he looked at me and just held up seven fingers – that was back in 1999. He had worked it out. He knew he had to equal Eddy Merckx's record and get five. Most people would say: 'OK, I've equalled Merckx, now I've got to get six to beat it.' But for Lance Armstrong six is not enough. It's only one more. For Lance it has got to be two more.

"But I think the 2004 Tour was Lance's most complete Tour win. My feeling was that that was the one Tour de France where you saw the Eddy Merckx in him. The desire to win, the hunger, the cannibal in him was greater that year than any year before or after. I think if Lance had raced a few more years and not retired you would have seen a lot more performances like that. He had so much to give and he was incapable of holding it back."

Since first meeting in 1992 Watson and Armstrong have continued their friendship and professional relationship, and together they produced the *Images of a Champion* book. "That was good fun because the book was his idea in the first place," Watson says. "I was doing him a favour, and at the same time he was doing me a huge favour by asking to do the book with me. It was entertaining trying to track him down and get his opinions on pictures. I did a lot of the work myself, then Lance would have the very final choice with the last selection. It was also quite challenging because he was constantly travelling, but it gave me a much better insight into Lance the man than I would have had otherwise.

"I would describe Lance, away from the public image, as very ordinary – not in a disrespectful way, more in the way that he is down to earth. He is very interested in other people and what they are doing, he likes to chat to other people and he won't refuse an autograph. Ordinary is probably the wrong word, humble or normal is probably better. Through no fault of his own he became a star, he has handled it very well and he has very good people around him who make sure his image – if not angelic – is pretty good. Probably the best way to understand it is that his stardom is a business."

Lance's Psychology

With Professor Ian Maynard, sports psychologist, Sheffield Hallam University

The difference between winning and losing in modern top-level sport is increasingly being seen as having less to do with outright physical ability – because so many top athletes are already at the peak of fitness – and more about the mental approach they might take. In addition to that, the psychology of sportspeople isn't confined simply to the moments when they are competing, it has just as big a role to play in the way athletes train, rest, and prepare for competition.

Cycling is a sport that is unrivalled in the way it tests its participants' psyches, and the Tour de France, as a sustained three-week event, puts mental as well as physical pressure on riders like few other races. To become a top-level cyclist there is no alternative other than to put the miles in on the bike. That means hour upon hour of solitary riding. That may be fine for amateurs who perhaps want to forget the stresses of work or family life, but who would want to be forced to do it all year round, rain or shine?

"The initial thing that makes unbelievable cyclists is physiology: if they have the heart and lungs and the right kind of internal capacity," says Professor Ian Maynard. "But I think it is probably the mental perspective that makes the difference in the long term, in terms of being able to deal with making it to the top and having the strength needed. To endure in events like the Tour de France it takes an awful lot of mental toughness to produce the performances each day that, at the end of three weeks, gets you to the top of the podium. A team leader has to be fantastically fit, fantastically focused, to be able to do it minute-on-minute over three weeks. If he or his team misses a breakaway then it could be the end of his Tour challenge. The Tour is exceptional in the way that it makes its competitors think.

"There are potentially numerous psychological things that are required by any top athlete. Essentially, mental toughness really is what it's all about: the ability to deal with the challenges, the adversity and the failures and come back and still give 110 per cent and stay positive and focused. It's really all about that ability to stay positive even when things aren't going very well. I think most people can cope with the easy times but it's the tough times that make the difference between the good and the great."

During his seven-year reign at the top of cycling, Lance Armstrong often looked unafraid or unchallenged by anybody, and so perhaps would not need this mental toughness. Not so, says Maynard: "Spectators may not have perceived any massive challenges to Armstrong during all of that time but to do what he did year-on-year is something quite exceptional. I'm sure on a daily basis there were many challenges there, at least in Armstrong's perception of events. I suppose it's really all about our definition of an expert: somebody who makes things look easy. I think Armstrong sums up that definition quite well in what he did."

So what events would have gone into creating the psyche of someone who could perform like that athletically and psychologically? Top of the list, Maynard says, are the experiences from Armstrong's childhood, his family's relative lack of affluence, and his lack of a father figure. "For me this is one of the most important aspects in how you develop mental toughness. Obviously the two factors are nature and nurture. Yes, you have to choose your parents carefully, in that you need to have inherited the right physiology, but the kind of environment you are brought up in will also mould the mentality you have. It's repeated so often across a lot of sportspeople – you find that people who have had adversity in their life and have had to deal with it can transfer those abilities and traits into a sporting scenario. They actually use these learning experiences in the most positive way. It might not be great to experience such things at the time, but these people can find the silver lining in the dark cloud and work their way forward.

"I wouldn't say if you've got any up-and-coming sportsmen, just chuck them in the deep end of adversity, but sports psychologists now use adversity with a lot of athletes. We now put them under pressure, so that they can get used to dealing with a form of adversity. It's not quite like being brought up without a parent, but it's part of the mentality that they have to get used to."

The fact that Armstrong was an only child, who was doted on by his mother, would also suggest he might be more prone to selfishness than people who grew up with other siblings. Maynard says, for a sportsman, that may not be a bad thing. "For many of the top sportspeople I work with there are a lot of what we might perceive as negative traits that come to the fore, in terms of selfishness and obsessiveness and things like that. I suspect that being an only child would to some extent enhance that. You would be quite selfish because you wouldn't be used to dealing with other siblings. And if parents only have one child to focus on then that child could well end up being spoiled in some respects. I'm not saying that is the case with Armstrong, though.

"On the other hand, only children get an ability to deal with isolation. Whereas other kids have got their brothers and sisters to play with, only children tend to be able to spend time by themselves and not get too depressed, which may help with things like long-term training. And although selfishness wouldn't be a positive attribute in society, it is a very positive attribute in sport. You have to do what it takes and sometimes that's not very nice, but that's what you have to do to be a winner."

Probably the next great milestone in Armstrong's life after childhood was the discovery that he was suffering from cancer, and then he overcame the disease. Maynard says that that experience would have had a massive effect on Armstrong's mentality. "Something like cancer affects people in lots of ways. It's interesting because some sports psychologists are just starting to look at a factor called 'resilience', and they're actually working with cancer survivors as part of that research. I'm not extrapolating that out to include Armstrong's experience, but it would invariably change people's perspectives on life. In fact, even with something like cancer, if the person can regard it as a challenge rather than a threat, those people tend to have better survival rates.

"To have overcome something like cancer can have a massive effect on your confidence as a person. What I'm looking for as a sports psychologist is a thing I call 'robust self-confidence'. In other words, self-confidence that is going to be there on a daily basis. Even if you have a bad day on the bike, you get up the next morning and you're ready to ride again, you're not depressed because of your bad day yesterday. It's really the ability to bounce back, and it's vitally important. So overcoming a life-threatening illness like cancer makes you a much stronger person afterwards."

But Armstrong's formative years and experiences with cancer are not the whole story, and Maynard believes he would still have had to employ a range of sports psychology techniques to keep him focused for his Tour victories.

"Fundamentally you cannot stay fully focused for three weeks on end, there have to be gaps in the circumstances," Maynard says. "But the way you deal with a lot of it revolves around the idea of taking one day at a time, one stage at a time, one climb at a time, one kilometre at a time. Breaking down the challenge into usable chunks is the way most top cyclists will retain their focus, rather than fixating on the massive challenge that the Tour is as a whole. Then the little pieces combine to build up to the stage, to build up to the week, to build up to the three weeks, to build up to going down the Champs-Elysées in the yellow jersey."

One of the most important places to utilise such a mental approach isn't in the race itself, but in Armstrong's training regime. "Guys like Armstrong do have to spend six to eight hours in the saddle every day for an awfully long period in the build-up to the Tour. You think of the pressure of dealing with it mentally: the miles and miles of training roads that they have to pound. There has to be a certain type of mentality there, but I'm sure Armstrong must also be using mental skills in order to deal with it, because if you just focused on: 'Oh dear, I've got another eight hours of cycling to do today,' it would soon grind you down."

Whatever sports psychology techniques Armstrong uses to get him to the peak of fitness, he also displays some aspects to his psyche which are quite unlike many other top-level sportsmen. He seems to thrive on riling the press and his rivals, sometimes causing himself more trouble than he needs. In his second autobiography 'Every Second Counts', Armstrong says: "I began looking for reasons to be aggravated on the bike; I catalogued each expression of skepticism, every disbelieving remark and put them to good use... I'd always been underestimated, and I knew how to put it to good use."

Maynard says that this approach, if used in the right way, can work perfectly. "What a great athlete would do is perhaps rely on the media to get them upset, but then they use that anger to drive them internally. The great athlete would actually turn the source emotion around to make something positive out of something negative. When you feel the whole world is against you, which perhaps Armstrong has felt at times in his career, then you have to turn that feeling around so that it drives you on. I suspect Armstrong is quite often motivated by the ability to stick two fingers up to the press or whoever else."

Rather ironically, this might mean that when French newspapers or other areas of the media have tried to upset Armstrong or put him off his game, they simply succeeded in inspiring him to higher heights. "I'm sure accusations in the French press would have been one of the things high up on Armstrong's list of factors that allowed him to dig deeper every day," Maynard says. "The fact that he was racing in France's greatest sporting event, and he was able to tell the vast majority of their media where to go, I think he could harness that as a fantastic source of motivation. But it wouldn't be something that I as a sports psychologist would tell him to go and do: to alienate the French media.

"Having said that, once you've got that alienation then you have to interpret it in the right way or it could become quite depressing. For most of us, to be the target of newspaper articles every day would usually get us down, but Armstrong seems to have taught himself to turn it around. When he's digging deep or going through the pain threshold, that's what will drive him on."

Armstrong also has an amazing capacity for letting his emotions – pride or anger – overrule his brain. There have been a couple of notable examples when displays of pure spite have come to the fore, with probably the most famous coming during stage 18 of the 2004 Tour when Filippo Simeoni attempted to break from the peloton and join an earlier escape group. To everybody's incredulity Armstrong, then comfortably in yellow and just two days from his sixth Tour title, escaped the main pack to chase Simeoni. The reason why Armstrong reacted in such a way was very personal, and to many race observers it was bizarre to see the yellow jersey allow a private disagreement influence his race tactics.

"In the Simeoni case Armstrong was taking his life in his hands when he didn't really need to," Maynard says. "That's the kind of drive that creates winners. But for me as a psychologist I also start to wonder what is going on inside Armstrong's head. There was nothing logical there, he's obviously being driven by his emotions which, a lot of the time, are very negative. Spite is not really a common motivator. But the fact is Armstrong has the athletic ability to deal with it, so in one sense it's fantastic really.

"It's very difficult to put your finger on it, but there are a lot of things that Armstrong has said and done which are actually quite contradictory to what somebody would normally do if they wanted to get to the top of their sport and stay there. He's done some things in spite of common sense, and he's got away with it. It's sometimes very hard to explain, but the ability to be able to do that, when everybody is thinking: 'What the hell is he doing that for?' and then still go on and win is amazing."

Maynard says that in terms of sports psychology, one of the most interesting areas of focus isn't with Armstrong himself, but with his rivals and the way they react to him. Most years during his reign as Tour champ Armstrong would break away on the opening mountain stage to gain an advantage, and even when his rivals knew Armstrong would attack, often they could do nothing about it. This immediately gave Armstrong the psychological edge.

"I would hope that the better rivals would know Armstrong's attack was coming and look upon it as a challenge and be determined to live with it," Maynard says. "But I suspect the vast majority of them probably started to see him as a bit of an enigma, hold him up there, and think that whatever they did Armstrong would still win. Once you've got to that stage in sport then you've broken the opposition. That's basically what everybody tries to do, whether it's Tiger Woods or Lance Armstrong or triple Olympic gold medallist Ben Ainslie, who I have worked with a lot. Once the opposition starts to think they have got no chance against you, then you have won.

"It often takes four, five, six years to build up that kind of mentality where everybody thinks you are invincible. For example, in sailing people will even get out of Ben Ainslie's way because they realise he will beat them anyway. Once he is past they can then concentrate on sailing to win second place. I suspect the same is true of Armstrong. A lot of his rivals will have given up just by the fact he is there anyway, but the true greats will be challenging him."

To some extent the hold or mystique that Armstrong had over professional cycling returned with him when he came back to competition in 2009. But in Armstrong's own psyche he may have needed to reinvigorate his personal mental strength after three years out of racing.

"In retirement Armstrong's mental strength may have weakened because he hasn't practised being focused day-on-day, which you have to do when you are at the top physically," Maynard says. "During his time away he may have lost the edge. I'm not saying it would be gone forever, because if it's in your psyche then it tends to be there forever, but I suspect it was harder for Armstrong to find it again; to get the same drive that he had in the past. That said, from what I have seen in interviews with him, I think there are lots of other things going on behind the scenes in his psyche – I would say he looks as if he is almost unnaturally driven.

"It would be fascinating to try to understand somebody like him. He's weird and there's a lot of things about him that you'd say: 'That's not normal,' but he just uses them in a positive way."

2005: Seventh Heaven

With George Hincapie, Armstrong's US Postal/Discovery Channel team-mate 1999-2005 and the only rider to accompany him on all seven of his Tour de France victories

The 2005 Tour de France was always going to be special because, win or lose, it would be Lance Armstrong's last crack at the greatest prize in cycling. In fact, the 2005 Tour would be Lance Armstrong's last professional cycling race of any kind – or so everyone thought at the time.

So how would somebody who already had the record number of Tour wins, and who was committed to retiring from the sport immediately after the event, raise their game enough to be competitive?

And what about his team, now out of the colours of US Postal? Many commentators were saying Armstrong's decision to ride the Tour was simply due to a clause in new sponsor Discovery Channel's contract which stipulated that, in return for the big funding, the world must see Armstrong at the Tour with the Discovery name across his chest. Was that really a good enough reason for Armstrong to try for a seventh win? And now there was a whole new breed of young riders coming through – of a different generation to 33-year-old Armstrong.

Armstrong revealed his reasons for retirement at a press conference earlier in the year: "I've been doing this for nearly 14 years, I've been a professional athlete for almost 20 years. The body doesn't just keep going and going and going. So my time has come and there are many, many other things that I want to do in life. This has been a dream of mine. Whenever I watch sport, whatever sport it may be, I love to watch the guy go out on top. I would love to try and do that."

Despite the talk of retirement some things had stayed the same, and returning to support Armstrong for a seventh time – the only team-mate to accompany him on each of his Tour victories – was American strongman George Hincapie.

"I spent most of May in America preparing for the Tour," Hincapie remembers. "I had done the Classics season earlier in the year then I came back home. I joined Lance for our first mountain training camp at the end of May. Then I did the Dauphiné Libéré with Lance. I had a very good Dauphiné that year, winning the prologue and the last stage. Then Lance and I trained in southern France together. So I didn't spend a huge amount of time with Lance before the Tour, but I certainly spent some time with him.

"Lance had been talking about retirement for a while. He told me personally about his decision before the press conference where he made it public, which I think was at the Tour de Georgia. But Lance's imminent retirement didn't really have any bearing on how the team prepared for the Tour. It was pretty much the same team. Sometimes over the years we had new riders join the team, which can create a different ambiance among the squad, but Lance and Johan Bruyneel always did a good job in choosing riders that everyone got along with."

In the off-season Armstrong had lost one of his key lieutenants, Floyd Landis, who had moved to be team leader at Phonak. But Armstrong had strengthened his Tour squad with some new names, not least the man who had won the 2005 Giro d'Italia, Paolo Savoldelli, and Discovery Channel's great young hope Yaroslav Popovych. He could also rely on the support of his most trusted helpers: Chechu Rubiera, Manuel Beltran and Jose Azevedo. It wasn't all good news, though. One key component of 'Team Lance' who wouldn't be racing was perennial hardman Viatcheslav Ekimov, who had crashed at a training camp in Austin and broken his collarbone.

On the face of it, Armstrong's preparation for the Tour was mixed. He had pulled out of Paris-Nice in March with one of the weakest excuses possible: a sore throat. Then he was unimpressive at the Classics and had a pretty poor Tour de Georgia time trial, before finishing fourth – for the second year running – at the Dauphiné Libéré.

But Hincapie says that everybody within the Discovery Channel team was as confident as ever about their chances at the Tour. "We were always really motivated for the Tour and we knew how important the Tour was to the team. We also knew that the rest of us were all going to continue racing, so if we could help Lance win the Tour again it would only be good for our careers. Having said that, Lance and I were probably closer in that last Tour simply because I had been with him in all his Tour-winning years. He knew that his time was coming to an end so it felt like he was trying to get every last bit out of riding before he stopped.

"The team spirit going into the Grand Départ was pure excitement. We were all fired up. I really wanted to win a stage of the Tour that year and start with a good opening time trial."

Armstrong needed strong support because there were plenty of riders stacking up to spoil his farewell party. Ivan Basso was back, one year more experienced, and accompanied by a stronger CSC support squad. Landis was leading the Phonak team. Illes Balears's young Spaniard Alejandro Valverde was threatening to make life hard in the hills. And Jan Ullrich returned with a strong T-Mobile squad that again included Andreas Klöden and the tough Kazakh Alexandre Vinokourov. Ullrich appeared to be in reasonable shape, although his confidence must have taken a knock when he crashed through the rear screen of the T-Mobile team car while practising the opening time trial a day before the start of the 2005 Tour. Ullrich was cut and shaken, but he would start the race.

Hincapie says that Ullrich was seen as a major rival as usual but Armstrong's other prospective challengers weren't being discounted either: "Ullrich was always a threat but in 2005 Lance was really worried about Basso. Vinokourov was also a worry because he was getting stronger every year and he was one of the best attackers in the bunch. But all those guys had chinks in their armour: some of them didn't time trial that well, or some hadn't proven themselves over three weeks. There was definitely some concern because it's not a given that you are just going to win a Tour de France, so those guys were always on the radar. But Lance was always very self-focused and more worried about his form than anyone else's."

Ullrich's last-minute crash may have been unfortunate but Armstrong himself had an interesting final lead-up to the Grand Départ. After giving his obligatory sample for the pre-race dope test, he was then later selected to be the only subject of a further pre-race random dope test as well. It was a parting gift of sorts from the French Ministry of Youth and Sport.

The 2005 Tour de France started with a full opening time trial stage on the Isle of Noirmoutier, just off the Vendée coast and where Alex Zülle had all but lost the Tour back in 1999. A race debutant, CSC's David Zabriskie, set the early pace, covering the 19-kilometre course in 20-51. That figure was still standing atop the time sheets when Ullrich, Basso and Armstrong took to the course. Armstrong looked as cool and as calm as ever as he waited to set off down the start ramp, but almost immediately there was a moment of upset as he pulled his right shoe out of his clipless pedals. Soon, though, he was tucked into his aerodynamic position and on his way.

With Ullrich not too far up the road, this was one of the final chances to compare the different techniques of two men who had dominated cycling for almost a decade. Ullrich pushed on with his relatively slow, grinding but ultra-smooth pedalling motion, while Armstrong was all action, his legs whirling at high speed. At the half-distance time-check it was Armstrong whose technique was paying dividends, going through just three seconds down on Zabriskie, however neither Ullrich nor Basso were in the top 10 at that point.

But spectators didn't need a time sheet – the story of the stage was visible on the road. Armstrong was catching Ullrich and had reduced the German's minute head-start to just a few seconds by the halfway point. Soon he was on Ullrich's wheel, and then he rocketed past. Ullrich glanced to the side, perhaps psychologically already watching his Tour disappear in the distance.

Basso came home having done pretty well for somebody who was not a noted time triallist: posting a time of 22-17 and putting him in a provisional 18th place. But the big story was whether Armstrong could take the stage. He powered into the final few corners but the excitement of catching Ullrich seemed to have taken its toll. As he pushed on to the line it became obvious that Armstrong would just miss out on the victory. His time was 20-53, two seconds slower than Zabriskie. Then almost immediately Ullrich's time flashed up on the screens: 21-59. Although he had been caught, beaten and demoralised by Armstrong it was still good enough for 12th place.

Zabriskie led the race, Armstrong was second at two seconds, Ullrich's team-mate Alexandre Vinokourov was third at 53 seconds, and Hincapie was fourth overall at 57 seconds.

Despite going all-out to take the opening stage victory himself, Hincapie had just missed out on the glory: "I had won the prologue at the Dauphiné, which was a bit shorter than the Tour time trial, so I was hoping to win at the Tour as well. I thought I had a chance. There were some wind issues, I suffered with a bit more wind than the riders that started earlier. Zabriskie and Lance would have beaten me anyway but I might have beaten Vino, so the best I could have done was third. Lance, though, was really excited by the fact he had managed to catch and beat Ullrich in the time trial."

Stage two ended in a sprint and due to a split in the peloton Ullrich managed to claw back nine seconds on most of his rivals. Stage three also went down to a bunch gallop but there were no major changes to the overall classification.

Stage four was a 67.5-kilometre team time trial, from Tours to Blois, and the Tour organisers had decided to revert to the traditional way of scoring team time trial results – giving the riders the time deficits accrued on the road rather than standardised time differences depending on placings, as used in the 2004 Tour.

By the time all the teams had taken to the course the Liberty-Seguros squad had set the early marker to beat with 1-11-32, but the big guns were lining up to shoot them down. At the second checkpoint, at 46 kilometres, CSC had set the fastest time, with Discovery Channel just six seconds slower and T-Mobile a further seven seconds behind. Of these it was T-Mobile who finished the stage first, crossing the line in 1-11-15, 17 seconds quicker than Liberty Seguros and going to the top of the provisional rankings. The Phonak squad of Floyd Landis arrived soon after, only managing to record the third fastest time at that point with 1-12-10. Then came Discovery Channel. It was obvious Armstrong and his team had turned up the wick over the final portion of the course, and they recorded an impressive 1-10-40, 35 seconds quicker than T-Mobile.

But out on the course the team of yellow jersey David Zabriskie still had a slim chance to win the stage, and they were pushing themselves to the limit. Then Zabriskie pushed himself beyond the limit. As the squad negotiated the twists and turns in the streets of Blois, Zabriskie's front wheel slipped away from him. He slid across the tarmac, coming to rest against a roadside barrier. The remainder of the team pushed on, trying to get their real leader Ivan Basso home as quickly as possible, but their time of 1-10-42 was two seconds slower than Discovery Channel.

"The team time trial went perfectly for us," Hincapie remembers. "It was a really fast day, as we rode down the Loire valley we had a massive tailwind. Team time trials are always super stressful and we had won the previous two editions so there was extra pressure on us. Obviously it was important to get Lance an advantage on his rivals if we could. The fact that we beat CSC by just two seconds and they crashed resulted in a big shouting match in the press, with people saying CSC would have won. But it's debatable. If you watch the video of the stage the rest of the CSC team didn't wait for the guy who crashed. And in any case that's part of the team trial – you have to be the fastest team, but you also have to stay upright."

Overall there were big changes. Armstrong was in yellow, 55 seconds ahead of Hincapie. In third was CSC's Jens Voigt at 1-04. Of the overall favourites Vinokourov was seventh at 1-21, Basso was 10th at 1-26 and Ullrich was 14th at 1-36.

In an ironic twist, Armstrong wasn't keen to have the leader's jersey so early in the Tour, but his second-placed team-mate, Hincapie, would have loved to have been in yellow: "Any rider wants to have the yellow jersey and that year I was feeling particularly good, so I did sort of regret being so close to yellow but not having it. At that point Lance didn't want to have the yellow jersey, it was still a little early in the race for him, so I would have probably appreciated the jersey more. Even a day in yellow for me would have been a big deal. But the way the race went it wasn't like I could have done anything different to get myself in yellow. I had done the best prologue I could have done and the best team time trial, so I was happy with second place overall."

Stage five headed over flat terrain and finished in a sprint, then stage six rolled over a relatively lumpy course. A solo break from Française des Jeux's Christophe Mengin was joined by Alexandre Vinokourov and Fassa Bortolo's Lorenzo Bernucci in the final kilometres, just a few seconds ahead of the main pack. But under the final-kilometre banner, on a rain-soaked corner, Mengin lost the front of his bike and slid into the barriers. Vinokourov and Bernucci sneaked their way through, but Mengin's crash sparked a chain reaction in the bunch, with rider upon rider sliding into the barriers at the same point.

Bernucci took the stage win just ahead of Vinokourov with riders from the rest of the field arriving seven seconds later. Because the mass pile-up happened in the last kilometre the remainder of the peloton were all credited with the same time. Overall the big mover was Vinokourov. Armstrong still led the race with Hincapie second at 55 seconds but Vinokourov was up to third at 1-02.

"I think it started raining towards the end of the stage," Hincapie remembers. "There was a small climb before the end and there was a breakaway that we were catching. Everybody went down on the last corner – it was a pretty dodgy finish, downhill. But really it was a typical first-week Tour stage, where everybody was feeling good and risking their lives to be at the front. I was shaking my head as we crossed the line because I couldn't believe how dangerous it was, and I was happy just to make it through in one piece."

Stage seven travelled across the Franco-German border but it was an Australian, Davitamon's Robbie McEwen, who won the sprint finish. Hincapie says there was always a slight change in the atmosphere around Armstrong when he competed in front of German fans. "In Germany the crowds weren't too happy with Lance because their favourite was Ullrich. I remember when Lance did the time trial up Alpe d'Huez the year before, I think there were even threats against him. The police warned us that we had to be careful because there might be some crazy fans out there, and the team was definitely scared on some stages. So there were the typical crazy fans spitting or yelling at Lance in Germany, but he was always really focused and it didn't really affect him."

There was something of a sting in the tail to stage eight with a serious second-category climb, the first real uphill challenge of the 2005 Tour, facing the riders near the end of the route. Rabobank's Peter Weening led the way on the climb with a group of three chasers behind him. But among the favourites at the front of the main bunch it was Vinokourov who was stirring things up. The Kazakh rider attacked repeatedly but Armstrong was wise to the moves, matching each burst of energy. Gradually a select group of riders formed around Armstrong, who was without any Discovery Channel back-up, and each rival took it in turn to attack the yellow jersey. First Klöden went up the road, to no reaction from Armstrong. Then it was open season. Rabobank's Denis Menchov went, then Vinokourov, then Basso, then Valverde, and all the while Armstrong stuck to the wheel of Jan Ullrich. The group reformed with Ullrich and Armstrong joining on at the back, but by then Klöden was off the front with a 15-second advantage.

Klöden had had a very poor first half of the season so wasn't really seen as a threat to Armstrong overall, despite his second place in the 2004 Tour. But he joined Weening just before the summit of the climb and the pair worked together on the 15-kilometre downhill stretch to the finish at Gérardmer. Weening pipped Klöden to the line by a matter of millimetres, while Valverde led in the chasers 27 seconds behind. But perhaps most serious for Armstrong was the fact all of his team-mates went missing in action on the day's one major climb.

"Stage eight was really a bit of a shocker," Hincapie remembers. "Nobody knew how hard that last climb was so our climbers just missed the split and the front 30 guys or so got away, and Lance was left by himself without any team-mates. I was actually feeling really good that day but I was in a breakaway for the first 70 kilometres of the stage with Jens Voigt and we had been going full gas, so I paid for my effort by the end. So that was my excuse. I had an excuse but I don't know what happened to the other guys. The performance that day was definitely a little bit of a concern for the team.

"When things like that happened Lance wouldn't make a big thing of it. He always believed in us. He wasn't upset or anything, he just said: 'We've got to do better than that, guys.' He's not the type to go ahead and yell at you. He knew we were doing the best we could and he was very understanding."

Despite the problems on stage eight Armstrong still led the race, Jens Voigt was second at one minute, Vinokourov was third at 1-02, Basso was up to fifth at 1-26 and Ullrich was sixth at 1-36. Klöden's exploits had lifted him to ninth, at 1-50.

Stage nine featured six climbs including the first-category Ballon d'Alsace. Rabobank's Michael Rasmussen, who was already wearing the polka-dot jersey, seemed to be following the 'Richard Virenque handbook of winning the King of the Mountains' by attacking early on the stage and taking maximum points over all six of the day's summits. Behind him Crédit Agricole's Christophe Moreau and CSC's Jens Voigt broke away from the main bunch, which today had Armstrong's Discovery troops leading it with complete control.

"There was definitely a deliberate show of force by us in the days following stage eight," Hincapie remembers. "On stage nine we did a climb towards the end of the stage, and we all stayed near the front and we rode at a higher tempo than we normally would have done, just to show that we were still the same team, we had just had a bad day the day before, but there was no reason to underestimate us."

Despite Discovery's high tempo Rasmussen held onto his lead all the way to the finish to take a heroic solo victory. Moreau and Voigt arrived together 3-04 after Rasmussen, but that was enough to put Voigt in yellow, with the Armstrong group crossing the line three minutes later. Overall Voigt led, 1-50 ahead of Christophe Moreau in second place. Armstrong was third at 2-18 with Rasmussen fourth at 2-43, Vinokourov fifth at 3-20, Basso seventh at 3-44, Ullrich eighth at 3-54 and Klöden 11th at 4-08.

The riders then had a rest day before the race headed into the Alps on stage 10 for the first true mountain stage. There were only two climbs on the route, but they were two biggies: the Cormet de Roselend and then the climb up to the summit finish at Courchevel. As was the custom, Armstrong's troops set the pace for most of the stage, trying to put as many people in trouble as possible. By the time the Armstrong group of overall favourites hit the lower slopes of the climb up to Courchevel the bunch had been whittled down to just the best riders. Discovery's Yaroslav Popovych and Armstrong were setting the pace with the other favourites in close attendance. The one person missing was Vinokourov, who had cracked and was dangling off the back of the group.

At one point, with Popovych leading the way, Armstrong drew alongside him and appeared to have a word in his ear. Almost instantly both Discovery Channel riders exploded in a sprint up the mountain. The small pack splintered even more leaving just Armstrong, Basso, Rasmussen, Davitamon-Lotto's Cadel Evans, Valverde and Valverde's Illes Balears team-mate Francisco Mancebo at the front.

Armstrong took a short breather, falling to the rear of his group and taking the chance to stretch his back, before resuming a fierce pace again. Evans and Basso dropped away, leaving just a quartet – Armstrong, Rasmussen, Valverde and Mancebo. With less than two kilometres to go Armstrong flicked his arm, asking somebody else to do pace-setting and Rasmussen took over at the head of the pack. Through a tunnel and under the final kilometre banner it became apparent that the fight was now on for the stage win. Armstrong had a two-minute advantage on Ullrich on the road, but the American wanted more. Rasmussen made a tentative effort only to be countered by Valverde, while Armstrong just watched. Then he exploded. Valverde latched on to his back wheel and matched him pedal stroke for pedal stroke until 50 metres from the finish, when the Spaniard cut around him and lunged for the victory. Armstrong knew he was beaten, and extended a hand in congratulations as the pair crossed the line.

Rasmussen and Mancebo crossed the line nine seconds later. Basso arrived at 1-02 while Evans, Landis, Klöden and Ullrich arrived together at 2-14. Vinokourov finally arrived 5-18 down. The overall standings had seen another massive change. Armstrong was back in yellow, Rasmussen was second at 38 seconds, Basso was third at 2-40, Valverde was fifth at 3-16, Ullrich was eighth at 4-02 and Klöden was ninth at 4-16.

Armstrong spoke to the press after the stage: "Somebody asked me this morning: 'What do you expect?' I said we're going to see surprises... There were surprises, there were poor performances and there were exceptional performances. New faces, new names, new characteristics that we have to watch for. It's dangerous for us because we don't know those guys as well as we know the Vinos and the Bassos and the Ullrichs."

Looking back now, Hincapie says the Discovery Channel team wasn't really too concerned about the new names coming through: "In terms of stage wins Valverde and Rasmussen posed a worry, but Valverde had never shown he was an incredible time triallist, and nor had Rasmussen. So we always knew that even if they won the stages, as long as Lance was close he would get time back in the time trials. And they were also never really able to ride away from Lance. When guys like that won, Lance was either there with them or he simply wasn't concerned about keeping them close, so it wasn't a big deal.

"But stage 10 was definitely the stage where Lance asserted his authority. And it wasn't just Lance, the whole team rode awesome to Courchevel and basically blew up the race on the last climb. By the time Lance attacked there were only a few guys left with him, so the whole team really impressed everyone that day."

More climbs were on the horizon on stage 11 but, although the course took in the summits of the mighty Col de la Madeleine, the Col du Télégraphe and the Col du Galibier, the finish was downhill, so it was unlikely to have as much effect on the overall standings as if it had been a summit finish. On the road, and with his Tour challenge now in tatters, Alexandre Vinokouorv took a punt on an early attack and was joined by two of the Phonak team's better riders: Oscar Pereiro and Santiago Botero. The trio led the way over the first major climb, the Madeleine, then Vinokourov and Botero were allowed to fight among themselves all the way to the finish. In the end Botero couldn't match the Kazakh national champion's pace and Vinokourov took a well-deserved stage win. The Armstrong group appeared 1-14 later.

Overall there were two main changes as Botero moved up from 11th to sixth at 3-48 while Vinokourov jumped from 16th to 12th at 4-47, but the time gaps between Armstrong and the other big favourites remained as they were.

Stage 12 headed away from the true mountains into the rolling Provençal landscape, and it was Bastille Day, so French hearts were heavy with expectation. There was bad news for Armstrong though as his loyal domestique Manuel 'Triki' Beltran crashed out and had to abandon the race. But for the home fans things looked good – Cofidis's David Moncoutié escaped from a small breakaway group to race into Digne les Bains alone and win the stage. The main field arrived over 10 minutes later and there were no changes to the top of the overall standings.

Although stage 13 finished with a bunch sprint, Valverde's abandonment from the race with a knee injury meant that everybody behind him moved up one place on the overall standings, but the time differences between Armstrong and his rivals remained unchanged.

Then it was into the Pyrenees on stage 14 with a mammoth 220.5-kilometre trek to Ax 3 Domaines, the scene of Armstrong's last show of weakness when he lost 19 seconds to Jan Ullrich at the 2003 Tour. On paper the day looked like it would start easily with four low-category climbs in the first half of the route, before the road ramped up to take on the hors catégorie Port de Pailhères and then, after a long descent, up another tough ascent to the summit finish at Ax 3 Domaines.

On the Port de Pailhères the T-Mobile team decided it was time that it made its move on Armstrong, attacking with Guiseppe Guerini, Vinokourov and Ullrich. Armstrong latched onto the back of the trio before Vinokourov attacked again. Quite bizarrely Ullrich then seemed to pace the yellow jersey back up to his own Kazakh team-mate. The initial attack was a brave effort by the German squad, finally taking the fight to Armstrong, but the American seemed capable of answering every move.

By the time the leaders reached the final climb Vinokourov had been dropped, Gerolsteiner's Georg Totschnig was leading alone, and Armstrong was being closely followed by his regular two shadows, Basso and Ullrich. The yellow jersey trio worked together, sharing pace-setting duties as they hunted down Totschnig, while behind them Rasmussen climbed alongside Francisco Mancebo. With just over two kilometres to go Totschnig had a lead of 1-50. Behind him Armstrong had made his way to the front of his small group, and rose out of the saddle to increase the pace as they entered the barriered section of the route. Ullrich couldn't keep up and cracked but Basso remained glued to Armstrong's wheel.

At the line Totschnig celebrated a glorious stage victory, but the big battle was happening a minute further down the road. Armstrong led Basso through the final corners, then sprinted hard enough to distance the Italian by a small margin. The yellow jersey took second place 56 seconds behind Totschnig, Basso was a further two seconds back and Ullrich came in fourth, 20 seconds after Armstrong. Rasmussen finished eighth at 1-47. Overall Armstrong had increased his lead on second-placed Rasmussen to 1-41, Basso was up to third at 2-46 and Ullrich was fourth at 4-34.

Although happy with his ride, Armstrong had his eye on the following day. "The stage tomorrow will continue to sort out the race," he said. "It'll sort out the places for the podium, it could even sort out the top step of the podium. It's such a difficult day that, well, I can tell you that I'm tired now so I don't know if I'm going to be perfect for tomorrow."

Stage 15 was indeed another big day that crossed one second-category climb, four first-category climbs and featured a hors catégorie summit finish at Pla d'Adet. Armstrong may have been cagey about his chances, but there was good reason to suspect he would be more motivated than usual. The first climb of the stage would be the Portet d'Aspet, the scene of the death of Armstrong's Motorola team-mate Fabio Casartelli. Armstrong even wore an armband for the stage that said, simply, 'Fabio'.

After the first descent a breakaway formed of 16 riders, which had been whittled down to just six by the time they reached the slopes of the Col d'Azet, the penultimate climb. Sixteen minutes behind them came the group of the yellow jersey and the other race favourites. With 26 kilometres to go Basso attacked from the Armstrong group, drawing Ullrich with him and then Armstrong. As always Ulrich seemed unable to instantly follow Basso's fierce attacks, but his steady trundling kept him among the trio, while Armstrong appeared to effortlessly match whatever Basso could dish out. For the second day running the trio cruised on together, up and over the summit of the Col d'Azet.

By the final climb the leading group had been reduced to just four riders – Armstrong's loyal team-mate George Hincapie, Crédit Agricole's Pietro Caucchioli, Phonak's Oscar Pereiro and Rabobank's Michael Boogerd – with Basso, Ullrich and Armstrong following around seven minutes behind. Basso attacked again, Ullrich couldn't respond, but Armstrong eventually decided to sprint across the gap and join the Italian.

In the front group Caucchioli went on the offensive. Pereiro reacted and carried on straight past Caucchioli with Hincapie shadowing him. At four kilometres left to race Pereiro and Hincapie had a gap and were looking to decide the victory between themselves. Through an incredible sea of orange-clad Basque fans the two stage leaders ploughed upwards. Pereiro, the purer climber of the two, tried to raise the pace to drop Hincapie, knowing that the big American had the far superior sprint finish. But Hincapie could see his chance for a stage win and looked easily able to keep pace with Pereiro.

By the final kilometre Pereiro and Hincapie had left the claustrophobic orange-lined slopes and entered the last barriered part of the route. Hincapie looked comfortable, still tracking Pereiro's wheel, turning around to check there was no threat from behind, and waiting for his moment. With 300 metres to go, all of it still uphill, Pereiro tried to make his move but Hincapie was too strong. In an instant he was past the Spaniard, sprinting out of the saddle to the line. Hincapie put his hands up in front of his face, shook his head incredulously and allowed himself a smile – a man known best for one-day racing and committed team work had won one of the toughest mountain stages the Tour de France had to offer.

In 10 years of riding the Tour it was Hincapie's first stage win, and it was the first stage win for any of Lance Armstrong's US Postal or Discovery Channel team-mates. Pereiro crossed the line six seconds later.

Understandably, Hincapie remembers the day well: "My job was to help control all the initial attacks in the beginning of a stage. The day before I knew I had been feeling good, and I knew that if I could slip into a breakaway I wouldn't have to do much work. I knew that there was a really good opportunity for me to get in a breakaway on that stage, and possibly go for a stage win. But at first, when I got in the breakaway my job was just to be there and let the team have a presence in the break. It would always be better if the team could have one guy in a break because then it would be up to other teams to work to chase the break if it started to look dangerous.

"So I just happened to feel really good that day. I went across to the breakaway, and it was a good strong break. I was able to sit on – not work – for most of the day, and once we got 18 minutes on the peloton Dirk Demol – our directeur sportif at the time – came on the radio and said to me: 'You guys aren't going to get caught, you can go for the stage.' That got me all excited and ended up working out."

Hincapie says his excitement increased as the line grew nearer: "In the last kilometre I was pretty sure I was going to win the stage, just because Pereiro seemed overconfident to me. By the way he was riding he seemed to think he would be able to just ride me off his wheel. He didn't think I would be able to hang on to him all the way to the line. He didn't seem to be riding very smart. He was super strong, unbelievably strong at that time, but I was feeling like I was probably on the best day of my career; one of those days when you are in the zone and you just feel better than ever. And I was doing a good job of bluffing. On every climb I would pretend to be hurting a lot more than I was, and I think I did a good job of fooling everyone.

"I was so emotional after I won, it was a dream come true. I just thought about when I was a child imagining winning a Tour stage, where you have time to look back and put your hands up. And especially winning on top of a mountain like that, it's just amazing. It's emotional because you start thinking about everything you have been through and what you have done to get you to that point."

Still, the immediate joy was replaced by more practical matters. "It's so hectic when you win a stage of the Tour and you're on top of a mountain because you have to go to dope control and then drive back down the mountain. So by the time you get to the hotel it's several hours later. But Lance sent me a message as soon as I got in the car saying how proud he was of me that I had finally managed to win a stage at the Tour, and he was just very happy for me."

Basso and Armstrong appeared 5-04 after Hincapie, while Ullrich came in over a minute later at 6-28. Frustratingly for Ullrich, who was trying to secure a podium place overall, Rasmussen had managed to claw his way back up to him and crossed the line just four seconds later. Overall Basso had climbed to second place, 2-46 behind Armstrong. Rasmussen was now third at 3-09 while Ullrich was fourth at 5-58.

The final day in the Pyrenees headed over two big climbs – the Col de Marie Blanque and the Col d'Aubisque – but there was some respite for the riders in the fact that the last big climb of the day happened two-thirds of the way into the stage. A four-man breakaway was allowed to escape featuring Davitamon's Cadel Evans, Lampre's Eddy Mazzoleni, Illes Balears's Xabier Zandio and that man Oscar Pereiro again. The quartet led the race over the Col d'Aubisque then managed to hang on all the way down to the finish in Pau. Evans, desperate to improve on his 11th place overall, kept the pace high through the last kilometre and set up the final sprint which – in a show of some kind of cosmic justice after his disappointment the day before – Oscar Pereiro won. The bunch of favourites arrived 3-24 later, meaning that Evans had jumped four places overall into seventh, while ahead of him there were no changes among the standings of the race favourites.

Hincapie says that the final wave goodbye to the mountains was a big sign that Armstrong was on his way to a seventh Tour victory, but they still had to be careful: "When we left the mountains we were pretty confident Lance had the race won, but you are never absolutely confident until you cross the line. Lance could crash or get sick, but in terms of anybody being stronger than him, probably when I won stage 15 on that last real mountain day, that was the sign the challenge to him was over."

Stage 17 saw Discovery Channel's Paolo Savoldelli take the win from a four-man breakaway. Back in the bunch, despite being 20 minutes behind Savoldelli, all hell broke loose. Vinokourov attacked, Ullrich joined him, and the result was a shake-up of the main pack. A group of 10 race favourites, including Armstrong, Ullrich, Rasmussen, Mancebo and Vinokourov came home at 22-28, but 20 seconds behind them came another group that included Leipheimer, Landis and Evans. Overall the top six remained as they were but Vinokourov's aggressive display had allowed him to leap Evans and Landis into seventh place.

Savoldelli's victory helped improve morale yet further among the Discovery Channel team. But despite dominating the race, Armstrong still didn't have a stage victory at the 2005 Tour to his name.

"The fact Lance hadn't won a stage, despite putting time on his rivals, wasn't a major concern to him for most of the race, but I know it was by the end of the Tour," Hincapie says. "But there were no jokes that Savoldelli and I had managed to win a stage but Lance hadn't. Savoldelli's stage win was kind of similar to mine, in that we were happy to have him in a break, making other teams get nervous and making them have to do the work of catching. But at that point Lance had been doing an amazing Tour, he had shown he was the strongest guy, so we didn't really give him a hard time over the fact he didn't have a stage win."

Stage 18 should have been a simple transition stage on the way to the grand finale in Paris, but a vicious climb five kilometres from the finish – in fact, the steepest climb of the whole Tour, the Côte de la Croix Neuve – looked to give the riders a final challenge. Liberty Seguros's Marcus Serrano escaped from a three-man break to take the victory while, almost 12 minutes back, the group of favourites had its own battle. Basso led the charge on the Croix Neuve and splintered the pack, with Armstrong in close attendance, then Evans, Ullrich and finally Vinokourov. Armstrong took over pace-setting duties up and over the summit, which had the effect of dislodging Vinokourov, who ended up dropping back to join Rasmussen. At the line Evans had the temerity to pass Armstrong, with Ullrich and Basso also recording the same time, 11-18 behind Serrano. Vinokourov and Rasmussen arrived at 11-55.

Overall Armstrong remained 2-46 ahead of Basso, Rasmussen was still third but now at 3-46, and Ullrich was homing in on a podium place in fourth at 5-58.

The final chance for any escape artists to get their faces on the television occurred on stage 19 and in the end T-Mobile's Giuseppe Guerini won from a four-man break. The main field arrived four and a half minutes later, so there were no changes to the overall standings.

Going into the stage 20 time trial Lance Armstrong faced the prospect of setting a new personal record – he was potentially going to win a Tour de France without actually winning a stage. But Hincapie remembers Armstrong being particularly fired up for the final race against the clock: "At that point Lance knew this was going to be his last Tour de France and he was very, very motivated. Even though there was not much of a chance of Basso in second place catching him on the overall, he was solely focused on winning that time trial so he could have another stage win at the Tour before he retired."

The leading early time on stage 20 was set by the 2004 Tour's best young rider, Illes Balears's Vladimir Karpets, who set a benchmark figure at 1-14-51. But among the big names it was Rasmussen who was making waves, for all the wrong reasons, as he tumbled off his bike at an early roundabout. With Basso also on the course, Armstrong took to the start ramp for what was planned to be his last time trial in professional cycling. Almost smiling as the final seconds were counted down, in a flash Armstrong was on the road and up to speed.

At the finish line CSC's Bobby Julich had bettered Karpets's time by over a minute and a half with a 1-13-19. Out on the course, though, more important things were happening: Ullrich was riding well while Rasmussen was having a nightmare and, as things stood, the T-Mobile leader had overtaken the Dane for third place overall. Basso was also on a good ride and had set the fastest time at the first checkpoint, with Armstrong seven seconds adrift at the same part of the course. The contrasting fortunes of Basso and Rasmussen were seen in stark reality as the CSC rider caught and then had to weave his way round the Rabobank team car, which had stopped to help Rasmussen, who had a puncture. Soon Rasmussen was on his way, but it wasn't long before he was off his bike again, this time in not such a controlled way, as he crashed head first into a ditch.

Basso's early pace looked to have been a bit too high as he started to slow, while back down the course Armstrong caught and passed the hapless figure of Rasmussen. At the line Vinokourov, who had been storming around the course, managed to record a new best time of 1-13-02. A little while later Ullrich improved on Vinokourov's time by almost a minute with a 1-12-09. Basso crossed the line with a 1-13-40, meaning his second place overall was sealed. Then came Armstrong, battling all the way to the finish and making good on his wish to leave the Tour in no doubt who was the best. His time of 1-11-46 was just 23 seconds quicker than Ullrich, but it was good enough to win the stage. And Michael Rasmussen was the last to finish, finally arriving with a time of 1-19-33.

For his part, Hincapie had ridden well and finished eighth on the day: "I was really focused on my own performance. I was feeling really good and wanted to do the best time trial I could. It was a really tough time trial. There were two third-category climbs and it ended up being hard. I finished eighth, but if you look at my history I had been in the top 10 of the final time trials for the previous five or six Tours. It's funny, towards the end of the Tour everybody is so tired, but even though nobody feels great I am still able to do a good time trial. I think that I am just able to push myself through that, and I am always motivated at the last time trial. You are so close to finishing the race that I see it as just one last effort to try to get a good result."

Overall, there were some big and probably final changes. Armstrong now held the yellow jersey by 4-40 from Basso with Ullrich securely in third at 6-21. Rasmussen's terrible time trial had dropped him to seventh at 11-33.

Accompanied by his three children Armstrong spoke to the media after the time trial: "I wanted to go as hard as I could, I wanted to represent the yellow jersey and prove that it was on the strongest rider in the race, but quite honestly I wasn't sure I could do it. I thought Jan would be strong and then when I got to the first check and saw that Ivan was seven seconds up I thought: 'Oh boy, this could be an interesting day.'

"I turned things around and ended up winning, so it was a surprise. It's nice to be done, to be retired and move on in life."

Mind you, Armstrong wasn't quite done yet, there was still the next day's processional run into Paris to get through.

Stage 21's final jaunt onto the Champs-Elysées wasn't an entirely placid affair with Vinokourov particularly animated, and a slippery, wet road surface adding to the excitement. On one corner Discovery Channel riders Yaroslav Popovych and Hincapie slid to the floor, and Armstrong only just managed to avoid crashing, although all three were able to continue.

"That last day to Paris shows exactly what can happen at the Tour," Hincapie says. "That's what everyone means when they say the Tour isn't won until the line is crossed. I crashed and Popovych crashed, it was raining and it was definitely a scary moment."

The race saw the usual attacks and counter-attacks on the Champs-Elysées and it looked likely to end with a bunch sprint. Then, with just three kilometres left to race, Bouygues Telecom's Laurent Brochard and Alexandre Vinokourov attacked. Brochard fell back but Vinokourov was joined by Française des Jeux's Bradley McGee and together, incredibly, they managed to get a gap on the sprinters. Up to the line it was a two-man sprint between the Kazakh and the Australian, but Vinokourov had too much aggression and crossed the line first, his arms open wide. With all the race leaders finishing in the bunch it meant there was no change to the overall standings, with the notable exception of a 20-second bonus for the stage win allowing Vinokourov to leap over Levi Leipheimer into fifth place.

More important than that, though, was the fact that Lance Armstrong could enter retirement as a seven-time Tour champion. We would never see his like again... or so his fans thought.

Hincapie also had plenty of reason to celebrate. Not only had his team leader won the race, and he had won a stage for himself, but Hincapie had finished in an incredible 14th place overall: "I was very proud to finish 14th overall, especially when you consider that on the days when I was doing my job, once my work was finished I would just sit up and crawl to the line. So to finish that high up overall made me very proud.

"It's always a joy to reach Paris, even if you're not winning the race. Everybody suffers the same in the Tour de France. Whether you finish last or you finish first, everybody goes through the same amount of suffering. So there's joy just in getting there. But the joy for me – having won a stage and being part of seven Tour de France overall victories, which nobody had ever done before – was huge on a personal level. I was very happy, I had family there, and there were tons of Americans who had come out to see Lance's last Tour de France. Then we had a huge party. Days like that you remember for the rest of your career.

"The celebrations after the final stage that year were huge, they were massive. I think there was something like 600 people at the party, which was bigger than ever. It was at a really nice venue – the Ritz Hotel in Paris. The team really kicked it up a notch for the final party. There was great food, and video, and there was a stage where they introduced everybody. It was a much bigger production than it had been in other years."

As the only rider to accompany Armstrong on all seven of his Tour victories, Hincapie is uniquely placed to put that final Tour win in context: "All Lance's Tour wins are special in their own right. I would say the 2003 Tour was the most exciting just because it was Lance's worst year and we were always on the brink of not knowing what was happening. But 2005 for me was most gratifying for personal reasons. I don't know how Lance felt about it. I think he was just super motivated to do something nobody else had ever done. Not only was he about to create history in the sport of cycling but he had also done so much for cycling in America, and also in raising awareness for his cancer foundation."

With Armstrong enjoying success right up to his retirement, many people asked if his decision to quit the sport was absolute. Hincapie says there were no doubts at the time: "People were always joking with him about changing his mind over retirement. People would say to him: 'Are you sure you don't want to come back and win eight?' And he would say: 'No, I'm sure.' I was very understanding of his decision to quit. We had been professional riders for about the same amount of time at that point and if I had accomplished as much as he had I probably would have stopped too. The only reason I haven't stopped is that I still feel like I want to accomplish a couple more things in cycling.

"For me it was always very exciting and meaningful being with Lance for all of his seven Tour wins. I always looked at it that here I was helping a guy achieve history. I never looked at the situation and wished it was me making history, or even thinking that it could be me, because to me there is no other athlete like Lance Armstrong. To me he is a freak of nature. He is just the toughest, most focused, most detail-orientated athlete that I have ever met. The way he deals with what goes on in his life is very impressive to me. I don't know if I would want to be in that position, and I don't think I could be in that position, so I always had a lot of respect for Lance."

Before he could start partying, or disappear off on holiday, Armstrong had one last job to do in Paris and gave a speech from the podium on the Champs-Elysées. "The first thing I would like to say is this podium is really a dream podium," he said. "This guy [Ullrich] is a guy that has challenged me and our team on all levels for a long time. He is a special rider and a special person. Ivan is... it's tough to race with Ivan, he's too good a friend. He is perhaps the future of the Tour de France. So next year Ivan perhaps this is your step of the podium, or Jan perhaps this your step. I'm out of it so it is up to you guys.

"I couldn't have done this without an excellent team, and the best sponsor in the Discovery Channel. We have absolutely the best programme in the world, the best trainer, the best soigneurs, the best mechanics and I owe them everything. A lot of great people and a lot of great years have gone into this.

"Finally, the last thing I'll say is to the people who don't believe in cycling, the cynics and the sceptics. I'm sorry for you. I'm sorry you can't dream big, I'm sorry you don't believe in miracles. But this is one hell of a race, this is a great sporting event, and you should stand around and believe. You should believe in these athletes and you should believe in these people. I'm a fan of the Tour de France for as long as I live and there are no secrets – this is a hard sporting event and hard work wins it.

"So, vive le Tour, forever."

The Retirement And Comeback Business

With Paul Kitchin, senior lecturer in sports management and marketing at
London Metropolitan University

So Lance Armstrong had won his seventh Tour de France, then he said some nice things on the Champs-Elysées, and disappeared out of the world of professional cycling – in theory at least. Armstrong's first job was to go on a well-deserved beach holiday with his three children and girlfriend Sheryl Crow. But any domestic bliss he may have found was quickly shattered on August 23rd when *L'Equipe* ran a story saying that six of Armstrong's samples from the 1999 Tour had been retrospectively tested and were found to contain EPO. Armstrong issued a statement saying the story was just another example of the European press out to get him, and two weeks later he even suggested to his local newspaper, the *Austin American-Statesman*, that he was considering returning to cycling in 2006 just to "piss the French off".

However angry he was, the episode wasn't really going to affect his retirement plans and Armstrong had plenty of other irons in the fire, not least catching up with his family and friends. For a man who doesn't like sitting still, he certainly moved pretty quickly in one direction. On August 31st, 2005, while on a holiday in Sun Valley, Idaho, Armstrong proposed to Crow. Speaking about it on 'The Oprah Winfrey Show' three weeks later, Armstrong explained how the moment happened: "We took this boat... It ran out of gas in the middle of the lake, and so I thought, you know, we're stuck here, I may as well ask her now."

The plan was for the couple to get married the following spring, but things didn't work out and on February 3rd, 2006 – just five months after getting engaged – Armstrong and Crow announced that they were to split up. Just to compound matters, in a cruel twist of fate, Crow was diagnosed with breast cancer less than two weeks later.

With plenty of money in the bank, time on his hands, and a status as one of the most famous (ex)sportsmen in the world, Armstrong quickly became a contender for the title 'America's most eligible single man'. In the three years that he was retired Armstrong was romantically linked with New York fashion designer Tory Burch, then 21-year-old actress Ashley Olsen, then fitness model Kim Strother, and then film star Kate Hudson. In truth, the tabloid gossip columns linked Armstrong to almost any woman who was captured in the same photograph as him.

Armstrong appeared to revel in his A-list celebrity status and made new friends or cemented old friendships with some major Hollywood stars, like Matthew McConaughey, Jake Gyllenhaal and Owen Wilson. In fact the relationship between Armstrong, Gyllenhaal and McConaughey led to perhaps the most interesting gossip column story during Armstrong's retirement: that the three were gay. Photographs of the trio cavorting half-naked in the Miami sun sent the celebrity rumour mill into overtime, but Armstrong explained that they were just good friends.

Armstrong's business ventures also went from strength to strength. He opened his own signature sports clubs, run by the 24 Hour Fitness company. The Capitol Sports and Entertainment management company, of which Armstrong continued to have a stake, helped resurrect the Lollapalooza music festival in 2005 and saw its Austin City Limits event grow consistently. And Armstrong even opened his own bike emporium in Austin, named Mellow Johnny's.

But perhaps the most ambitious of Armstrong's business ventures during his retirement only came to light after his comeback. In March 2009, the *Wall Street Journal* ran an article claiming that, in 2006, Armstrong put together a plan to create a company that would control professional cycling. In the autumn of 2006 at a Manhattan bar, Armstrong, his agent Bill Stapleton, hedge-fund manager David 'Tiger' Williams, and Jake Gyllenhaal, apparently talked about how professional cycling could do with a central organising company to make the most of the sport. Armstrong said any new organisation would need to control the Tour de France if it wished to succeed, and then, according to the *WSJ*, he set about collecting potential investors for an attempt to buy the Tour. As far as we know, the project has not got any further.

In terms of Armstrong's own personal choice of athletic pursuits he switched disciplines and took up running. He completed his first marathon in New York City on November 5th, 2006, finishing in a time of 2-59-36. "I can tell you, 20 years of pro sports, endurance sports, from triathlons to cycling, all of the Tours – even the worst days on the Tours – nothing was as hard as that, and nothing left me feeling the way I feel now, in terms of just sheer fatigue and soreness," Armstrong said at a press conference afterwards. Still it didn't stop him coming back to do the race again in 2007 – recording a time of 2-46-42 – and he raced at the 2008 Boston Marathon, where he finished in a time of 2-50-58.

Armstrong also continued working for the cancer cause. The Lance Armstrong Foundation reached its 10th anniversary in 2007, and in its first decade the LAF raised $180 million. The LAF's former main fundraising event, the 'Ride for the Roses' held annually in Austin, Texas, was expanded in 2006 to become the 'LiveStrong Challenge', and grew to be formed of four events held across the USA.

Finally, in Armstrong's retirement, there were constant rumours about a prospective political career, perhaps beginning with a shot at becoming the Governor of Texas. Armstrong was also on President Bush's Cancer Panel for some time, although he was also vocally critical of the relatively small amounts of federal money spent on cancer care in the United States. And just before Christmas 2007 Armstrong visited US service personnel in Iraq and Afghanistan, which could be seen as a strange trip for a former cyclist to make, but a politically expedient trip for anybody with ambitions of high office.

But even with politics, the cancer cause, running challenges, business ventures and family life all vying for his attention, Armstrong didn't completely cut ties with the sport that made him famous, and another of the companies that he had a financial interest in, Tailwind Sports, continued to run the Discovery Channel cycle team. But without Armstrong riding, and suffering from the residual effects of repeated drugs scandals that were blighting pro cycling – none of which actually involved Discovery Channel riders – Tailwind Sports had incredible trouble finding a new sponsor to replace Discovery Channel when the television company stopped funding the team at the end of 2007.

Although Armstrong took a personal interest in trying to attract new sponsors – he was spotted at the 2007 Tour de France encouraging and advising Alberto Contador from the team car – and although Contador eventually won the race, it wasn't enough to save the Tailwind Sports cycle team, which was forced to fold.

But if Tailwind Sports was having problems, it was nothing compared with the Tour de France. Although the Tour organisers would perhaps be unwilling to admit it, sports management expert Paul Kitchin believes their race was always going to suffer when Armstrong retired in 2005.

"I think any major sporting event might lose out when the champion sportsperson goes," Kitchin says. "Whether it's a golf tournament or a tennis tournament there is always a state of flux while people work out where the next challenger is going to come from. Before Tiger Woods it seemed like there were different guys every year challenging for the US Open, there was no consistency. Then Woods came in and dominated the sport. Then there was Roger Federer in tennis, who has since been replaced by Rafael Nadal. So that sort of situation, where there's a bit of anxiety once a top-level champion goes away, isn't unique to cycling.

"If you take a top cyclist who retires after years of dominance, like Armstrong, you sort of get this longing for someone to be the next great champion. It wasn't like he was deposed by another rider who could then start his own era from a position of dominance. I think the race always benefits from the presence of a key competitor. Before there was Armstrong there was Miguel Indurain and Bernard Hinault and Eddy Merckx; fantastic competitive cyclists that were able to win the Tour over many years. Armstrong happens to have the record for the most race wins but really he is just the latest incarnation of the 'champion rider'."

Even so, many people interested in cycling saw the 2006 Tour as the start of a brave new era. With no Armstrong to dominate the race it meant cycle fans could have a real battle among equally matched competitors, with the two top pre-race favourites being Ivan Basso and Jan Ullrich. But that battle was never to be. In May 2006 Spanish police arrested five people for possible doping offences. One was Manolo Saiz, the general manager of the Liberty Seguros team. One other was perhaps less well-known, but even more important in the world of professional cycling: Dr Eufemiano Fuentes, the man who helped the best riders cheat.

Fuentes had previously been the team doctor at ONCE and Kelme, but by 2006 he had supposedly stopped his involvement with cycling and ran a clinic in Madrid. Concerned that Fuentes was helping sportsmen dope, Spanish police launched an investigation, called Operation Puerto. As well as arresting Fuentes they raided his clinic and found drugs, doping equipment, and 100 bags of blood, all labelled with codenames. In total it was suspected that 200 athletes worked with Fuentes, 56 of which were cyclists, and pro cycling felt the full force of the scandal.

Over the next few weeks, as the investigation developed, names of some of those implicated with Fuentes leaked out to the press. The Liberty Seguros and Comunidad Valenciana squads were the first teams to be linked to Fuentes, and Saiz found that his Liberty Seguros main sponsor withdrew its funding shortly after the news was released. Luckily for Saiz a group of five Kazakh companies under the collective banner Astana – the name of Kazakhstan's capital – came in to replace Liberty Seguros as sponsors. Meanwhile Comunidad Valenciana had its invitation to compete at the Tour revoked.

As the Tour grew nearer other teams were affected. Rumours that Jan Ullrich might have been involved with Fuentes prompted the T-Mobile team to ask that all its riders sign a declaration stating that they had had nothing to do with the Spanish doctor. The Phonak team went one step further and suspended two of its riders under suspicion: Santiago Botero and Jose Enrique Gutierrez. Yet still there was no full official release of which riders the police suspected had links with Fuentes.

Two days before the start of the 2006 Tour that all changed when the Spanish investigators revealed the names of the 56 cyclists involved. Among those implicated were the two biggest names in cycling: Ullrich and Basso. On the eve of the 2006 Grand Départ T-Mobile suspended Ullrich and Oscar Sevilla – who was also named – and Team CSC followed suit with Basso. The Tour organisers demanded all the riders officially named in the Operation Puerto investigation be withdrawn by the teams, which meant that the Astana squad had to cancel its involvement simply because it didn't have enough riders – six as required by race rules – left to compete. In total 13 riders were prevented from taking the start line. Still, with the scandal out of the way before the start of the Tour, things could only get better...

The race itself was super exciting, with Phonak's Floyd Landis fulfilling many people's expectation as the race favourite. He had hung around the overall top-five positions in the first couple of weeks, and finally took yellow on stage 11.

Then, on stage 14, the Phonak team allowed a breakaway that contained Caisse d'Epargne's Oscar Pereiro to escape and gain 30 minutes on the rest of the overall contenders. Pereiro took over yellow, while Landis lay just 1-29 behind him in second place. The next day finished at Alpe d'Huez and things went as expected for Landis, who retook the yellow jersey by 10 seconds.

Then the Tour went crazy. First, on stage 16, Landis dramatically ran out of energy on the final climb, finishing the stage at a snail's pace over 10 minutes behind the winner. This dropped him to 11th overall, 8-08 behind Pereiro, who was again leading the race. Then on stage 17, on the 2006 Tour's final day in the mountains, Floyd Landis simply rode away from the main bunch with almost 130 kilometres, and five climbs, still to go. He swept up all the other riders ahead of him on the road, and pushed on for a solo victory. His margin of victory was 5-42 on CSC's Carlos Sastre, but he had regained even more time on his other overall rivals, lifting him to third overall. He was just 30 seconds behind Pereiro in yellow, with Sastre in second. With Landis being a far better rider against the clock than Pereiro and Sastre he easily gained enough time at the Tour's final individual time trial on stage 19 to take control of the yellow jersey for good. Then, in Paris, Landis won the eighth Tour de France victory in a row for America.

But just a few days later the result was in tatters. It was revealed that Landis had failed a dope test for testosterone at the end of that amazing stage 17 solo ride. An already dubious Tour became almost completely irrelevant. Landis protested his innocence and the case seemed to rumble on forever, with statement after statement and appeal after appeal. The eventual conclusion was that Landis was banned for two years, and Oscar Pereiro was belatedly awarded the 2006 yellow jersey. But that situation, combined with the continued rumblings of Operation Puerto, meant many people involved with professional cycling and the Tour realised the sport needed change, and soon, if it wanted to continue as a viable business.

The 2007 Tour started with a feeling that nothing could be as bad as the previous year. For much of the race Rabobank's Michael Rasmussen and Discovery Channel's new signing Alberto Contador battled each other for the yellow jersey, but that was only after Cofidis's Cristian Moreni failed a dope test for testosterone on stage 11 and he and his entire Cofidis team left the race. Then

Astana's Alexandre Vinokourov won the stage 13 time trial but also failed a dope test, this time revealing he had had a blood transfusion before the stage, and so he and the rest of the Astana squad quit the Tour. And then came the big one. As the race neared Paris it was revealed that Rasmussen had missed four dope control tests – two each for two different regulatory bodies – over the past two years, and had lied about his whereabouts to his Rabobank squad. Despite leading the Tour by 3-10 to Contador, Rasmussen was sacked by Rabobank, and never started stage 17. Contador held onto his advantage and took his first Tour win, the eighth for directeur sportif Johan Bruyneel in nine years.

As we know, that Tour success was of no help when it came to Bruyneel's attempts to secure new sponsorship for the Discovery Channel team, and the squad disbanded at the end of the year. But a new opening for Bruyneel appeared from an unlikely source. With a raft of scandals having hit the Astana team in the course of 2007 the sponsors decided it was time to overhaul the squad's management and eventually the newly-unemployed Johan Bruyneel was enticed to start the team almost from fresh.

The problem Bruyneel had was that, although his new Astana squad was only a distant relative to the team that competed at the 2007 Tour de France, the race organisers did not want a squad called Astana competing in their event in 2008. It meant that some of the biggest names in cycling in 2008 – Andreas Klöden, Levi Leipheimer, and not least the then-reigning Tour champion Alberto Contador – never took to the start line of the most famous bike race in the world.

Maybe because of that the 2008 Tour de France was rather exciting – had Astana been allowed to compete it is likely they would have dominated the race. In the end CSC's Carlos Sastre just edged the overall victory by 58 seconds from Silence-Lotto's Australian hero Cadel Evans. But more important than the victory, perhaps, was the fact the race wasn't tarred by massive doping scandals – just a number of smaller controversies, including the disqualification of double stage-winner Ricardo Ricco of Saunier Duval for failing a test for a new version of EPO called Mircera.

While these events weren't good news for the Tour de France, the 2008 edition of the race had a much stronger focus on which riders and teams were doing things right, rather than which ones were cheating, and there seemed to be a new future for professional cycling.

Then a monster from Tour de France history rose from the deep. On September 9th, 2008, Lance Armstrong posted a shaky, low-grade home movie on his website. With just his head in shot, complete with stubbled chin, he issued a pretty informal statement. "Hey everybody. I know there have been a lot of reports in the media today about a possible return to racing. I just wanted to let you know that after long talks with my kids, the rest of my family, a close group of friends, I have decided to return to professional cycling in 2009. The reason for this is to launch an international cancer strategy based on the fact we lose eight million people around the world to this disease, more than AIDS, malaria and tuberculosis combined. I will announce the entire initiative, as well as the other plans for the comeback on September 24th at the Clinton Global Initiative in New York City. Until then, take care and live strong."

Initially some thought it was a hoax – was Armstrong having a laugh at professional cycling's expense? Quickly it became obvious the programme to win an eighth Tour de France was all too real. An exclusive interview with Armstrong was published on *Vanity Fair*'s website the same day, which went some way to explaining what was afoot. Written by Armstrong's near-neighbour, the respected historian Douglas Brinkley, the article revealed just how seriously he was taking the new challenge, including asking his long-time coach Chris Carmichael to organise a new training regime for him. Brinkley's interview also explained that Armstrong's idea to come back came after he competed at the Leadville Trail 100-mile mountain bike race in August, where he finished second. "Leadville, this kind of obscure bike race, totally kick-started my engine," Armstrong said. He also revealed that he would once again team up with his old directeur sportif, Johan Bruyneel.

As Armstrong promised, more concrete details were revealed two weeks later in New York at the opening session of the Clinton Global Initiative. Flanked by former US president Bill Clinton and New York mayor Michael Bloomberg, Armstrong set out his vision for the year ahead. He announced that he couldn't guarantee a Tour de France win, but he could guarantee a major summit on cancer in Paris after the race had finished. He lectured the audience on the worldwide death rates from cancer, then said he wanted to promote his cause across the world, spreading the message through the medium of bike racing.

It was certainly a very worthy vision, but Kitchin feels there was more to Armstrong's comeback than just that: "I could understand him wanting to return to cycling, not necessarily to reinvent himself, but to get his name re-established in cycling again. There's also the doping aspect – maybe he felt that subsequent discussions about drugs had tarred his image. Or perhaps he is just a natural-born competitor and that after time away he felt it was right to return because he needed to prove his ability to himself.

"I see his comeback as a sort of reincarnation. I think Armstrong is aware that he is his own brand, and his relationship with Sheryl Crow and the ensuing media profile that came with that added a new aspect to it. Whether he got to the point where he felt: 'Well that's exhausted without me cycling, I need to get back into it,' I don't know. Perhaps he felt he needed the bike to help keep generating his public interest and rejuvenate his public image. Of course he might just have had a mid-life crisis – just because you're a champion athlete it doesn't mean you don't experience all the issues the rest of us do!"

If that was the case it was shaping up to be a pretty exhausting mid-life crisis. Armstrong said he would start his season at the Tour Down Under in Australia, in late January 2009. He also revealed officially that he would be joining Bruyneel at the Astana team. That meant he would be in the same team as the best stage racer in the world, 2007 Tour de France, 2008 Giro d'Italia and 2008 Vuelta a Espana champion Alberto Contador. Armstrong said he wouldn't be claiming a wage from Astana, instead using the opportunity to be part of their team to spread his message around the globe.

Finally, Armstrong mentioned somebody else sitting on stage with him that day – the anti-doping expert Don Catlin. Armstrong said that Catlin – the founder of the testing laboratory at UCLA for the 1984 Los Angeles Olympics and the first person to discover and crack designer steroids – would have free rein to test whatever he wished, and the results of those tests would then be put on Armstrong's website. From the minute he announced his comeback Armstrong seemed well aware of the questions that surrounded his seven Tour wins, and the inclusion of Catlin in his comeback plan was designed to show that he would be whiter than white.

As well as the open approach to dope testing, Armstrong also said he would turn over a new page in his relationship with the press. This meant in early October he undertook a flood of interviews, some with publications he had refused to speak to for years. He also announced some more of the races he was planning to compete at, including, incredibly, the Giro d'Italia – an event he had never raced at any point in his career.

Among Armstrong's new team things were not all rosy, though, and there were some unhappy noises coming from one key party – Alberto Contador. When the triple Grand Tour champion first heard the rumours of Armstrong's comeback he could hardly hide his concerns. "With Armstrong some difficult situations could arise in which the team would put him first and that would hurt me," Contador said. But by December, and Armstrong's first training camp with the Astana team, the Texan was going out of his way to explain his role in the team – even if some parts of the media were sceptical.

"I came into this completely open, loyal to Alberto, the team and the unwritten laws of cycling," Armstrong said. "I have a lot of respect for this man. I can't say it any simpler. This guy is the best cyclist in the world. I came to Astana as a volunteer."

With Armstrong's strange status among the Astana squad confirmed by the man himself it was no surprise to see that he wore a different kit design when the team took to the roads of Tenerife to train. Not for him the blue, white and yellow shades of his colleagues, instead Armstrong opted for the black and yellow corporate colours of his LiveStrong foundation. It certainly made him stand out, and the black also hid some of the extra weight Armstrong was carrying.

Things then went a bit quiet over the Christmas period as Armstrong continued to work on his conditioning. But there was one interesting piece of Armstrong news, as media sources reported that Armstrong and his new girlfriend, Anna Hansen – a cancer charity employee – were expecting a child. Perhaps even more of a shock was the news that the baby had been conceived naturally, something Armstrong – who believed he had been made infertile from his cancer treatment – thought was impossible.

On January 18th Armstrong officially started his comeback season at the 2009 Tour Down Under. Although he was reportedly paid a staggering US$1million to compete (some sources even claimed his appearance fee could have been as high as US$2million), Armstrong certainly gave the race organisers their money's worth of publicity, with media from across the globe attending the race for a glimpse of the world's greatest Tour cyclist. From a racing point of view Armstrong finished 29th overall with a solid if unspectacular ride. However, there could be no denying he grew in confidence and strength as the week developed.

The next step on Armstrong's comeback was the first major American race of the year, the Tour of California, between February 14th to 22nd. Even before he had turned a pedal in anger Armstrong was back in the news – he had decided to drop his highly publicised dope-testing programme with Don Catlin, citing logistical and expense problems. Instead he said he would be part of the Astana team's in-house testing system and would post results from this and any other test he may have on the web. On the bike, in California, Armstrong was looking leaner and stronger. He finished the prologue in 10th place, then came fifth on the opening road stage and spent most the week in the top five in the general classification. Armstrong only came 14th in the main individual time trial, although that was still good enough for seventh overall. His real role at the Tour of California was to act as a domestique de luxe – which he did with great efficacy – for Levi Leipheimer, who went on to win the race.

As well as the racing Armstrong was still spreading the cancer message with gusto, and that part of his image makes him unique, says Kitchin: "I think Armstrong's cancer story gave him – and it sounds terrible putting this in a business term when it is such a terrible disease – that unique feature, a unique selling point, that other riders have never had. And his success after having the disease has just made him a fantastic ambassador for talking about cancer.

"I saw a press conference at the 2009 Tour of California when Armstrong reacted to being questioned by *Sunday Times* journalist Paul Kimmage. Doping issues were coming up but Armstrong simply has a huge amount of credibility to put down accusations. The words Kimmage used – previously describing Armstrong himself as a 'cancer' – weren't exactly going to win Kimmage any friends, but Armstrong is able to say with credibility: 'You insult everyone with this disease by criticising me in this way.' So Armstrong was able to deflect the main issue, which was a question on doping, by focusing on Kimmage's words.

"So in some ways Armstrong can use his association with cancer to manage his PR output, and many people won't question it. And after seeing how he treated

Kimmage few people would have the balls to do it again.

"I also think the LiveStrong brand – with its yellow wristbands and everything else – has transcended cycling and by association Armstrong has as well. I think LiveStrong will continue to be connected with a guy overcoming adversity in terms of cancer much more than it will be connected with a guy on a bike. I think it's bigger than cycling and bigger than Armstrong, but if LiveStrong gets bigger it doesn't hurt him in any way, if anything it reinforces his credibility. Incidentally, to see the power of the Armstrong brand, it's interesting to know that just 10 days after the spat between Armstrong and Kimmage, one YouTube video of the episode had had 36,000 hits."

Armstrong's racing schedule, which continued to chop and change on a sometimes daily basis, then headed east, to Europe. First he flew to the Côte d'Azur to do some training and scouting missions for the Giro and Tour time trials. Then on March 21st he took part in the 'Sprinters' Classic', Milan-San Remo. Although Armstrong only finished 125th out of 162 finishers, he remained upbeat. "What a race! Fast, crazy, but great," Armstrong wrote on his Twitter feed. "My legs felt good. Bad position at start of the Cipressa [final climb] so my day was done. Good to get in close to 190 miles on the bike, too."

Next on Armstrong's itinerary was the Tour of Castilla y Leon in Spain, a five-day stage race beginning on March 23rd. But before the first day had finished disaster struck. Armstrong was one of six riders to be involved in a crash 20 kilometres from the stage finale, and he was the only one to be injured. His collarbone was broken. Armstrong's old team-mate Victor Hugo Pena was nearby when the accident happened.

"I felt really bad when Lance crashed at Castilla y Leon," Pena says. "I was riding just behind him, and when I saw him crash I went up to him and said: 'Hey man, come on.' But he said: 'I'm finished.' He knew that he had broken his collarbone."

Initially Armstrong was downcast after the incident. "In 17 years as a pro, I have been lucky to avoid one of the most common cycling injuries. The crash has put my upcoming calendar in jeopardy, but the most important thing for me right now is to get back home and rest up and begin my rehab," he said. But after undergoing surgery back in Austin – where he had a five-inch stainless steel plate and 12 screws inserted into his body to repair the collarbone which had fractured in four places – Armstrong seemed reinvigorated. "Obviously the Giro is on people's minds and that's about five weeks away. I think the Giro is still very doable," Armstrong said on his website. The surgeon who operated on Armstrong, Dr Doug Elenz, suggested though that his kind of injury normally takes eight to 12 weeks to heal.

In the following weeks it looked increasingly likely that Armstrong would compete at the Giro, but what looked more in question was his main comeback goal, the Tour de France. In early April the French anti-doping agency (ALFD) released a statement saying that Armstrong had behaved strangely during a random dope test on March 17th while he was training on the French Riviera. Armstrong provided hair, urine and blood samples, which all produced negative results, but the ALFD claimed Armstrong delayed things for 20 minutes and had also taken a shower before providing the samples; the ALFD said that its rules state that an athlete must remain under direct and permanent observation when samples are requested.

Armstrong defended himself, saying: "We asked the tester for evidence of his authority. We looked at his papers but they were far from clear or impressive, and we still had significant questions about who he was or for whom he worked." Once the tester's identity had been established with the governing body of world cycling – the UCI – Armstrong said he offered the samples immediately.

Armstrong publicly suggested it was all a sign that the French cycling establishment did not want him to compete at the 2009 Tour de France. Eventually, though, the whole situation blew over.

After a five-day warm-up race in Mexico at the end of April, Armstrong was on the start line of the Giro on May 9th, and the world was eager to see what shape he was in. The race began promisingly with the Astana team finishing third in the opening stage team time trial and by the end of stage three Armstrong was up to the heady heights of fifth overall. Stage four ended on a climb and Armstrong wasn't quite able to keep pace with the best, losing 15 seconds. He then lost another three minutes on stage five's final climb up to Alpe di Suisi. But Armstrong remained upbeat: "The first half of the Giro is not going to be my half. I can't expect to be in the front."

True to his word Armstrong grew obviously stronger as the race developed, often working hard on the hills to set the pace for Astana's designated team leader Levi Leipheimer. Perhaps the most exciting moment came on stage 17 when Armstrong launched an audacious move to try to link up with eventual stage winner Franco Pellizotti. Armstrong didn't quite have the legs to do it, but it showed his mindset was aggressive.

By the time the Giro finished in Rome Armstrong was 12th overall – not bad for a rookie.

Away from the actual racing there was another story involving the Astana team. For a large portion of the Giro the team wore jerseys with the sponsors' names faded out, due to the fact the team's wages hadn't been paid. The situation was eventually resolved, but not before a great deal of public speculation that Armstrong would find a new sponsor to take over instead. In fact, there was a very real suggestion it could be Team LiveStrong riding at the 2009 Tour rather than Astana.

Armstrong returned to America for final preparations for the Tour and soon there was some really good news for his family – on June 4th baby Max Armstrong was born. But even the birth of his fourth child couldn't interrupt the road to the Tour de France too much. On June 22nd he won the first race of his comeback, the Nevada City Classic, a one-day race in the Sierra Nevada foothills. Armstrong had tasted that winning feeling again. Next stop, France.

So the former biggest name in cycling was coming back to the biggest race in the world – it sounded like a match made in heaven. But Kitchin believes that in terms of his commercial brand value, Armstrong was taking by far the biggest risk. "I don't think it would have done Armstrong any good if he had come back and wasn't competitive any more. The general public may have thought they liked the idea of his comeback but then they may have been disappointed if he didn't live up to expectations. If he failed to perform he might find himself open to the accusation that this is his true performance in an era where dope-testing has become even more stringent. The accusations of doping have bugged him for some time and if he didn't ride well at the Tour people might think that, with all the rigorous testing, this is the real Lance Armstrong. That wouldn't be brilliant for his brand, although his brand is a lot more complex than that."

And for all the Tour organisers' often begrudging statements about Armstrong, Kitchin believes that in a business sense they had a lot to gain from Armstrong's reappearance. "I think in general terms, and especially in the suburbs of North America, Armstrong is the bigger brand because he has the human interest story – the man who overcame cancer and was a successful sports star after that. In cycling and sporting terms the Tour is still bigger than Armstrong, even though as an individual rider he gets so much attention. The Tour is always eager to show itself as being bigger than any one rider, but the Tour needs Armstrong, especially if he is riding professionally anyway. If Armstrong was actively competing and he didn't go to France in July, then the Tour would be missing the man to beat.

"I actually think it was mutually beneficial to both the Tour and Armstrong that he competed at the event this year. I think if Armstrong came back to professional cycling then he really had to go back to the sport's biggest event. There may be a long-running tension between him and the Tour parent company, ASO, so it wasn't guaranteed to be a fun time for him, but the Tour was never going to miss out from having Lance Armstrong racing in it. And if it turned on a few more TV sets then that could only be good for the Tour."

2009: A Champion's Return

Even aside from the presence of Lance Armstrong in the 2009 Tour de France peloton, the race itself was always going to be fascinating with a truly unique route. The riders would start their journey around France with a long opening, and hilly, time trial in Monaco, before heading west and even visiting Spain on stage six. The first real climbing challenge would appear at Arcalis on stage seven then there would be two more days in the Pyrenees, followed five days later by three days in the Alps, then a final individual time trial and, just to round things off, a penultimate mammoth day up Mont Ventoux before the final ride through the streets of Paris.

With just two individual time trials on the cards, most pundits were saying this was a race for the climbers, and top of the pre-race favourite list was Armstrong's team-mate, and the supposed Astana team leader, Alberto Contador. In addition to Armstrong and Contador, Astana also boasted Levi Leipheimer and Andreas Klöden, both of whom were podium contenders. The 2008 Tour de France champion Carlos Sastre, accompanied by his new Cervélo Test Team squad, was one of the threats singled out in particular by Armstrong before the race, while Sastre's former team-mates, Saxo Bank's Frank and Andy Schleck, were also seen as likely overall rivals. Finally Australia's very own 'eternal second' Cadel Evans was also seen as a potential winner, even if he did have a weak Silence-Lotto squad to help him.

But make no mistake, whoever else was planning to be on the start line in Monte Carlo, all the pre-race hype was about just two men: Contador and Armstrong.

If nothing else the weather conditions for the opening 15.5-kilometre individual time trial looked likely to throw a cat among the pigeons and rain was forecast for later in the day. With Johan Bruyneel being wise to the possible upset that a downpour could cause it was decided that Armstrong and Leipheimer would set their times early in the session. The route for the time trial took the riders up a climb that reached a gradient of 10 per cent to the summit of the mountain, which also signalled the halfway point of the course, before facing a difficult, technical descent back into the streets of Monte Carlo. Armstrong set off as the first rider for Astana and powered his way to the top of the climb, setting the fastest marker at 11-39, before reaching the finishing line with the provisional leading time of 20-12. But with 161 riders still to finish, it was unlikely to last until the end of the day.

The first person to beat it was the rather surprising figure of Columbia's 24-year-old Tony Martin with a time of 20-05. Then Leipheimer came home with a 20-02. A fair while later it was another Astana rider, Andreas Klöden, who took over the position at the top of the leaderboard with a time of 19-54.

And then the big guns started to come out. Britain's time trial expert and multi-Olympic gold medallist Bradley Wiggins of the Garmin team took to the course and finished in 19-51, putting him provisionally first. Then came the pre-stage favourite, Saxo Bank's time trial superking Fabian Cancellara, who dropped like a stone from the summit midpoint to record a simply astonishing time of 19-32. Contador, a natural climber who had developed his time trialling ability to the point where he now wore the red and yellow of the Spanish time trial champion, went through the halfway marker five seconds quicker than anybody else, but he couldn't match Cancellara's descent and finished in a time of 19-50, not good enough for the win but comfortably second. Cadel Evans recorded a time of 19-55 to go fifth, and then finally reigning Tour champ Carlos Sastre finished in a time of 20-38, only good enough for 21st.

So, perhaps expectedly, Cancellara was in yellow. Contador lay second at 18 seconds but he had firmly established himself as the leader of the Astana squad. Third was Wiggins at 19 seconds. Despite his time at the head of the provisional standings earlier in the day Armstrong only lay 10th at 40 seconds. Even more significantly, though, with Contador, Klöden and Leipheimer all ahead of him, it meant Armstrong was only the fourth best rider from Astana. And Team Saxo Bank's highly-rated Schleck brothers, who many expected to figure later in the Tour were placed 18th for Andy and 67th for Frank.

After the stage Armstrong was far from downhearted: "The stage was very technical, and it was hard to find the right rhythm, but I'm happy with my ride. I didn't expect to win or take the yellow jersey. It wasn't a super, super performance, but not bad. I was nervous, which is logical. It's a long time since I had that emotion... I'm happy. Even if we don't win I'm having a good time, and I want to be here."

Stage two finished as expected, with a bunch sprint won by the fastest man in the world, Columbia's Mark Cavendish. But stage three really caused some unforeseen excitement. In the final 30 kilometres, with fierce winds constantly battering the peloton, the rampant Columbia squad took to the front to chase a breakaway group and prepare the way for another Cavendish win. But such was the tempo that Columbia set, the peloton ended up splitting, with 28 riders racing away at the front, and everybody else losing touch behind.

All nine Columbia riders kept pushing on in the front split, and among them were Astana's Yaroslav Popovych and Haimar Zubeldia doing their bit to keep the speed high. Yellow jersey Cancellara hung around the middle of this bizarre breakaway group, right next to, amazingly, that man Armstrong. Crucially Contador wasn't there, he had been left behind in the main group, as were the rest of the overall favourites. Although it wasn't quite as dramatic or as significant, the split in the peloton had faint echoes of the Passage du Gois incident back on the second stage of the 1999 Tour, when Armstrong stayed ahead of a crash and built himself a gap on all of his overall rivals.

So all thoughts turned to what Armstrong would do next. Any suggestion that he was just going to bide his time, remaining in the group as an inactive member, was quickly dismissed as he sent both Popovych and Zubeldia to the front to help the Columbia boys keep up the infernal pace. By the finish line – which saw Cavendish take his second stage win in succession – the advantage the front group had on the rest of the peloton was 41 seconds. It meant that Cancellara was still in yellow, Tony Martin was second at 33 seconds, and Lance Armstrong was third at 40 seconds. Contador, meanwhile, had slipped to fourth at 59 seconds. Significantly, with the team time trial coming the next day, it meant that if Astana were to win by a big enough margin, Armstrong could be back in yellow.

At the finish Armstrong reflected on events: "It wasn't a day that you would look at and say it was a critical day. It was relatively flat, although you could see that it had a lot of open areas and a lot of seafront and on those days you've just got to stay up front. I don't know what it does for the overall, 40 seconds is 40 seconds, but it changes the dynamic going into tomorrow's team time trial. I've preferred to stay out of the drama and polemics of who is the leader of the team – I've won the Tour seven times so I think I deserve a little bit of credit. Alberto is a great rider too and we've got it going with two leaders but that doesn't mean you can't take advantage of opportunities like today."

Armstrong couldn't say it much more clearly: he was here to win.

So to the team time trial, 39 kilometres based around Montpellier. Although Astana was the strongest team of individuals on paper, there were plenty of strong, cohesive squads out to challenge them. And technical ability was going to be hugely important, with a particularly tight and twisty course

Team Garmin were the first of the strong time trial squads to set a significant result with a time of 46-47. Then yellow jersey Cancellara, inspired by wearing the race leader's tunic, pulled his Saxo Bank squad all the way to the line to record a time of 47-09, good enough for second at that point. But it meant that if Astana were to finish in a time of 46-29 or less then the yellow jersey would be changing hands.

Out on the course the Astana riders were looking quick and efficient with massive pulls coming from Klöden, Leipheimer and Armstrong himself as they raced to the line. At the final time-check Astana had set the quickest marker – 17 seconds ahead of Garmin and crucially 41 seconds quicker than Cancellara's Saxo Bank squad. Armstrong was provisionally in yellow on the road. As they approached the finish the remaining six Astana riders weaved through the last few corners with Contador – highlighted by his unique Spanish time trial champion colours – leading from the front. They crossed the line with a time of 46-29. They had done it, just. Astana were the stage victors and Armstrong was in yellow.

Or so they thought as they celebrated back at their team bus.

In fact, with the overall gap between Cancellara and Armstrong being so tight, race commissaires decided to re-examine the opening time trial stage to establish an exact time difference. What they ruled was that Cancellara still held the yellow jersey by 22 hundredths of a second. "That's precision Swiss timing," Cancellara, champion of Switzerland, joked afterwards.

Armstrong wasn't quite so eager to crack a joke, but equally he wasn't overly distraught by the outcome and he talked bullishly after the stage. He also publicly acknowledged for the first time at the Tour that things could get tense inside the Astana squad.

"That was closer than I thought," Armstrong said. "I figured Saxo Bank would easily be close to us if not better than us. But that's the way the ball bounces sometimes and we were close but not today. I think I can be close to winning the Tour. We still have to see how the others are. In terms of the overall classification today was important: Evans lost two minutes, Sastre lost a minute and a half – those things count. So it helps, but we have a delicate situation within our team. We'll dance around that, and see what happens at Andorra. Johan will have to manage the situation. Alberto came to win and quite honestly so did I."

Contador, meanwhile, with 16 stages still to race, was already growing tired of the in-house battle: "How many leaders in Astana? How many of us are there? Nine – so there are nine leaders. This whole thing about the leaders is a bit tiring, it's boring me. I think the race will put everyone in their place and nothing else."

Overall Cancellara led the race with Armstrong in the same time in second place. Third was Contador at 19 seconds, fourth was Klöden at 23 seconds and fifth was Leipheimer at 31 seconds. Britain's Bradley Wiggins lay sixth at 38 seconds with Andy Schleck 20th at 1-41, Frank Schleck 25th at 2-17, Sastre 29th at 2-44, and a very disappointed Cadel Evans – who was left despairing at the performance of his Silence-Lotto team time trial squad – 35th at 2-59.

Despite the fact that stage five saw more splits in the peloton caused by the wind, and stage six witnessed multiple crashes on a rain-soaked course into Barcelona, the race favourites marked each other so there were no major changes in the overall. The Astana team looked particularly impressive, ruling the peloton from the front.

Stage seven would be the first true chance to see whether Armstrong could still climb Tour mountains with the best, although – despite the course being long and featuring a few categorised hills en route – the only major challenge was the final 10-kilometre climb to Arcalis. Somewhat ironically, the only person to have won at Arcalis before was Armstrong's greatest rival, Jan Ullrich, who took the stage finish there in 1997 on his way to his overall Tour victory.

When the riders took to the road memories may not have returned to 1997, but race observers were certainly being reminded of the early 2000s, with the Astana squad doing a passable impression of US Postal or Discovery Channel and controlling the peloton with an iron fist. Just like the classic Armstrong-era years, a small group had been allowed to get away early on in the stage and nine riders paving the way ahead of the peloton. Although they enjoyed a gap of over 14 minutes at one point, by the time they entered Andorra with 40 kilometres left to race, the gap was slowly being whittled down. At the bottom of the final climb the break's advantage was around six and a half minutes.

With a little less than six kilometres remaining, France's young Tour debutant Brice Feillu of Agritubel decided to attack his five remaining breakaway companions and set off up the hill alone. Back among the main field things were splintering even more and strong pulls at the front by the Astana domestiques - riders like Yaroslav Popovych and Sergio Paulinho - were causing a selection and succeeded in dropping yellow jersey Cancellara. The unrelenting pace also had the effect of quelling potential attacks by any of the pre-race overall favourites on the early part of the climb.

While Feillu sailed serenely to the finish, back among the big names there was finally some action. Cadel Evans who, after his team's disappointing time trial on stage four, had declared he would break the habits of a lifetime and actually go on the offensive, was as good as his word and put in a fierce effort that split the bunch further. A group of only 20 or so riders – including Armstrong and Contador – jumped on Evans's wheel, with Armstrong in particular looking alive to attacks and seemingly having the power to hunt them down.

With less than two kilometres left to race, the fuse of the 2009 Tour was truly lit as Contador decided he had had enough riding in, literally, Armstrong's shadow. He exploded out of the diminished group from just behind his American team-mate. Armstrong watched him go, then, like a good team player, just sat on as Evans and Britain's Bradley Wiggins put in turns to bring the Spaniard back. With Cancellara a long way down the climb, both Armstrong and Contador had a chance to assume yellow, but Contador simply danced away, fully justifying his reputation as the best climber in the world.

He took the line 3-26 after Feillu, while Evans, Armstrong, Leipheimer and company arrived 21 seconds later. However, by a strange quirk of fate, it became apparent that neither of Astana's main men would be in yellow. One of the early breakaways, Ag2r's Rinaldo Nocentini, had been 2-54 behind Contador overall at the start of the day, but he finished three minutes ahead of Contador at the stage finish. It meant Nocentini was in the overall race lead by just six seconds. Contador was second and, adding to the crowding at the top of the overall standings, Armstrong was third just two seconds behind Contador. Cancellara, suffering terribly on the final climb, arrived 9-16 after Feillu.

Who was the leader at Astana now? Nobody knew. Contador may have made the headlines, but Armstrong was quietly looking stronger than at any point in his comeback so far.

"It was a spontaneous attack. I saw some dangerous general classification rivals around who didn't look too comfortable and since our team is very well placed I attacked and I gained a few valuable seconds," Contador explained afterwards.

Armstrong's post-stage chat to the media was not quite so straightforward: "I think it worked out. It didn't go according to the plan we had earlier but it was a fine day and I think overall we're fine... I didn't expect Contador to go by the plan, so no surprise. I have a lot better legs than at the Giro, but when you've got a rider away my obligation is to the team."

Quite understandably, the next morning, before the start of stage eight, both of Astana's leading men were in high demand from the press. But to be fair to them, both Armstrong and Contador looked relaxed. "Yesterday I felt good. It was a truly formidable climb so I am happy with the result," Contador said, but he refuted any suggestion his attack was designed to take the overall race lead. "Our objective was to gain time on riders like Evans and Andy Schleck who we were most fearful of," he insisted.

After the drama of the first day in the mountains, stage eight was always going to be a disappointment, but it wasn't completely without action. Cadel Evans was particularly animated and formed part of an early breakaway, although he fell back into the grasp of the main bunch, which was again being pulled along by the Astana team. Then Andy Schleck tried to attack on the final climb – the Col d'Agnès – before he too was rounded up by the Astana boys. At the head of affairs a four-strong breakaway led the race all the way to the line, with Caisse d'Epargne's Luis Leon Sanchez taking the victory. Armstrong, Contador and the other overall favourites arrived in a bunch 1-54 later, so there were few changes to the overall rankings.

Despite the fact that stage nine's route went over two giants of the Pyrenees – the Col d'Aspin and the Col du Tourmalet – there was little excitement among the favourites. A 70-kilometre descent to the finish scuppered any plans of attack among the big names, although Armstrong rode aggressively from the start and briefly sent hearts racing with a burst of speed on one climb. Bbox's Pierrick Fédrigo won the stage from Liquigas's Franco Pellizotti, 34 seconds ahead of the yellow jersey group. So, after three days in the Pyrenees, Nocentini was still leading the race by six seconds to Contador, with Armstrong third at eight seconds. Leipheimer was fourth at 39 seconds and Wiggins, quite unexpectedly, was still lingering in fifth at 46 seconds.

With the Tour's first rest day came the chance for Alberto Contador to try to clear the air about the situation in the Astana team, and specifically about his relationship with Armstrong.

"I don't feel any tension in the team," he said. "I don't feel alone – I have important people around me... It's true that Armstrong has a media impact no other cyclist does, and these things make these things grow. It would be better for us if there were not so many questions about this. The Tour is a tiring race and you can't waste energy on things that don't concern the race... The situation of the team is normal, like for any other rider in any other team on the race. We eat together at the table and are together on the bus. Often the tension seems higher from the outside than it really is. All the riders in the Astana team are professional enough to work for all four main riders, I have no doubts about this."

Armstrong also spoke to the press, but his take on the situation seemed to be a little different: "The honest truth is that there's a little tension," he said. "Alberto is strong, and he's very ambitious... If he proves to be the strongest in the race, there's nothing I can do." But while the Texan may have been guarded about his chances in this year's event, he also gave a very strong hint that he would return to compete at the Tour in 2010.

Back to the racing and Mark Cavendish continued his amazing performance by winning the sprint finishes on stages 10 and 11, then Saxo Bank's Nicki Sörenson won from a rare successful breakaway group on stage 12. The only point of significance for the overall competition was Leipheimer and Cadel Evans being involved in a crash with less than three kilometres remaining at the end of stage 12. Both Evans and Leipheimer remounted and made it to the finish, although Leipheimer wouldn't start the next day having broken his wrist in the fall.

Stage 13 headed back into the mountains, or at least the medium mountains of the Vosges region. And despite the fact that many race commentators were suggesting the day would see the reignition of the overall battle, the stage finished with all the favourites together. But the day wasn't entirely without interest, and the subdued battle on the climb of the Platzerwasel – the day's only first-category climb – saw first the Astana team set the pace and reduce the group, and then Saxo Bank turned up the wick. Throughout the climb, though, Armstrong and Contador lurked near the front, and both looked pretty comfortable. Saxo Bank's Heinrich Haussler won the stage from a breakaway and Nocentini, who also looked in control throughout the day, retained his yellow jersey. There was no major movement at the top of the overall standings.

Stage 14 saw a 12-man breakaway succeed with Katusha's Sergey Ivanov taking the stage victory. But again the day had some unexpected high drama. Alongside Ivanov for most of the stage was Columbia's George Hincapie, one of the most popular riders in the peloton and the highest placed rider overall in the break. At the start of the day Hincapie lay 28th on the general classification, 5-25 behind Nocentini, and for a large portion of the day the breakaway had more than a 5-25 gap on the peloton. So it looked like Hincapie would be in yellow come the evening.

But as the race neared the finish in Besançon strange things occurred. Nocentini's Ag2r squad understandably led the chase to the line, trying to protect his yellow jersey, but they were given significant assistance by the Garmin team, who, on the face of it, should have had no interest in the overall situation. Tensions between Hincapie's Columbia team and the Garmin squad – two rival American-based organisations – had been strained throughout the Tour, but on the road to Besançon it seemed to turn into all-out war. In the end the peloton arrived 5-20 after Hincapie, meaning he had missed out on the yellow jersey by just five seconds. And capping a terrible day for Columbia, the peloton's sprint to the line was won by their figurehead Mark Cavendish, who tried to delay the sprint to such an extent that race judges ruled he had blocked green jersey rival Thor Hushovd. Cavendish was disqualified, and in the process he saw his chance to win the green jersey evaporate.

Overall Nocentini was still in yellow, but Hincapie had moved up to second place at five seconds. Contador was third, still at six seconds, and Armstrong was now fourth at eight seconds. The gaps between all the other big names remained the same.

Finally, on stage 15, race fans were sure to see another major shake-up among the Tour favourites with a tough day in the hills and a nine-kilometre summit finish at Verbier. For most of the stage a 10-man break led the way and the Astana team remained in complete control of the peloton, but by the start of the climb Lampre's Simon Spilak had escaped his nine breakaway colleagues to lead the race and back in the peloton it was riders from Garmin and Saxo Bank setting the pace.

Soon the big names – the Schleck brothers, Armstrong, Contador and, incredibly, time trial specialist Wiggins – had risen to the front and ridden away from the rest of the peloton. As expected it was a Schleck – Frank – that started the fireworks by attacking, but he was immediately chased by Contador and Armstrong, and the pack regrouped.

Eventually Contador just couldn't hold himself back any longer and he exploded away from the small group of favourites. Andy Schleck tried to chase but couldn't bridge the gap and ended up stranded between Contador and the others while his brother Frank, Armstrong and Wiggins rode to their own pace behind and were caught by other important riders – Klöden, Evans, Garmin's Christian Vande Velde, Liquigas's Vincenzo Nibali and Roman Kreuziger, and eventually Cervélo's Carlos Sastre.

Klöden came to the front and set the pace for Armstrong, but with just under four kilometres to go, Wiggins put in a surprise attack. Frank Schleck quickly matched the Briton and brought him back into the group. Frank himself then decided to attack, taking Nibali and Wiggins with him, while Armstrong and

Klöden struggled behind. Then Evans and Sastre put in a charge and also dropped the Astana pair.

At the front Contador was riding on imperiously, elegantly dancing his way to take the victory. Andy Schleck arrived 43 seconds later. But behind him things had splintered big-time in the final kilometres. Nibali arrived next at 1-03, then Frank Schleck, Wiggins and Sastre at 1-06. Evans was seventh at 1-26 and Klöden eighth at 1-29. Then came Armstrong, powering himself around the bitterly steep last corner. He had lost 1-35 to Contador.

Overall things were very different. Contador was in yellow, 1-37 ahead of Armstrong. Wiggins, the surprise of the Tour, was up to third at 1-46, with Klöden fourth at 2-17. Andy Schleck was fifth at 2-26 and his brother Frank was 10th at 3-25. Sastre was 11th at 3-52.

As had become the norm in this Tour, Armstrong was completely honest with the press at the finish: "I didn't know what to expect. It's been so long since we had a finish like this. This was as hard as I thought it would be – it was a lot harder than Andorra... I give myself a 'B minus' I guess. It'll be hard to win the Tour now. A day like this really shows who is the best, and I wasn't on par with what is required to win the Tour. For me that's the reality, that's not devastating news or anything."

Contador, though, was hedging his bets: "I haven't won the Tour today but I have taken a big step. There's a long way to go and the last week is going to be very difficult."

After the exertions on the road to Verbier the riders had a well-deserved rest day, then it was back into the fray for stage 16, another monster featuring two major climbs, although no summit finish. A large group of 21 riders got away early on with Astana again ruling the yellow jersey group, but by the time the race reached the final climb – the Col de Petit Saint Bernard – Liquigas's Franco Pellizotti and Silence-Lotto's Jurgen Van Den Broeck had leapt away from the shrunken breakaway group at the front, while Saxo Bank riders had come to set the pace in the pack of favourites behind.

Suddenly Andy Schleck attacked among the yellow jersey group, taking his brother Frank, Contador, Nibali, Klöden and Wiggins with him. But Armstrong had missed the acceleration and was left behind. Frank Schleck took to the front and lifted the pace trying to isolate Contador, but it didn't work. Then Andy Schleck attacked again, but to no effect.

Back down the road, Armstrong was just riding tempo, allowing others to set the pace in his group, and unwilling to pull some of Astana's overall rivals back up to his team-mates Contador and Klöden. Then, in a display almost as explosive as Andy Schleck's initial attack, Armstrong burst away, seemingly happy that his rivals didn't have the strength to follow him. He sprinted up the hill in a show of quite incredible power. Using the same high-cadence, out-of-the-saddle pedalling technique that took him to seven Tour victories, Armstrong closed the gap to the Contador group within just a couple of kilometres. At the summit of the Petit Saint Bernard Contador, Armstrong, the Schleck brothers, Klöden and Wiggins were together in a group of overall favourites, while a quartet of Pellizotti, Van Den Broeck, Euskaltel's Mikel Astarloza and Cofidis's Amaël Moinard still led the way on the 30-kilometre descent to the finish.

The tricky, twisting, technical plummet quickly claimed one victim as genial hardman Jens Voigt of Saxo Bank experienced a terrible crash at the back of the Contador group, fracturing his cheekbone and suffering heavy concussion. But it did not hinder the rest of the group's progress. At the finish it was Astarloza who took the stage win, with his breakaway companions arriving six seconds later. The group of Contador and Armstrong arrived en masse 59 seconds after Astarloza. The biggest loser was Cadel Evans, having a simply terrible Tour, who finished 2-56 after Contador and put the final nail in the coffin of any overall hopes he may have had left. Because most of the favourites finished together there were, against expectations, no significant changes at the top of the overall standings.

At the finish Contador suggested it was Wiggins and not Armstrong who had come to the forefront of his concerns: "If I can gain any time I'll gain it on everyone. But the most dangerous rider in the time trial is Wiggins. He's putting in an excellent ride. He's very strong in the mountains, so if I can take a bit more distance from him, I will."

Armstrong, meanwhile, was happy to be performing at his best again on the biggest stage: "That acceleration felt a little bit like the old Lance but I still maintain that I can't accelerate like these young kids can now. So, maybe today in the back of my mind I just wanted to ride my own race at my own tempo, like I didn't do the other day and I got left behind. We'll see tomorrow – tomorrow will be an up and down day, a day of attrition. Hopefully I'll be there."

But away from the racing there were other moments of interest for the Astana squad. First, one of the team trucks was searched by Swiss police as the race crossed the border from France – nothing untoward was discovered. Then it was reported that Johan Bruyneel would quit as manager of the Astana team. And then, on Lance Armstrong's Twitter page, the American stated that in two days' time, after the final individual time trial, he would reveal the details of a new team he would be leading – presumably with Bruyneel as manager – in 2010.

Stage 17 was another battle through the mountains, with five major climbs en route to Le Grand Bornand. The mountain worrying most of the riders was a new climb for the Tour de France – the Col de Romme, which was only 1,300 metres high but most of that appeared at a gradient of 10 per cent. After the Romme came an old favourite, the Col de la Colombière, before a descent down to the finish.

Certainly, at the start of the stage, Armstrong knew who he was going to watch. "The Schlecks will be very, very aggressive today," he predicted.

That said, it was the rather more bulky figure of Thor Hushovd who set the early pace, leading the race alone over the first climbs as he claimed points at intermediate sprints to further secure his hold on the green jersey. Behind him came a large group of escapees, and behind them came the peloton, this time being marshalled by the Saxo Bank squad while Astana waited in the wings nearby.

On the Col de Romme, Quick Step's Carlos Barredo and Silence-Lotto's Jurgen Van Den Broeck led the race while back in the yellow jersey group Sastre attacked, to little reaction from the other favourites. Gradually Contador, Armstrong, Klöden, Wiggins, both Schlecks and Caisse d'Epargne's Rigoberto Uran cruised up to the wheel of Sastre who simply couldn't create a decent gap. Frank Schleck attacked, only to see Armstrong immediately follow him. Then Andy Schleck burst away, splitting the bunch momentarily before it regrouped. A game of cat and mouse ensued, with the Schleck brothers attacking, only to be matched by Contador and Klöden while Armstrong and Wiggins hung onto the back of the pack.

Finally the Schlecks' vicious increases in pace had an effect, with Andy and Frank drawing Contador and Klöden clear of Wiggins and Armstrong. Having initially let the quartet disappear up the road, eventually Armstrong had enough marking tempo alongside Wiggins and attacked to try to regroup with his Astana team-mates. But the seven-time champion couldn't shake off Garmin's British star and he had to ease off the pace again. The Contador foursome led the race over the summit of the Col de Romme with the Wiggins and Armstrong group reaching the same point 1-03 later.

A descent followed then the riders took on the final challenge of the day up the Col de la Colombière. At the front the Schleck brothers continued to be shadowed by the twin Astana threats of Contador and Klöden, while 1-30 down the road, Wiggins set the pace for Armstrong and now Nibali. Against all logic Contador put in a ferocious attack but he couldn't distance the Schleck brothers. In fact, all he succeeded in doing was to drop his own team-mate. In the group behind, Armstrong finally broke away from Wiggins with another full-gas sprint up the hill. By the summit Klöden was 1-15 behind the Contador-Schlecks trio with Armstrong a further 50 seconds in arrears.

On the descent to the finish Armstrong was joined by Nibali and together they succeeded in catching Klöden, while at the front it appeared that Contador had come to some agreement with the Schlecks. In a display of formation riding Frank was allowed to take the stage win, followed immediately by Contador and brother Andy. Then, 2-18 later, came Nibali and Armstrong, with a shattered Klöden crossing the line nine seconds later. Wiggins, who away from the television cameras had put in a brave ride, came in next at 3-07.

Overall there were big changes. Contador had a gap of 2-26 to the rider in second place, which was now Andy Schleck. Frank Schleck had moved up to third at 3-25 while Armstrong had dropped down to fourth at 3-55. Klöden was fifth at 4-44 and Wiggins was sixth at 4-53. But with the individual time trial coming the next day, those placings were far from fixed and Armstrong, Klöden and Wiggins were all still within touching distance of a podium place.

At the finish Armstrong explained his day: "Again I just tried to be conservative on the Col de Romme. I didn't go with those initial attacks and then I got stuck behind, and when you're 30 seconds back there's nothing you can do – you've got to just sit on. I was a little concerned with Bradley Wiggins in the time trial tomorrow so in the last kilometre up the Colombière I decided to jump away... It would be nice to get on the final overall podium so I'll go as hard as I can in the time trial and go up the Ventoux as fast as I can."

But, despite relative calm breaking out within Astana following the emergence of Contador's obvious superiority, Armstrong still couldn't resist a bit of stirring. Asked what he thought about Contador's attack that resulted in Klöden being dropped, Armstrong replied: "I have no idea what that was all about. I wasn't really paying attention, I was just staying with Wiggins and Christian Vande Velde, but, er, [grimacing] I'm going to bite my tongue on that one."

The second and final individual time trial, in what had been a very sparse Tour for solo challenges, had the potential to mix everything up once more. The 40.5-kilometre course was a largely flat affair around the shore of Lake Annecy, with just one third-category climb about two-thirds of the way into the stage. With changeable weather conditions it looked like riders further down the starting order, the highest riders on the general classification, would face the biggest handicap, while the earlier starters enjoyed drier roads.

With that in mind, it was perhaps no surprise to see that as the favourites took to the course it was the performance of Fabian Cancellara that sat at the top of the leaderboard with a time of 48-33. But the rider who all the big names really feared was Britain's Bradley Wiggins. Famously respected as a time trial supremo, in this Tour the Brit had proven he could match almost everyone in the mountains. The big question was: could he still race against the clock? And what did Armstrong, Klöden and the Schlecks still have to combat him?

Of the top six riders overall Wiggins was the first one to take to the road, hammering his way around the increasingly blustery course and managing to finish in a time of 49-13. Then came Klöden, normally another great time triallist but whose exertions on the road to Le Grand Bornand the day before looked likely to have left him spent, but who finished in a creditable time of 49-24.

Immediately after Klöden came Armstrong, who had started fast, setting the second quickest time so far at the first time-check, but who then started to falter on the climb. Riding a custom-painted Trek machine – with the design created by Japanese artist Yoshitomo Nara – there was little doubt that Armstrong was putting everything he had into this performance, openly suffering at points out on the course. But unlike the experience that most race-watchers had grown used to during Armstrong's seven years of dominance, this time he simply couldn't match his rivals. His time of 50 minutes exactly would only end up being good enough for 16th on the day.

With the inspiration of Tour podium places on offer, both Schleck brothers produced solid performances. Frank arrived first with a good, if not amazing time of 51-04, which would put him 35th. Then Andy finished with an impressive 50-15, good enough for 21st place on the day.

And then came Contador, who had seemingly taken a leaf out of the 'Lance Armstrong Guide to Grand Tour Winning' and confirmed he really was the best rider in the race. Despite the damp conditions, despite the pressure on his shoulders, despite not having the build of a traditional time triallist, Contador flew around the course, setting some amazingly fast markers at the stage checkpoints. His final time of 48-30 was good enough to win the stage, and, short of a disaster on Mont Ventoux two days later, it effectively sealed his 2009 Tour overall victory.

On the general classification things had had yet another shake-up. Contador was safely in the yellow jersey, now 4-11 ahead of Andy Schleck. Armstrong's effort in the time trial had lifted him to third at 5-25 and Bradley Wiggins was breathing down his neck in fourth place at 5-36, with Andreas Klöden just a further two seconds behind in fifth. Frank Schleck's relative lack of time trialling ability had dropped him to sixth overall at 5-59. So the top two steps on the final podium looked reasonably well fixed, but with only 34 seconds separating Armstrong in third and Frank Schleck in sixth it seemed Mont Ventoux, on the penultimate stage, would be the decider.

After the time trial Contador was talking like a true team leader: "I'm very happy. I knew I was going to be contesting the stage win and when I saw I had the fastest time at the 18-kilometre checkpoint I knew I would be fighting for victory and right at the end, by very little, I got it. I don't plan to go for glory on Mont Ventoux. At times you have to defend the jersey and if I can help my team-mates onto the podium, even better."

Despite not doing the perfect ride, Armstrong, too, had reason to be cheerful: "I suffered. I probably started too hard and maybe I was just empty from yesterday. I felt good at the beginning, but of course there was a tailwind so maybe everybody felt good. But I guess the end result was OK as far as the GC goes."

While Armstrong's immediate future - his battle to reappear on the Tour podium - was obviously at the forefront of his mind for most of the day, once the stage was done he turned to rather longer-term plans. Armstrong announced to the world that the American electronics giant RadioShack – and not Nike as had been widely expected – would be the title sponsor for his new team in 2010. "To compete for an American team with the world's top cyclists, supported by the best coaches and staff – I couldn't be happier," Armstrong said.

Interestingly his involvement wouldn't be confined to the bike, and an accompanying press release claimed Armstrong would represent RadioShack in running and triathlon, as well as cycling. And with Team RadioShack having already submitted their application for a ProTour licence, the statement said the intention was to have Armstrong racing for the squad at the 2010 Tour de France.

But that was all for the future and there were still three stages left to complete in the 2009 Tour. Despite a tough second-category climb that finished just 16 kilometres from the finish of stage 19, Mark Cavendish showed just how strong he had become as an all-round bike rider and made it over in the lead group, and then won the sprint – his fifth stage win this Tour.

Then came the final battle for the overall classification, and what a battleground – Mont Ventoux. So often the scene of high drama in the history of both the Tour and Armstrong himself, this incredible mountain had the opportunity to determine the latest chapter in the career of the American. Could he cling on to his third place overall and seal a quite incredible return to racing?

The stage to the bottom of the Ventoux was a largely flat affair and a group of 16 riders had been allowed to escape earlier in the day. As the main field hit the opening slopes of the mountain the leaders had a gap of 4-50, but among the favourites at the front of the peloton things started to heat up. With a fierce wind battering the competitors, the Astana and Saxo Bank workers came forward and set a pace that succeeded in splitting the peloton in two. Then Garmin riders took over at the front to lift the tempo higher still.

At the front of the race a group of three riders – Juan Manuel Garate of Rabobank, Tony Martin of Columbia and Christophe Riblon of Ag2r – had escaped their fellow breakaway members and were pushing on through the lower forested slopes of the Ventoux. Back among the big names all of the top six riders overall were marking each other and all of them were looking cool. Armstrong, behind his LiveStrong-colour sunglasses, seemed particularly impassive.

Frank Schleck was the first to attack, and Armstrong was immediately on his wheel. Then Andy Schleck burst out of the saddle, to be matched by Contador. The pair made a gap, only to see Armstrong attack Frank Schleck, which brought the whole group back together. Still in attendance was Bradley Wiggins, desperate to hang onto his fourth place overall, if not better it, but Klöden was yo-yoing off of the back of the group.

The game of cat and mouse between the Schleck brothers and Armstrong and Contador continued, with Andy Schleck trying to inspire his brother to drop Armstrong, but the American wouldn't be shaken. Eventually Andy Schleck and Contador disappeared up the road, leaving Armstrong, Wiggins, Frank Schleck and Klöden left to battle it out between them. Wiggins came to the front of their small group and upped the pace, but Armstrong just kept watch.

Still leading the way were Garate and Martin. But behind them, by the time the big names reached the moonscape of the Ventoux's barren second stage, Contador and Andy Schleck had fallen back into the clutches of the Armstrong group. Through a quite incredible corridor of spectators, the most famous riders in the world battled their way up the Ventoux.

With just over four kilometres left to race the Schleck brothers attacked once again, with Andy setting the pace for Frank, and Contador, Armstrong and Wiggins quickly on their wheels. Klöden, though, disappeared, and then Wiggins, in obviously difficulty, started to dangle off the rear of the group. At the front Garate took the stage victory just ahead of Martin. Then 38 seconds later came

Andy Schleck, Contador and Armstrong. Frank Schleck followed them a few seconds later, but the bravest ride of the day came from Wiggins, who arrived just 20 seconds after Frank Schleck and so held onto his fourth place overall by the slimmest of margins.

On the general classification, barring an accident on the way to Paris, it confirmed what most people had known for quite a while: that Alberto Contador was the 2009 Tour de France champion. Andy Schleck was second at 4-11 and Armstrong third at 5-24. Wiggins remained fourth at 6-01, Frank Schleck was fifth just three seconds further back at 6-04, and Andreas Klöden was sixth at 6-42.

At the Ventoux's summit Contador was very pleased with his performance, both on and off the bike: "My legs responded well and, while I was watching my rivals, I was also looking out for Lance to see if I could help him onto the podium. And in the end we even dropped Frank Schleck, so we kept the race under control all day. I had to ride two races [this Tour], one on the bike and one in the hotel. But my conscience is clear and I am very happy with what I have achieved."

Armstrong was equally satisfied: "It was kind of simple: follow Wiggins and follow Frank Schleck, and I had the legs to do that... I have never seen so many people on the Ventoux – hell, it seems like half of America showed up... But hey, I can't complain. For an old fart coming in here and getting on the podium, it's not so bad."

So the Tour came to its final celebratory stage to Paris, where Contador and his Astana team could drink in their success, the plaudits and the customary champagne. Strangely, on what is typically a day of great bonhomie, the Astana boys seemed not to have read the script and television cameras weren't able to spot any sign of Contador and Armstrong congratulating each other, or indeed sipping bucks fizz in each other's company. What race watchers did see, though, was Armstrong riding another exclusive bike - a Damien Hirst 'Dead Butterfly' design Trek Madone - at the very front of the peloton for most of the stage while being courted by riders of all teams. He may not have won the Tour but Armstrong looked for all the world like the king, and the fact that he would soon have a team of his own again meant many riders were happy to grab a quick chat with a prospective employer. Contador, meanwhile, remained anonymous in the bunch.

After seven laps of the Champs-Elyseés Mark Cavendish came good on his promise to win the final stage in Paris with his sixth victory of the 2009 Tour. And with no unexpected events befalling the overall top men it meant Contador took yellow for the second time in his career, Frank Schleck was second and Lance Armstrong was third.

From the final Tour podium, Contador enjoyed his success while alluding to the difficulties behind the scenes: "I'm delighted to have won my second Tour. It's been especially difficult for me, but victory is even sweeter because of that. I only want to thank everyone and now I'm going to enjoy victory."

But with the press Armstrong was candid in his appraisal of the last three weeks: "The race was decided at moments that were really individual moments. There was never a time where I lost a minute or two because of my team. I lost time when it was man to man and I wasn't as strong as I needed to be. That's the way we want sport to be. I did my best and I'll be back next year and we'll see if these old legs can go a little faster."

Whatever happens in 2010, the fact remained that Lance Armstrong, at the age of 37 years and 10 months, after the best part of four years away from professional cycle racing, had managed to come back to the sport and finish on the podium at the Tour de France. Statistically it was his worst performance at the race since he contracted cancer. But emotionally and symbolically it could be seen as his greatest ride, where he showed many of the qualities that had been missing during his seven years of domination: humility, dignity, pain and humour. And rather than travelling the world making enemies, which was often the result of his earlier career, Armstrong had succeeded in spreading his cancer message and making new friends, including many of the French press and public. Contador may have become the unquestionable victor of the Tour de France, but Armstrong showed he was one of the race's eternal champions.

So that was that, for a couple of days.

The Tour may have been done and dusted but the Armstrong-Contador rivalry that had been bubbling away under the surface for three weeks, and the preceding eight or nine months, hadn't died out by Paris.

Initially Armstrong was full of praise for his team-mate. Then, just one day after the end of the Tour, Contador held a press conference back in Spain: "The situation was tense and delicate because the relationship between myself and Lance extended to the rest of the staff. On this Tour the days in the hotel were harder than the days on the road... My relationship with Lance in zero. I think that, independently of what his character is, he is still a great champion, he has won seven Tours and played a big role in this one too. But it is different to speak at a personal level. I have never really admired him that much or ever will, but of course as a cyclist he is a great champion."

Armstrong was quick to hit back on his Twitter feed – which had become the most direct source of news from the American during this Tour – saying: "Seeing these comments from AC [Contador]. If I were him I'd drop this drivel and start thanking his team. Without them he doesn't win." Then he followed it up with: "Hey pistolero, there is no 'I' in team." Before ending the verbal fisticuffs with: "A champion is also measured on how much he respects his team-mates and opponents. You can win a race on your own, not a Grand Tour."

And with Armstrong and Contador riding in rival teams for 2010, but both almost certain to face each other again at the Tour de France, it looks set to be another chapter in the Lance Armstrong story that will entertain the public for a little while longer.